Mobile phones: The new talking drums of everyday Africa

Langaa &
African Studies Centre

Mobile phones: The new talking drums of everyday Africa

Mirjam de Bruijn, Francis Nyamnjoh & Inge Brinkman
(editors)

Langaa Research and Publishing Common Initiative Group
PO Box 902 Mankon
Bamenda
North West Region
Cameroon
Phone +237 33 07 34 69 / 33 36 14 02
LangaaGrp@gmail.com
www.africanbookscollective.com/publishers/langaa-rpcig

African Studies Centre
P.O. Box 9555
2300 RB Leiden
The Netherlands
Phone +31 72 527 3372
asc@ascleiden.nl
www.ascleiden.nl

ISBN: 9956-558-53-2

Contents

List of photos

Preface

Collaboration is central in scientific work and this volume illustrates the collaboration that can be realized by the social sciences and the humanities. It is a collaborative effort between junior and senior scholars and between African and European scholars, and a joint publication by both an African and a European institute. In this respect, the book also represents a new phase in collaboration between the African Studies Centre (ASC) and Langaa, being the first book to be published jointly by these two institutes.

This co-publication would not have been possible without the excellent editing of Ann Reeves. Mieke Zwart did the type setting of the manuscript. We would like to thank them both for their help and endless patience. The book's origins lie in the 'New Social Spaces: Mobility and Communication Technology in Africa' panel discussions that were held at the AEGIS (ECAS) conference in Leiden in 2007. We are grateful for the financial assistance given by the African Studies Centre and the Celtel telephone company, as well as the intellectual contributions of participants and presenters at that panel.

The mission of Langaa Research and Publishing Common Initiative Group (Langaa RPCIG), headquartered in Bamenda, Cameroon, is to contribute to its country's own cultural development and the cultural renaissance of Africa. This is being achieved by promoting innovative research and publications and by enhancing collaboration in the social sciences and the humanities in Africa and among African and non-African social researchers, writers and cultural workers. Langaa seeks to facilitate dialogue between research and policy on cultural production and promotion in Africa.

The ASC is the only academic research institute in the Netherlands devoted entirely to the study of Africa. Its primary aims are to undertake scientific research on Sub-Saharan Africa in the social sciences and the humanities and to promote a better understanding of African societies in the Netherlands. The ASC's research is well embedded in national and international African Studies scholarship. The Centre has a research department and an extensive library with the most specialized collection on Africa in the Netherlands in the fields of the social sciences, the humanities and law. Its collection is accessible via the online public access catalogue.

An excerpt from *Married but available*, a novel by Francis B. Nyamnjoh

(…) Lilly Loveless noticed that her cell phone was not with her. She must have left it in the taxi. They screamed for the taxi to stop, but the man did not seem to hear them. They immediately took another taxi to follow, calling her phone as they did, from Britney's phone. After chasing for half a kilometre or so, they lost track of the taxi and gave up.

"The phone is now history," said Britney.

"But it rings when you call it," replied Lilly Loveless, marvelled. "Can't the taxi man just answer the call and allow us to tell him we are chasing him for the phone?"

"You must live in a dreamland," said Britney. "Is that what happens where you come from?"

"What do you mean?"

"Here in Mimboland we thank God for being lucky when we pick something like that. The reasoning is simple: If you really needed it, you wouldn't lose it."

"That's cynical."

"But true. It is the responsibility of the rich to take care of what they value."

"What makes the taxi man think that I am richer than him?"

"Simple. You let go of your phone. If it really mattered to you, it would still be with you as we speak.

"I give up," said Lilly Loveless, angry with herself for not being careful enough. Yet, how could she have thought that an apparently friendly taxi man sharing jokes with them would be a lion in sheepskin with her cell phone? She felt terrible. All her phone numbers were gone, making her feel naked, without ties and vulnerable. She felt as if a vital part of her person had fled.

"I need a new phone right away. Could you take me to a cell phone retailer to buy another?" she pleaded with Britney. "My mom would worry herself to death if she can't reach me by phone."

They boarded another taxi to Global Mobile Connections, the most popular cell phone dealer in town. It was a very big shop with phones and accessories of all shapes and sizes, from the most basic and cheapest to the trendiest and costliest.

To mitigate her frustration for losing her phone, Lilly Loveless decided to ask the proprietor a few questions about his business.

"This is an impressive shop you've got here," she started with a compliment.

"I'm trying my best," replied the shop owner. "There's little to complain about. Business is booming, we thank God."

"So cell phones are very popular?"

"Popular?" he laughed. "They've revolutionised the landscape in Mimboland," he told her. "Since graduating from Mimbo two years ago, I haven't looked back. All I needed was the initial push by my parents to kick start the business. It took a single trip to Dubai and I was able to triple what my parents lent me, and in less than no time, had paid them back. Today I'm my own boss with three employees…"

"Like someone who interacts on a daily basis with clients and also with cell phone users out there, what can you tell me about cell phone use in Mimboland?"

"My best customers are women. They go for the latest, slickest and most expensive. When I go to Dubai, it is them I seek to please the most. When a man walks in and wants a phone for a woman, I know instantly, just as I know if he is buying for himself, although even men seem to give up on the bigger the better when it comes to cell phones." He laughed as if there was much more to what he said.

Lilly Loveless recalled the words of a politician back home in Muzunguland who declared some years back that the cell phone is one of those rare items for which men are ready to compete on who has got the smallest.

"So tell me what phone I'm going to buy now," Lilly Loveless challenged, teasingly.

"That's easy. You are paying for it yourself, and you are Muzungu, so I swear you'll go for the cheapest Nokia, Motorola or Samsung," he laughed, his fat jaws quivering with underpinning comfort. "That's what amazes me about you the Muzungu. You make all of these things, yet are so frugal and crafty in your consumption of them. We make nothing and we don't have the kind of money Muzungu have, but we settle for kingly consumption of what we can't even repair or maximise use of. If it isn't the most expensive in the world, and if it isn't coming from abroad, we aren't going to touch it. Beggars with the choices of kings, we are!"

"You are right," agreed Lilly Loveless. "I'll go for your cheapest Nokia, not because I don't like a sophisticated phone, but just because all I want is a phone that works, and in any case, I would hate having to lose an expensive phone yet again."

Lilly Loveless paid for the phone, bought a new sim card and airtime, and as one of the shop assistants was busy configuring her new phone under Britney's supervision, she continued her conversation with the shop owner.

"Tell me more about cell phone use here in Puttkamerstown," she urged.

"I don't know the percentage of ownership between men and women, but I can say that most of the women who own phones get them from men, who also feed the phones regularly with airtime. The interesting thing is that usually when you transfer airtime electronically to a lady, you get a very quick call or an SMS from her to thank you for the airtime. Thereafter, you don't hear from her again and the next time she calls you is to tell you that her airtime is finished and she wants to have some more."

"So whom do they call with this airtime? Shouldn't it be for you who have supplied it?"

"That's the question the men are asking."

"Who are these men buying phones and airtime?"

"Boyfriends, husbands, Mbomas... Sometimes somebody gets into a serious crisis with the wife or girlfriend because he has refused to buy her a phone or to pay for airtime."

"What perceptions of cell phones are popular?"

"The cell phone is considered a luxury and as a tool of prestige, but also as something with much practical value. But because it is expensive to run, you sometimes find people with cell phones who go for months without making a single call. Still they are proud of their phones and usually they want to display it for people to notice that they have a cell phone. Although their bags and pockets are empty and indeed actually safer, people often prefer to carry their phones so others can see and admire or envy them."

"How exactly do they expose these phones?"

"They carry it in their palms or they hang it on their neck. I sell pouches and lots of accessories for that purpose. They display it where it would be very visible for anyone to see. You need to see people at workshops, conferences, churches and other public occasions, refusing to switch off their phones. Sometimes in church, phones interrupt prayers with funny ring tones, despite notices pasted all over asking members of the congregation to switch off their cell phones. Just last Sunday, my pastor asked if those who leave their phones on during service are desperately waiting for an urgent call from Satan. Women are particularly guilty. When they are not busy displaying their phones for others to admire, they leave them on and put them deep inside their handbags such that before they get to take the call, they have disturbed almost everybody around. People hardly respect notices and instructions telling them to put off their cell phones. To them, it is like being asked to switch off one's ambitions for prestige and social status."

"What do you have to tell me about ring tones?"

"Ring tones have gone wild these days, and tastes vary as much as human character. In general though, people prefer tones that are melodious, that are music, not simply signals. Once they buy their phones, they usually ask us or technicians to give them a rich variety of ring tones that they think are attractive and unique. If they get their fancy ring tones, sometimes they like to put the ring tones very high and to let the phone ring for long to attract passers-by to know that they are receiving a call. You have to be important and well connected to receive a call, you know?"

"What do you mean by that?"

"I remember when cell phones were still relatively new, students would arrange with others to beep them in lecture halls so they could pretend to be receiving important calls from family or friends abroad."

"Really?"

"Absolutely. Also, when there were not that many ring tones to choose from and everyone wanted the privilege of receiving a call, there was much anxiety when the phone rang in a public place. The tendency was for everyone to rush for their phones. Even today, women especially are always very anxious, as if they sit in permanent expectation of the phone ringing. They rush to unzip their bags and remove their cell phones even before they've ascertained that it is their ring tone. In certain instances, some people carry several phones by different service providers on them. You need to see them totally confused when one rings, worse still, if several ring at the same time."

"That's funny," Lilly Loveless giggled, visualising someone totally wired up, vibrating with a cacophony of ring tones. "So the phones are hardly on silent even when they have a silent feature?"

"No. Most people do not even know that the silent thing is there, and those who do don't care to use it, because to them when you receive a phone silently people do not know that you are around, and what is the point of being important, around and silent?"

"You are too critical for a businessman and dealer in cell phones," remarked Lilly Loveless.

"I went into business to survive, but my heart is with sociology," said the proprietor. "When I've made enough money, I intend to go to Muzunguland for further studies."

"So you want to fall bush?"

"You know about bushfalling?"

"Britney has told me all about it."

"It is the latest Gospel in town. Everyone is craving to fall bush. We believe in bushfalling, and are proud to be referred to not by name, but simply as bushfallers."

"How interesting," remarked Lilly Loveless, her mind not wanting to let go of the central theme of cell phones. "How many cell phones do you have personally?"

"I sell them, so I can have as many as I fancy. There are some with room for two or more sim cards, others with possibility for Internet, digital camera, word processing, graphics, games, Bluetooth, and so on. In general however, most people prefer to have two cell phones, since we have two main network service providers. They have one for this provider and a second for the other. This is understandable as both networks are hardly working well simultaneously, but I am sure people would still have two phones even if the networks were healthy all year round, just so others know that they can possess two phones. In some rare occasions, people who travel a lot and between countries could have a phone for each country, rather than having to juggle sim cards each time they travel."

"I understand that many people prefer phones from whitemankontri, is that true?"

"We Mimbolanders believe a lot in what comes from outside. Those of us who receive calls from whitemankontri like to dramatise the fact. Since most of the calls from abroad do not display the numbers of the callers, fraudsters use that feature to dupe lots of people locally, claiming that they are calling from Muzunguland, China, Dubai or elsewhere abroad. Due to the economic crisis we face here, many people tend to want to fall bush because they feel that once you are out there you will make it. Sometimes people with phones get very frustrated with calls from abroad, especially when these calls do not come along with promises of expected goodies. Most elderly people here link up and meet their children abroad thanks to cell phones. Remittances are negotiated and transferred thanks to cell phones, and bushfallers and their relatives or friends here at home can follow the transfer minute by minute, drawing the attention of one another to any hitches in the process."

Lilly Loveless intensified her note taking. She liked what she was hearing. This interview was worth the lost phone, she thought. "Any negative side to the cell phone?" she asked.

"The cell phone has its good and bad sides. Most unscrupulous people have used the cell phone to wreak havoc, just as some have used the phone to keep peace and deter crime. For young girls, they are mostly using the cell phone as a tool to grab things left and right, and also, to make themselves available for grabbing. When a woman gives you her phone number, she is actually giving you access to herself, and also as a way to pester you to send them airtime, this and that."

"How common is the beeping or flashing you mentioned a while ago?"

"When someone beeps me, I will never respond if I don't know them. My phone is strictly for business and important issues. I sometimes play with it, and may beep somebody once or twice only to attract their attention. The cell phone is still very expensive for Mimbolanders to manage. Even though the price per unit set is manageable, the airtime is still very expensive. Most people also feel that those abroad have easy access to cell phones. Usually, when you have relatives or friends abroad, you would want to request a cell phone from them. So most people have cell phones from abroad as gifts, and the tendency is to believe that those phones are superior to what we have locally, but that's not true, as you yourself can see from the stock I have here…"

At the end of their conversation, Lilly Loveless thanked the proprietor and his assistant, and left in a taxi, which dropped Britney off at her place, and continued with her further down the windy seven kilometres long road popularly known as the Anaconda Street.

* * *

Later that evening Lilly Loveless caught up with Bobinga Iroko at Mountain Valley to show him her new phone.

"Thanks for the bush meat," a young man told Bobinga Iroko, emptying his glass of beer and licking his fingers.

"It's the least I can do for a bushman," said Bobinga Iroko, as the young man stood up to leave. "Make sure your report on the attempted arson on the Mimbo Forest Conservation Project building is on my table first thing in the morning," he added.

"Others are bushfallers, he is a bushmeater," Bobinga Iroko told Lilly Loveless as she took a seat.

"What is bush meat?" asked Lilly Loveless, beckoning at the waitress to bring her the usual.

"Don't tell me you haven't eaten bush meat yet," Bobinga Iroko raised his eyebrows.

"What I see I eat, what I don't see I don't eat."

"Do you mean you wouldn't eat if you were blind?"

"Why can't you just answer simple straightforward questions straightforwardly?"

Bobinga Iroko laughed, and with his eyes closed, said: "'I see,' said the blind lady, sitting at the corner of a round table to place her order for Achu with yellow soup and red bush meat."

"And what is bush meat, for the blind and the sighted?"

"OK, bush meat is meat that hunters bring back from the bush," said Bobinga Iroko. "That's as straightforward as I can get," he added, with a laugh.

"How popular is hunting around here?"

"I don't know about around here, but where I used to come from until I got stuck in the city and its zero sum games someone who comes home with a leopard, a lion, an elephant or even an antelope is hailed and honoured with a red feather by the village chief."

Lilly Loveless wondered the extent to which this was still true, although she came short of asking Bobinga Iroko if people really hunt these days even in the villages. Instead, she asked: "Is bushmeating similar to bushfalling?"

"Have you fallen for a bushfaller?" Bobinga Iroko laughed in his usual jovial and jocular manner.

"Do you have a good looking, hardworking, long fingered smily, intelligent, bushfaller who laughs like you?"

"I'll arrange for a perfect clone," said Bobinga Iroko. "Bushfalling is like real hunting, which doesn't take place in your backyard," he added.

"What do you mean?"

"If you go hunting in your backyard, what you are most likely to catch is a neighbour's goat or fowl, in which case you are branded a thief and disciplined accordingly."

"If I understand you correctly, real bushfalling is that which takes you to a distant bush, and from which you bring back real game," said Lilly Loveless, taking out her notebook.

"Correct."

The waitress returned with a Mimbo-Wanda for Lilly Loveless, who filled her glass and said "cheers" to Bobinga Iroko. After a gulp, she opened her handbag and showed Bobinga Iroko her new cell phone, followed by a story of how she lost the old one.

Bobinga Iroko gave her a lecture on cell phones as instruments of exploitation.

"With the cell phone, men and women are able to schedule and reschedule appointments, and sideline the person they do not want at a particular moment," he told her.

"Also, the cell phone makes it easy for people to tell lies. Somebody would tell you, 'I'm in the house' when the person is in Mountain Valley having a nice time with your best friend. 'I'm coming in ten minutes', when he is actually going away from you. Some would say: 'Where are you?', and you could easily reply: 'Where would you like me to be?'"

"Let me understand you correctly," said Lilly Loveless, taking out her notebook. "You mean the cell phone makes it possible for people to want you to be where they want or where they don't want?"

"Absolutely," agreed Bobinga Iroko. "So it is very deceitful, at times. But again, it is also very useful in that, for those who know time management, instead of travelling for kilometres for an appointment or to send a message, you just tell the person that you will not be coming because that saves a lot of time and money. Creative in their use of the cell phone though they are in some ways, Mimbolanders are yet to master the cell phone as an instrument of expediency and purposeful communication."

"That's the same thing the proprietor of the cell phone shop said."

"Which means it must be true, right?" Bobinga Iroko laughed, faking mockery. "The cell phone has also proved very useful in rigging elections because the rigging of elections is the favourite pastime of our politicians," he added.

"I can well imagine how handy the cell phone could be to a polling official in the service of a government economical with democracy," agreed Lilly Loveless.

"And not to forget using the cell phone to eliminate critics, subversives and political opponents," added Bobinga Iroko.

"How do they do it? By planting a bomb in your cell phone? Or is it by calling you up and telling you to drop dead or else…?" asked Lilly Loveless, half teasingly.

"It is no laughing matter," Bobinga Iroko rebuked without sounding it. "We lost many a prominent son and daughter of this country through cell phone assassinations. Someone calls you up pretending to be interested in something else but actually seeking to identify your location so that it can be communicated to their squads of hired killers. Before you know it, someone has died mysteriously from a car accident, poisoning, break-in and assault by armed robbers, matters of the heart, etc…"

"I see," said Lilly Loveless, after noting down in her notebook. "In your own work as a journalist, how has the cell phone influenced things?"

"Good question," said Bobinga Iroko. "There is a very marked difference. Before the advent of the cell phone, we were using just the fixed phone, of which there were not that many. With the coming of the cell phone everything has been revolutionised. You are able to crosscheck information easily. The process of gathering news has been facilitated immensely by the cell phone, which has also enabled us to balance our reports. Initially, you get one side of the story, and even if you can't get the other side for want of mobility, you know all you need to do is get in touch with somebody who has the number of the person who has the other side of the story and then you crosscheck. So the cell phone has done a lot of good to the media even though it has also done a lot of harm."

"In what way has it done harm?"

"People take liberties with the cell phone. I for one am exploited."

"You, Bobinga Iroko, exploited? How?"

"If an event is happening around here, those from other news agencies in Mimboland, Muzunguland or elsewhere, have the habit of calling me up for information, and I find myself being a correspondent for news organs that have not placed me on any salary or a stringer's fee, but that are simply taking advantage of our esprit de corps."

"I see."

"Criminals have also used the cell phone to facilitate crime. I remember last year when I had to travel with a friend during the Ramadan period to Pawa-Town and at some point I said I didn't want to travel any longer because of the long delay we had at the motor park. Only my friend travelled, and they were robbed by armed robbers somewhere on the highway. The robbers were looking for somebody light in complexion, with sideburns and a twinkle in his eyes, and wearing a black shirt. This could only mean that somehow the people at the motor park had communicated through cell phones or through SMS to these robbers with the identity of this person and with an indication of how much money was on him, so they could pick him up and force him at gunpoint to hand over the money."

"Then there is also the issue of the use of anonymous calls when you write a story that is critical of somebody, he or she calls you anonymously to warn or threaten you, so that you have the impression that you are being trailed, and that at any moment something could happen to you. On many occasions I have received calls like that insulting me about a particular report although once in a while I also get calls congratulating me. But the insulting and threatening calls do not leave even the daredevils of our profession indifferent. So the cell phone to the best of my knowledge is a necessary evil."

"You are a courageous man with a big heart."

"Is that supposed to be a compliment?"

"What do you think?"

"Is it for me to think what you intend?"

"Difficult as ever, Bobinga Iroko... have you ever considered changing your name to 'Bobinga Iroko the Difficult'?"

"What is there to be gained?"

"A cell phone with a number only one person has besides Bobinga Iroko."

"And who might that person be?"

"Britney taught me about beeping or flashing a while ago, but how come you didn't reply when I beeped or flashed you to announce my new cell number?" asked Lilly Loveless.

"Normally beepers and flashers are low income people and generally women consider themselves to be low income so they beep even when they have far more than the men," Bobinga Iroko feigned tongue-in-cheekness. "I don't tolerate beeping or flashing," he added. "I only communicate with people whose numbers I have and with whom I have a prior appointment."

"That must be terrible for an investigative journalist," criticised Lilly Loveless.

"I have an official phone for official business," Bobinga Iroko defended himself. "And that number is very well known and regularly featured in the front page of The Talking Drum. With that number, I can do anything, but my private number is my private number. I have no patience with the abusive and reckless traffic in personal phone numbers by people who have no business giving out a number that was shared with them in confidence."

"I see," said Lilly Loveless.

"And with my private number, if I receive a beep, it doesn't matter who is there, if I don't know you I will never respond. You know how many people out there are just seeking for notice? So because I didn't recognise your new number, I couldn't avail myself to your beeps and flashes."

"Message understood," said Lilly Loveless. "And now that you've got my new number, do react when next I flash."

"It depends what mood I am in," replied Bobinga Iroko, a mischievous smile perching playfully on his face.

(…)

Taken from:
Francis B. Nyamnjoh (2009), *Married but available*, Bamenda: Langaa, pp. 123-130.

Introduction: Mobile communication and new social spaces in Africa

Mirjam de Bruijn, Francis B. Nyamnjoh & Inge Brinkman

Africa's communication landscape has undergone tremendous change since the introduction of mobile telephony. As the statistics show, mobile phones have spread remarkably fast across the African continent:[1] 1 in 50 Africans had access to a mobile phone in 2000 and by 2008 the figure was 1 in 3. This is a revolution in terms of voice communication, especially for areas where land lines were still rare at the end of the 20th century. Each chapter in this volume tries to show, in its own way, how this new technology is (re-)shaping social realities in African societies, and how Africans and their societies are, in turn, shaping the technologies of communication. All the chapters focus on the idea of appropriation of technology. Technologies are not seen as determining society as such, and there is no one-way direction in the relationship between technology and society. On the contrary, society and

---

[1] Africa: Telecoms Acceleration, Africa Focus, 17 May 2008. In 2004 Panos reported a huge gap between mobile telephony in the rural and urban areas of Africa. Most companies had invested initially in urban areas for commercial reasons. See Panos (2004) 'Telephones in Africa: Mind the Gap' (*Panos Media Brief*). For statistics about the country-by-country spread of mobile telephony: www.itu.int/ITUtelecome; and for ICT indications for 2007: www.tinjurl.com/3gvdkl. Statistics for 2007: Cameroon: total no. of phone subscribers: 3.267 million, 19.68 per 100 inhabitants, effective teledensity 24.45; Chad: 479,000 subscribers: 4.78 per 100 inhabitants, effective teledensity 8.52; Mali: 2.568 million subscribers; 20.81 per 100 inhabitants, effective teledensity 20.13 (Africa Telecommunication/ICT indicators 2008; ITU (International Telecommunication Union). See also Waverman *et al.* (2005).

technology are interdependent and are evolving in a dialectic process of cultural and social appropriation.

The book's contributors met at a workshop in the Netherlands in 2006 at which the social and cultural appropriation of the mobile phone in different settings in Africa was central. The call for papers invited the authors to consider the appropriation of the mobile phone and (in one case) the Internet in so-called marginal communities, and the mobility that develops in relation to the marginality of these communities. The relationship between communication technology, mobility and new societal forms in Africa were grasped alongside the concept of the mobile margins, i.e. social spaces in the margins of the state that are created by people's mobility.[2] Marginality refers to the kaleidoscope of perceived and real circumstances that cause people to feel disadvantaged and may include a lack or limited access to communication technologies and means of transport. As these mobile margins are not geographically fixed but are formed by strings of people, communication is a vital issue for the social fabric of such connections. It is in these geographical areas and social spaces that the mobile telephone is expected to make a difference, though the technology is often still an expectation rather than a reality. It also refers to the economic conditions of the people living in areas that are considered to be poor. We situate the existence of these mobile margins in the discussion about globalization and (dis)connecting the world (see Castells 2007).

The cultural and social appropriation of communication technology is a creative process that is well described in Horst & Miller's (2006) study of mobile telephony in Jamaica. Jamaica could be considered as a mobile margin, being a marginal space in geographic, economic and social terms and with a high rate of mobility among the population. Ways of appropriation of the phone, the social and identity marker the phone has become and also the economic opportunities it entails all form part of these new dynamics. It remains to be seen how specific the developing mobile phone culture is for these geographical areas and social spaces. The process of appropriation suggests that technologies acquire different meanings in different social contexts. It involves the contextualization of new ICT in the older processes and the dynamics of the introduction of new communication technologies. Weren't all technologies once new, Gitelman & Pingree (2003) ask? We are, therefore, interested in the link with similar technological 'revolutions' in the past and the chapters in this book all show how this appropriation of new communications technology is shaping society. New technologies are used as a means of social change

---

and development, and in the process they themselves are changed; hence the emergence of a mobile phone culture.[3]

From earliest publications on mobile phone technology[4] and our own observations in the field, we realize that rapid changes are taking place and what is a reality today will no longer be so tomorrow. For this reason, a scholarly publication of this type may become history by the time of publication. Research done in the first few years of the 21st century should already be read as history. It is for this reason that we started this book with an excerpt from a novel in which the mobile telephone is captured in its excesses and in which the fictionalized world becomes the reality of today. As Barber (1991: 1) stated: 'Literary texts tell us things about society and culture that we could learn in no other way.' This may be especially true in a situation where we are observing change in the making. The novel allows us to delve into reflections about the existence of a mobile phone culture and the social changes it makes but it is at the same time a critical reflection on the ideas that have been voiced to date in the literature on mobile phones and its (positive) effects on societal forms in Africa. This book, entitled "Mobile phones: The new talking drums of Acrica", critically reflects on social change and technological reform in an anthropological and historical perspective..

Mobile phone culture

Nyamnjoh's fictionalized account that opens this chapter draws extensively on mobile margins ethnography in Cameroon, and is as informed by stereotypes as it is by the reality of the appropriation of mobile phone technology in Africa.

The story of Lilly Loveless was written at a time when the mobile phone had conquered social communication possibilities in many urban spaces and was increasingly doing the same across rural Africa too. Lilly's story may help to illustrate realities around the mobile phone. As a satirical novel the story is of course fictitious, sometimes presented in conversations that are caricatured and designed to please the reader but, at the same time, they are meant to be a commentary on African societies and the way consumption and new technologies are appropriated in such a variety of forms. The story provides a window, though subjective, to various questions that concern the book's researchers and authors. To what extent do such artistic expressions refer to hopes, fears and the evaluation of a society's people, in this case in relation to the mobile phone?

One stylistic feature that Nyamnjoh uses is confrontation between the European researcher and the African citizen. For instance, in his picture of phone use, Euro-

---

[3] Goggin (2006), Katz (2006), introduce the notion of phone culture in the European and US context. It engages all the cultural and social reforms it brings, but also the inclusion in popular culture, in daily life etc.

[4] Dibakana (2002).

peans are portrayed as being frugal in their choice of mobile phone, even though they have produced them, while Africans are shown as extravagant and kingly consumers of what they do not produce, going for the slickest, the cutest and the most expensive, which they are not sure they will ever use to the full. Such excellence in sterile consumption is presented as being spearheaded by women, while men are made to appear as victims of female consumerism, expected as they are to finance the extravagance of the women in their lives. The mobile phone stands out as a status symbol, harnessed as such in different ways by different individuals and social categories. It is a whole new vehicle of identity and identification for all walks of life. The mobile phone, above all, is presented as an instrument of power, capable of positive and negative outcomes like a double-edged sword. Even if evil, the mobile phone is perceived as a necessary evil – something that has become and should stay as part and parcel of the communication landscape of Africa and Africans rural and urban, at home and in the diaspora.

Visiting researchers (like Lilly Loveless) and their local assistants (like Britney) are just as dependent on their mobile phones as they are on the air they breathe. Therefore, the moment Lilly Loveless leaves her phone in the taxi, she feels naked and terribly vulnerable, as if a vital part of her person has been lost. She is desperate to re-establish normality, making one wonder just how people managed to cope with life prior to the introduction of the mobile phone. Not only does Lilly Loveless feel lost without her phone, she feels stripped of her identity, networks and relationships, with the phone numbers of her contacts gone. She is helpless, at the mercy of uncertainties, and has a feeling of impotence that comes from being totally immobilized by time and space.

Here Nyamnjoh refers to an observed social reality, that the mobile phone with its capacity to compress and imbue with flexible mobility all the necessary phone numbers and hence the relatedness of its owners and users has rapidly grown to epitomize a person's relatedness and is the very indicator of life. Horst & Miller (2005) have turned this social fact into an interesting research tool: the content of a phone is a way to interpret a person's social network, both hidden and overt. For many people, it would seem that the mobile phone has become a necessary tool for the expression of identity and for keeping track of social relations in daily life (see Hahn & Kibora 2008). The contents of such an expression of identity and negotiation of social relation in social life may differ from context to context and even between people.

The shopkeeper explains to Lilly that relatedness via the phone is basically the same in the communicative purpose it serves, but that it differs from person to person in the way in which individuals and different social categories appropriate it. Men and women, so the shopkeeper tells us, differ in their phone cultures, their contacts, and in their procurement and relationship with the mobile phone as a technological tool. This part of the story refers to the question of whether and how the phone has become part and parcel of the social process of relating. Do these new forms of relatedness also imply hierarchical ways? The mobile phone seems to have become an intrinsic part of the negotiation process, not only because it is literally in between people and used to link them up but also because, as a gadget, it has a strong social and psychological value.

The shopkeeper in the story represents another important new avenue made possible by the mobile phone and its appropriation. The phone has an entourage and serves as an employer – providing a market and opening up possibilities for those who would otherwise be unemployed youth plagued by insecurities and uncertainties and desperate for the multiplicity of risks that beckon, including a longing for migration in search of purportedly greener pastures. The economy that has developed around the phone takes traders to Dubai, among other places, to find affordable brands of mobile phone and accessories for African consumers. The trade in mobile phones is not only flexible and mobile; it has also gained a positive status in many an African context, urban and rural, at home and further afield. The shopkeeper is a sociologist who is not at all unhappy with his new status as a smallholder of mobile phones and accessories. He clearly represents the high number of youths in Africa whose 'western' education has led them into an idle life. The wonders the mobile phone economy seem to hold for the youth are still questionable.

Here the story comments on the often-portrayed positive impact of the mobile phone economy as an employer for the youth. The mobile phone, through the social relationships it forges or entertains, and the economic possibilities it opens up, simultaneously challenges and reinforces the status quo, allowing for consolidation and renewal in ways not immediately obvious if treated in isolation or outside specific socio-economic contexts. In this way, the mobile phone reproduces social stratifications even as it is actively transforming them through the creativity and innovation that it provokes or condones. The shopkeeper's social itinerary is directly linked to his shop and the booming economy surrounding the mobile phone. This, however, can only happen because the phone has become a necessity for many people in the possibilities it offers them to communicate and in how it facilitates the production, reproduction and transformation of social networks, social status and hierarchies.

In Lilly Loveless's story, the brief discussion on bushfallers (those who go to another country to hunt, i.e. literally to return with big game) introduces us to another important aspect of the social possibilities of the mobile phone. This parody of distance is interesting in the light of our studies of mobile margins. The mobile phone compresses distance between people, as it does between Lilly Loveless and her mother and between bushfallers and those at home, thereby making it possible for people to cope in new ways with long periods of separation from family and friends thanks to the virtual or symbolic presence that the mobile phone provides. This new connectedness raises questions about the extension of social spaces and the de-essentialization of geographies in ways suggestive of a new politics of belonging that emphasizes flexibility over and above permanence. As the story shows, many people leave this economically deprived area in search of greener pastures abroad and far from their relations, and keep expectations alive in the same way that hunters in remote villages used to when they went on long-distance hunting expeditions. The new means of communication makes relating over distances easier, which is not perceived by all as positive, as ease of communication comes with heightened demands and expectations of remittances on the part of relations back home. In the face of the challenges of coping in the margins abroad, many bush-fallers feel the weight of the pressure of constant communication with folk back home who often do not understand the difficulties confronting them as economic migrants. The mobile phone that compresses distance also brings distance home to people and may lead to more of them moving to the purported world of infinite abundance that they have been deluded into internalizing (see Nyamnjoh 2005, forthcoming).

****

This literary text shows elements in the ethnography of the mobile margins that could be the starting point for academic research. Interesting parallels in Francis Nyamnjoh's story with the academic situation make it easy to link it to the practice of academic research. The character of Lilly Loveless is a researcher and many field-work issues are represented in the narrative. The questions it raises for social science research are linked to the possible changes that mobile telephony may develop for African societies that are encountering the globalizing world, economic crises, and new forms of relating. It certainly also questions the newness of this technology and its imbued social forms. These attitudes, relations and new social forms all build upon experiences and old forms of relating and society, and thus enclose continuities. Each of the chapters in this volume shows elements of these social changes and continuities. The chapters are located in different African contexts in various countries, regions and social groups and comparison will offer insight into the social and cultural processes related to the appropriation of the mobile phone. They also represent the current history of this era of communication in which the phone has become such an important tool. The phone's introduction is very recent but it has gained such speed and momentum that as we read in the story of Lilly we are observing change in the making, and the fluidities and flexibilities of human society.[5]

---

5   Gitelman & Pingree (2003: xii) in their exposée on the 'newness' of new media: 'There is a moment, before the material means and the conceptual modes of new media have become fixed, when such media are not yet accepted as natural, when their own meanings are in flux.' Similarly, because the mobile phone is 'new' in this sense and its meanings are still in flux that it has 'so many sides'.

The chapters

A book presenting studies in the social sciences and the humanities on new communication technologies, namely the mobile phone in Africa, needs to reflect on the role of communications technology in the practice of doing research. For the researcher Lilly Loveless in the novel, the importance of the mobile phone as her constant companion guiding her interviews and her mistakes cannot be underestimated. The fictional account is clearly based on the real-life experiences of researchers. Lotte Pelckmans's reflections on the mobile phone in her research and her survey among fellow researchers are therefore an indispensable element in the book. She started her MA research in 2000 and continued Ph.D reseach in 2005 in Mali. Bamako, the capital, had already been introduced to the new technology but the region where she conducted fieldwork in Central Mali only became connected in 2005. Pelckmans was thus observing changes in the making and became part of these herself. She stresses the immediacy of phone communication and the differences with all past technologies, including the fixed telephone, because it is direct, many people have access to it and there is an instant response. The phone helps when making appointments and can clarify immediate questions during the writing process too when one phone call to Mali from the Netherlands can be enough to provide missing information. Doing research without a mobile phone has become an unimaginable practice for her. How can one connect to informants in the chaotic urban forms of relating that she encountered in Bamako? Her anthropological fieldwork was conducted in several places that are connected through the families she follows in her research: Paris, Bamako and Douentza. The mobile phone proved indispensable in such multi-sited research and it has become possible to follow people in their lives from at a desk in the Netherlands. However following contacts and gathering information by phone also raises new ethical questions that she tries to answer. The phone has opened up a new era in the practice of ethnographic fieldwork. Research into the appropriation of the mobile phone should also detail the researcher's practices.

As Pelckmans remarks, the changes induced by the mobile phone are remarkable and its history is still very short. Walter Gam Nkwi's article highlights this point by sketching the history of direct voice communication in Buea, a medium-sized city in Anglophone Cameroon. It is interesting to note the importance the Germans, and later the British, attached to this direct voice communication (assuming the lines were working). This type of communication was essential for the governance of the colonies. Information from the European side could be received immediately and misunderstandings minimized. Nkwi argues that during the colonial time the phone remained a tool for the colonial elite and was primarily a tool of governance. This situation did not change after independence in spite of the installation of the national telephone company. The era of the mobile phone has, however, resulted in a democratization of access to voice communication (cf. Smith 2006) but it has done so in a very specific way. Similar to the reception of the fixed line that was appropriated in the economic and political logic of the time, mobile telephony has also had a specific economic and political logic. First of all, the spread of telephony was only possible because of market liberalization that allowed private telephone companies to enter the market and enabled the rapid introduction of new technology. Secondly, it was easily embraced in the local economy as another means of creating an income. Nkwi takes the Cameroonian town's uncertain economy as the leading logic behind the boom in mobile phones in Buea. Hierarchies and inequalities are reinforced and introduced with this new economic form that needs to be critically followed. The omnipresent mobile-phone business in the colours of the main providers has formed a new urban landscape and its impact on the local economy can be recognized in other parts of Africa too. The chapters in this book almost all refer to this phenomenon, in particular the chapters on Khartoum (Brinkman & de Bruijn), Zanzibar (Pfaff) and Tanzania (Molony). The international, national and local economic relations connected to the mobile phone are a major topic for future research (Waverman *et al.* 2005). And in this analysis we should not forget that, as was noted in Cameroon, the specific economic environment of local African economies is dictated by the world economy, to which African markets are considered peripheral. African economies are currently relying on foreign companies like MTN, Orange and Zain to develop their phone sectors and without investments from Ericsson and Nokia/Vodaphone these economies will not get off the ground. A political-economy approach to the development of these newly appearing markets is therefore necessary (Yu'a 2004). However what the articles in this book show is that, despite the unequal division of economies, African citizens are indeed appropriating the new technology in their own ways and, as the shopkeeper in Lilly's story explains, the mobile phone may open up new opportunities and create social as well as economic niches.

A booming economy and facilitating research cannot work without people who use mobile phones. But who are the users, the end-users and what do they communicate about and with whom? And what does the phone itself communicate in terms of identity? The phenomenon of the call box is discussed at length in Nkwi's article. People who are in these boxes not only work there but the very fact of being there relates to their social and economic status in the urban society of which they are part. An important discussion in relation to these boxes is the cost of phone communication: it is not cheap and the reason for the boxes' very existence is that they allow the ordinary phone user to call at minimal cost insofar as MTN and Orange allow their credit to be sold cheaply. Nevertheless, it is clear that this new form of communication does indeed rely on the depths of people's purses, which in a shortage economy may introduce newfound anxieties. But there is also another side to this apart from the monetary aspect. The mobile phone entails a specific form of communication, which is why some of the people in the Khartoum case study (Brinkman & De Bruijn) explained that the phone encourages people to lie. No exact information is exchanged, or lies told, about the place or situation of the person called. In the case of trade, this becomes an important aspect of the phone and its use. Thomas Molony, who did research among Tanzanian traders, emphasizes the lack of trust in a phone relationship. His main informant explained that he felt the use of the phone was, in fact, only a handicap in trade relations. This argument relates to the question about whether mobile phone communication fosters continuity or discontinuities in social interactions. For this specific trader it clearly entails such a discontinuity that he does not even embrace it at all. In other instances, such as Lotte Pelckmans's case, phone communication builds upon older practices, like fieldwork, or in the case of Buea's citizens on specific economic forms. Or as in the case of the Cameroonian healer presented by Wouter van Beek, the phone continues the practice of healing but incorporates those who are far away. Thus the phone enables the continuation of economic and social forms as it reshapes them.

Inge Brinkman and Mirjam de Bruijn's chapter presents the case study of Khartoum, Sudan. They give an overview of where the phone does indeed change, shape and continue older forms of social relationships. A clear example of reshaping relationships is in the specific form of gender relations in this Muslim society where men and women are supposed to live in separate spheres. The mobile phone, however, makes communication between the sexes easier, creating a social space where they can meet. It also enables women to organize their lives more independently while still taking the societal norms seriously. Women can call from their houses and meet their (male) friends without others knowing about it. These new practices are generating heated discussions in Khartoum society and are being reported in the media. People have strong opinions about the advantages and disadvantages these new opportunities hold.

Thomas Molony chose to present a trader who is not embracing the new technology in his business, as he holds it is contrary to the 'trade and trust' concept he takes as his leading principle. His argument also involves the other side of the coin: will those who embrace the new technology in their businesses develop new strategies to win the trust of their customers? It is an intriguing question that Molony puts forward by presenting a person who does not like using a mobile phone in business but will those who embrace the phone develop new forms of doing business? Will they ultimately be more successful? Will the core values of an economic relationship between traders and customers change? Molony conducted his study at the beginning of the 21st century and it would be interesting to follow his main informant in his recent decisions regarding mobile phone communication and trade. As already stressed, it is a rapidly growing and flexible process that we are observing.

Ludovic Kibora's study in Burkina Faso makes a comparison between rural and urban areas and focuses on text messaging, which is gaining increasing importance as a form of communication. This is a remarkable development in a society where oral communication is dominant and literacy is still the privilege of the minority, especially in the rural areas. His argument qualifies the existing stereotype about 'oral Africa', a notion that has been used to explain the success of the mobile phone in Africa. Clearly the orality both of Africa and of the mobile phone are overstated as new forms of literacy (i.e. text messages) are being employed in connection with the mobile phone.

Wouter van Beek's chapter is a case study of the appropriation of the mobile phone in healing practices in Cameroon. The mobile phone allows the healer to assist sick people who are originally from his area but are now far away, sometimes even in Europe or the States. It enables them to use the healer's own plants and herbs and to benefit from his precious advice. The mobile phone is a means of communication between the healer and people in distant places and it is also used to arrange payment for the healer for his services via a money transfer. The mobile phone has encouraged the healer and his patients to adopt a certain pattern and control system in the healing process. It is an example of a meeting of the social, the economic and the cultural.

The phone is, in itself, a mediator in society, not only because of its use of language and voice and text messages but as a thing in its own right, it expresses identities in society. Young people fashion the phone in different ways from the older generation. Julia Pfaff's chapter about the life of a phone in Zanzibar is illustrative in this respect. Her approach is based on the geography of things and her biography of the phone shows how they have indeed become social objects. In her chapter, the phone becomes close to being a real actor. It changes identity according to the specific person and the context in which it finds itself, where its social appropriation and vice versa become visible in the object itself: the SIM card it has, the messages sent, its position in the room, etc. We also explicitly encounter a phone culture where the phone becomes time management, an identity, receives names and is turned into a cultural object. In the case of Khartoum, the specific phone culture is ascribed to the urban nature of the culture and the fact that the phone has indeed become part of this urban culture. People cannot live without it, a sentiment evoked by Lilly Loveless. It also shows different uses across the generations as the phone plays a specific role in the life of the youth and in the creation of a youth culture. It was the youth who first embraced the new technology because they are more flexible in acquiring the new knowledge necessary for this technology. The studies in this volume all relate to the phenomenon of youth and technology as these technologies open up new ways of relating and provide access to new information. They also offer a way of acquiring a different identity. In Lilly's narrative, the young shop-keeper is not only young himself and engaged in the phone economy but also refers to the youth and the attraction phones have for them economically and the new ways of social relating they open up. In both Khartoum and Buea these phone reali-ties are being produced by the youth and their relationship with the phone is ex-plicit.

Jenna Burrell's chapter on youth in Ghana reminds us of another technology that has helped pave the way for phone technology, i.e. the Internet (cf. Miller & Slater 2000). She describes how the youth in Ghana are the city's Internet cafés' main visitors and their use of the Internet and their presence in this social space are interpreted as a manifestation of their youth culture. In these social spaces the youth meet, chat and formulate ideas about themselves and their identities and connecting to the other world and to faraway places has become an important notion.

The chapter on youth in Ghana and their Internet use refers to another impor-tant aspect of this new technology. Both the mobile phone and the Internet are technologies for connecting (or disconnecting) and as such they are related to forms of mobility. As Burrell shows, this relationship is problematic as mobility is not the same as being connected. It is also not true that these technologies are only being used to connect. Many elements are highlighted that relate to identities and social relations that are evolving within the immediate environment: new economic and social relations. The aspect of being hooked up, connected to another faraway world may also come into this picture but may not be the most important issue for the youth. Linking up via the Internet is however an important part of Ghanaian youth's frequent visits to Internet cafés and they do so in a variety of ways. Burrell shows that diversity in linking is related to the youth's possibilities for travel, such as during their studies, while for the majority it is related to ideas and anxieties and the wish to be linked to and ultimately part of that other world as an alternative to one's own world. It is like the example of the bushfallers in the story of Lilly Loveless. The bushfaller phenomenon is a story of anxieties but also of hopelessness among the youth in times of economic uncertainty, that finds its parallel in Burrell's ac-count of the youth and their Internet use in Ghana.

The chapters in this volume all show aspects of mobile phone and Internet cul-ture in so-called marginal societies, be it the linkage between the rural and the urban in Burkina Faso, the world of Khartoum's women, the youth in Ghana, traders in Zanzibar and Tanzania (who may not be marginal but are certainly mobile) or eco-nomic linkages as in the Cameroonian case. In all of these, we observe a reshaping of social relations in terms of continuities and discontinuities. Mobile technology does indeed change ideas about distance but it is also reshaping social and economic hierarchies in society. It may connect one where it disconnects another.

References

BARBER, K. (1991), *I could speak until tomorrow. Oriki, Women and the past in a Yoruba Town*, Edinburgh: Edinburgh University Press.

CASTELLS, M., M. FERNÁNDEZ-ARDÈVOL, J. LINCHUAN QIU & A. SEY (2007), *Mobile communication and society, A global perspective*, Cambridge, MA: MIT Press.

DIBAKANA J-A. (2002), 'Usages sociaux du téléphone portable et nouvelles sociabilités au Congo', *Politique Africaine* (85): 133-48.

GITELMAN, L. & G.B. PINGREE, eds, (2003), 'Introduction: What's new about new media?' In: L. Gitelman & G.B. Pingree, eds, *New Media, 1740-1915*, Cambridge: MIT Press, pp. xi-xxii.

GOGGIN, G. (2006), *Cell phone culture: Mobile technology in everyday life*, London: Routledge.

HAHN, H.P. & L. KIBORA (2008), 'The domestication of the mobile phone: Oral society and new ICT in Burkina Faso', *Journal of Modern African Studies* 46(1): 87-109.

HORST, H.A. & D. MILLER (2005), 'From kinship to link-up. Cell phones and social networking in Jamaica', *Current Anthropology* 46(5).

HORST, H.A. & D. MILLER (2006), *The Cell Phone: An Anthropology of Communication*, London/New York: Berg.

KATZ, J.E. (2006), *Magic in the air. Mobile communication and the transformation of social life*, New Brunswick, NJ: Transaction Publishers.

MILLER, D. & D. SLATER (2000), *The Internet: An ethnographic approach*, Oxford: Berg.

NYAMNJOH, F.B. (2009), *Married but available*, Bamenda: Langaa.

NYAMNJOH, F.B. (forthcoming) 'Notions of Bushfalling and Bushfallers in Cameroonian Diasporic Discourses'.

NYAMNJOH, F.B. (2005), 'Images of Nyongo amongst Bamenda grassfielders in Whiteman Kontri', *Citizenship Studies* 9(3): 241-69.

SMITH, D.J. (2006), 'Cell phones, social inequality and contemporary culture in Nigeria', *Canadian Journal of African Studies* 40(3): 496-523.

WAVERMAN, L. ,M. MESCHI & M. FUSS (2005), 'The impact of telecoms on economic growth in developing countries, moving the debate forward,' Vodafone Policy Paper Series No. 3.

YU'A, Y.Z. (2004), 'The new imperialism and Africa in the new electronic village', *Review of African Political Economy* 31(99): 11-29.

2

Phoning anthropologists:
The mobile phone's (re-)shaping
of anthropological research

Lotte Pelckmans

Never has so small a device been used so easily
by so many to do so much to so many
(Katz 2006: 129)

Communication technologies are increasingly playing a significant role in social and cultural interaction. Studies on the impact of information and communication technologies (ICTs) on social life are emerging but focus mainly on western, urban contexts. With their inspiring study about the use of the cell phone in Jamaica, Horst & Miller (2006) called for an anthropology of communication, an innovative field that needs more elaboration. However, their study focuses on 'Others' as communicators. But what about the interaction between those others and their researchers as mediated by the phone? This seems to have been ignored. So far, there has been no analysis of the impact of the mobile phone on anthropological research as such.[1] This chapter aims to address the consequences of the social appropriation of the mobile phone by both informants and researchers as end-users.

---

[1] The same goes for the impact of the landline phone on doing research. I have not seen any studies on this subject. Apparently these technologies to date have not been considered worthy of study in relation to research methods.

Research on virtual ethnography and the use of virtual methods in ethnography has been conducted (Miller & Slater 2000, Hine 2002, 2005, Horst 2002) but the focus has been on the Internet, text and virtuality, thus mainly on computers even though Internet access is significantly lower in most developing countries than access to mobile phones. Direct oral contact with people while on the move – a very specific feature of the mobile phone – is completely different from research within the textual and often place-bound context of the Internet. The need is, therefore, to study the potential changes to ways of interacting with informants and changes to traditional research methods as a result of the social appropriation of the mobile phone by social scientists.

'Many anthropologists maintain more or less continuous contact with one or some handful of informants by way of letter, telephone or E-mail' (Hannerz 1998: 249). This highlights how technological tools are increasingly channelling communication with anthropologists' informants. Global contact and communication has become dependent on such channelling tools and since 2000 many developing countries have appropriated a new communication tool: the mobile phone. As everywhere, landline phones preceded mobile phones and the phenomenon of being able to call or to be called is not new but the scale of mobile phone use is much larger than landline use. Comparison with the landline would therefore be inappropriate as the number of people having access to them and being affected is extremely different. In addition, the mobile phone has several extra qualities outweighing landline phones, with its nomadic aspect being probably the most appreciated.

Phone use in my multi-sided fieldwork on the (social) mobility of the Fulbe in rural, urban and transnational contexts has allowed me to connect with informants in new places anywhere and at any time.[2] Using the phone during fieldwork has made me aware of multiple and fluid social interpretations, practices and uses related to a seemingly universal object we call the mobile phone.[3] In the vein of Appadurai's study on the 'social life of things' (1986) in which the differences in the social lives of commodities are attributed to their appropriation in specific 'regimes of values', this chapter looks at the social life of the mobile phone not as a commodity but rather as a technology, a tool that can shape human interaction and communication. To put it simply, I will elaborate on the social life of phone-mediated communication and analyze how this shapes[4] research contexts and anthropological

---

[2] My communication by phone went up from just one contact with an informant maintained via landline communication in 2000 to at least half of my contacts, which were established and maintained via mobile phone from 2005 onwards. (Mobile phone networks first emerged in Mali in 2002).

[3] See Klein & Pinch (1996) for examples of social appropriations of the internal combustion engine designed for the motorcar. Also De Laet & Mol (2000) on 'fluid' meanings and interpretations of the Zimbabwe Bush Pump.

[4] The use of the mobile phone has several shaping potentials that work in two directions: the phone shapes and is being shaped by the researcher, his/her methodology and practices.

knowledge more generally. Most data referred to in this chapter are based on personal fieldwork experiences[5] and a modest email survey among colleagues.[6]

Trying to grapple with the changes the mobile phone has brought about in both the practice and production of anthropological knowledge, it would seem important to define the starting point from which these so-called changes are measured. This is, however, a complex endeavour in that the impact of ICT over the last few decades has often been reinforced by other parallel processes such as improvements in infrastructure and worldwide communication, and lower prices for travel in general. However, a main trend in the changes in anthropological research over the past decades is related to increased access to alternative and multiple fields. 'Access is perhaps the key issue, in so far as it conveys the notion of movement in space and time and the material, institutional and intellectual contraptions a given subject is in a position to embody' (Sökefeld & Warnier 2008: 222). The changes and shaping effects of the mobile phone discussed in this chapter cannot be separated from the broader socio-economic processes of an increasingly globalizing world.

Each section, however, takes an integral part of the anthropological encounter as its point of departure for discussing changes. The first section describes changes in relations as channelled by the phone in social life more generally since it is impossible to completely separate the impact of phone use on fieldwork from the general impact on social life. The second and third sections focus on changes in anthropological practice (methods) and theory (epistemology) respectively. Changes in the practice of anthropology are central to the second section: using the phone as a tool in data collection generates advantageous methodological alternatives to older techniques. Nevertheless, the possible disadvantages of phone-mediated information should not be ignored and are framed in classic ethnographic problems of authority and ethics. In the final section, epistemological changes as a result of time and space compression through mobile phone use are considered. The conclusion addresses the main question of reflexivity and whether and how anthropological research and knowledge production shape or are being shaped by appropriating the mobile phone in research communication.

---

[5] Fieldwork in Mali: six months in 2000-2001, 2005-2006 and 2007. Data about phone use in Mali was gathered by interviews with local people and marketing specialists from the phone companies Malitel and Orange in Bamako, June 2007.

[6] A written survey asking about anthropologists' personal experiences with their use of mobile phones in various fields on various continents.

Absent relating: The mobile phone's shaping of social relations

*In an interconnected world, we are never really 'out of the field'.
We take our 'home' with us when we do research: in our background,
our education, our social position*
(Gupta & Ferguson 1997: 35)

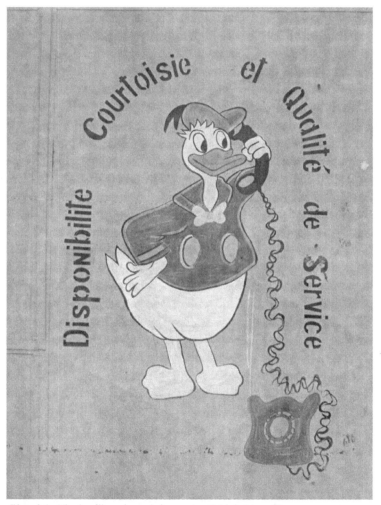

Photo 2.1   The landline phone is becoming "old-fashioned".

This section describes the shaping effects of the mobile phone as a 'total social phenomenon', impacting on many aspects of people's social life. Local cultural changes in social-relating practices necessarily bring about changes in the anthropological encounter too as the ethnographer is there, building up social relationships as everyone else does. Ways of relating to each other differ significantly from context to context and mobile phone communication does too (Horst & Miller 2006). In addition to the general shaping effects the mobile phone has brought about worldwide, in this section I briefly offer some examples of (cultural) differences in the local appropriation of mobile phones (e.g. flashing).

A general realm that has definitely been reshaped by the use of mobile phones relates to increased feelings of safety. Many acknowledge that the mobile phone has rendered certain situations safer and more practical. Cars breaking down in the middle of the desert are no longer life-threatening experiences. Before, one would have had to wait until a person happened to drive by (which in the worst-case scenario might have been days) but nowadays it is a question of simply phoning the nearest village and asking someone to bring a spare part to fix the car. Female researchers stress increased feelings of safety and are happier when taking taxis and make appointments after dusk because they have their cell phone to rely on should things go wrong. They are now less dependent on a male companion to accompany them. Katz (2006: 18) talks about 'personal empowerment: people can feel safer in public places. It has expanded the locales and times that people, especially women, can go, thus increasing people's freedom and mobility.'

Understanding socio-cultural ideas about public versus private spheres is a challenge. Most western researchers are socialized with the idea that while 'working' or discussing professional issues, their phone should be turned off unless the user is expecting an important call and announces this beforehand. Interpretations of the places and contexts in which the phone is allowed to intrude and can be used without offence differ from one cultural context to another.[7] My local host in Bamako was so often on her mobile phone that it was difficult to get to talk to her other than by phoning her, which is what I ended up doing if I needed to discuss something.[8] In extreme cases, the phone paradoxically renders access more difficult instead of facilitating it.

Professional life abroad seems to have been facilitated by mobile phone penetration. One reason why people experience phone presence as facilitation is because

---

[7] Studies by Cumiskey (2007), an American social psychologist, have shown that in America, in general, what is experienced as positive mobile phone use is phone use that facilitates face-to-face interaction and does not exclude those present. Negative mobile phone use is associated with use that excludes the person present and that indicates the user would much prefer to be spending time with the caller. I am confident that the same research would yield different results for Mali.

[8] There were four ways to try and reach her: on her Malitel number, on her Orange number (cheaper for calls abroad), on her landline phone and/or through Skype (she got connected to the Internet in December 2006). Some people even used to try to reach her on her best friend's phone because he is often around and would pass messages on to her. Even leaving a message on her voice mail was impossible, as more often than not it would be full.

they can keep in touch with their home situation. A university teacher[9] supervising students on fieldwork made the following remark: 'Fieldwork has become completely different for my students now that they are able to be in perpetual contact with home. This brings with it a structural existential and irrevocable change in the identity of the anthropologist/fieldworker.' Another anthropologist who often has undergraduate students on the first weeks of their fieldwork, remarked that before the introduction of the mobile phone, these first weeks were frequently difficult and the students felt alone and isolated in their new environment. Landline phones were expensive and complicated (the line would be bad or simply did not work).[10] These days, worried mothers can reach their 'poor child' in 'poor Mali' any time of the day to give them a pep talk and stay in touch. An interesting metaphor related to this perpetuity of contact with one's social network is quoted from Palen, Salzman & Youngs (2001) in Geser (2004: 12): the mobile phone as an 'umbilical cord'.[11]

Does the maintenance of this umbilical cord have consequences for the ethnographer's immersion and engagement with the local field context? Is 'going native' a practice doomed to disappear? Or does perpetual contact, on the contrary, constitute a positive development that stimulates the maintenance of personal balance for researchers, enabling them to put certain fieldwork situations into perspective and make a sharper analysis of them. There is the risk that maintenance of this umbilical cord might undermine people's self reliance, making them unable to operate alone and leaving them dependent on their phone as a source of assistance and advice. One is less exposed to the vagaries of chance and unlikely to be thrown onto one's own resources or to encounter adventure, surprise or the happiest of accidents.[12] In the end, it seems to be a double-edged sword and phone use might result in more and/or less involvement with/in the field and with the world more generally.

A topical example of local context-shaping phone use in, for example, West Africa is the practice of 'flashing' (in French: *biper*). It entails calling someone with the sole purpose of making the phone ring, without expecting the other person to answer. A Malian phone credit seller explained that flashing could be compared to

---

[9] Man, 45, cultural anthropologist, Francophone, West Africa.

[10] In 2001-2002, I often spent hours waiting at the *cabine telephonique* for my family to phone me.

[11] 'The cell phone now serves to cushion traumatic experiences in a foreign environment by remaining tightly connected to loved ones at home. Thus the mobile phone can function as a 'pacifier for adults' (Geser 2004: 12). Businessmen admit that because of the increasing possibilities to phone and be phoned 'Dark Africa' feels safer and less threatening, which is a very serious argument to encourage increasing engagement with Africa. Accessing Africa has become a more feasible and viable option. Penetration by companies is currently on the increase.

[12] Some of the people interviewed in Tokyo by Plant (2000: 62 and quoted in Geser 2004: 13) felt that there was now less chance that time would be spent standing and staring, for example, at the cherry blossom and being alone with one's thoughts or inner resources, which slows down the whole process of partial disconnection from one's own culture that a person needs to start orienting him/herself towards the new local culture, whatever and wherever that might be.

tapping someone's shoulder or winking at them as it is a means of confirming and/or reminding the other person that you are friends (*qu'on est ensemble*). Flashing is a practice that puzzles many foreigners at first as it is embedded in a context of different economic resources tied up with ideas about reciprocity, such as who takes care of or is in charge of whom (cf. Hahn & Kibora 2008: 95). For a researcher to engage in these practices, it is important to interpret them in relation to the (re)production of power relations. Depending on the social context of social hierarchies, flashing or being flashed can thus take on different meanings.

In Mali when someone flashes someone who is clearly better off, more often than not the flash is no longer a metaphorical 'digital blink' but should be interpreted as a request to phone back. The one considered to have money at his disposal is thus put in the position of the 'credit caretaker'. Just like migrants in Europe and local elites, researchers are considered wealthy in many research contexts and are therefore subject to numerous flashes. Some flashers are so persistent that new strategies to avoid them have emerged: taking several numbers with different companies, changing one's phone number regularly or giving a wrong number.[13] The cultural understanding and embodiment of flashing practices is a fascinating example of how the researcher is being shaped by phone use in the context s/he is living in. Flashing practices definitely influence and (re)produce power relations among people. It is a continual process and impacts beyond the fieldwork period provided one does not consciously withdraw from keeping in touch.[14]

Social hierarchies reveal not only *who* is in charge of phone credit but also *how* credit is purchased and exchanged. The redistribution of resources in families is – apart from food, transport and clothing – increasingly about the allocation of phone credit. Being such a central commodity, phone credit enters the realm of gift exchange. Further research on the redefinition of gift exchanges as mediated by phone would be interesting.[15]

Social hierarchies define what is discussed online and are related to people's social position. 'An important principle deriving from the particular tradition of orality is the hierarchisation of speech' (Hahn & Kibora 1998: 101, see also Ong 1992). Social hierarchies are translated not only in content (what can be discussed) but also by whom. Thus as a young, unmarried woman in Mali I was not always in a position to contact people directly. Someone might call a new informant he wanted me to meet about my research, thus facilitating my first phone-mediated appointment. Hosts can be very direct concerning their expectations about being informed of someone's whereabouts. Failing to do so is failing to respect your 'caregiver' and

---

[13] For examples of migrant coping strategies when dealing with persistent fellow countrymen, see Nyamnjoh (2005) and Diome (2003).

[14] After leaving Mali, those who consistently flashed me were also the ones I phoned and kept in touch with. They effectively ensured that I would not forget them.

[15] In general and more specifically, the shifts in gift exchanges between researchers and informants.

is a serious offence. In principle, the obligation to greet and maintain contact lies with those who are in an inferior status position, as is keeping in touch by phone. The transaction costs are, however, likely to be redistributed to those in positions of superior status.

An example of how a researcher's phone behaviour can be (re)shaped in spectacular ways by informants and vice versa is, for example, that as I write, I am receiving a text message from a Malian friend who tells me he is travelling to his native village (where I once stayed). If it was not for the low cost of the text message, the availability of the mobile phone on the road and his interest in keeping me posted, my friend would never have informed me, in Europe, of something while in the process of doing it.[16] Inversely, a fellow researcher[17] described how it was that by coming back home he became aware of his need to live up to the expectations of communicating with his Ghanaian informants. 'Ghanaians phone each other for nothing other than the sake of phoning and asking how you are. By doing this too, I improved my relationship with informants, also after I was no longer in the field. At the same time it creates a lot of expectations: I spent relatively a lot of time in maintaining contacts and people did not like it when I did not phone them for a week, even when I was back home in Holland.' Once home, this researcher found that continuing this way of communicating became much more difficult, as new demands obviously emerge from the changed context of price (expensive airtime), time (availability) and affinity (which tends to diminish over time when one is less grounded in shared experiences).

Since it is impossible to separate the impact of phone use on fieldwork from its general impact on social life, I have addressed some general changes and processes of phone-related shapings of relatedness in the anthropological encounter. The mobile phone is gradually becoming a tool of changing access to people and generates new forms of relating through appropriation in the economic realm (e.g. flashing, credit distribution), the socio-cultural realm (e.g. reshaping hierarchies and private-public division) and the personal realm (feelings of safety). These general changes also impact on fieldwork and anthropologists' ways of relating more concretely.

The phone as a research assistant shaping logistics and authority

How did the phone alter anthropological research practices? To be able to highlight these changes, I first define the practice of the anthropological encounter, i.e. fieldwork, in which participant observation is a central method. Fieldwork is a shared space of encounter in which self and the other emerge in mutual reflection and interaction (cf. Sokefeld & Warnier 2008: 224). Participation (often participant ob-

---

[16] In 2001 before the arrival of the mobile phone network, I would probably only have found out about his visit by discussing it face to face retrospectively on his return.
[17] Man, 27, cultural anthropologist, Anglophone, West Africa.

servation) is and will always remain a basic requirement of such an encounter, as it necessarily consists of a performative[18] mode of knowing[19] in which face-to-face contact is crucial. Although much has changed in ideas about fieldwork, with many 'variations on the regulative ideals of Malinowskian first field work' (Fabian quoted in Marcus & Okely 2007: 353), 'classic fieldwork has been increasingly interpreted as a variable component of a broader process of research' (Ibid.: 354) remaining 'a core modality' that should be relativized in terms of its functions and a blurring of its beginning and end (Ibid.: 355).

The advantages and disadvantages of phone-mediated research are questioned in this section and compared to those of face-to-face contact. Firstly, the advantages of new and/or changing methodologies and concrete research practices as a result of increased phone use are discussed and then the shaping of authority in information exchange is considered and leads to reflections on the possible disadvantages of phone use, raising questions about the ethics of online information and communication.

Phone-mediated methodologies and practice

What new phone-mediated methodologies are emerging as a result of phone use in research? What are the surplus options generated by the the mobile phone as an all-in-one technical device, physical object and multiple tool? An interview can be recorded anywhere, at any time and there is no longer any need to take any extra equipment. The phone has great potential as a recording, receiving and broadcasting tool. A researcher can record a seminar or speech in one place and broadcast it in another context to obtain feedback from informants. Mobile phones host many more applications than just telephony and generate new and flashy social-archiving practices for symbolic (love letters, showing how much attention you get with a full SMS box) as well as practical purposes (address books, transporting texts with a USB stick, storing music and pictures).

Regarding the advantages of phone use for concrete research practices, the introduction of the mobile phone has made it easier to obtain access, establish new contacts and get back to people without taking buses, cabs or motorcycles. On field trips in the past, a researcher had to meet people in person to check their availability for an interview.[20] These days, anyone can provide anybody with a phone number and contact people directly. Thus the mobile phone has the potential to significantly reshape a network of informants. Especially in an urban context where distances are time-consuming, this partial replacement of a research assistant by a mobile phone

---

[18] Performance, Fabian (1990: xv) argues, is not what they do and we observe, as we are both engaged in it.

[19] Both reflexivity and coevalness (sharing time with interlocutors on equal terms) are inherent to this performative way of knowing (cf. Fabian 1990: 4-10).

[20] During my fieldwork in Mali in 2007, at least two-thirds of my appointments were made by phone.

certainly has advantages.[21] However, this is not to say that everything has changed. One still needs an interpreter or assistant to know how to get somewhere and for (socio-cultural) advice on how to approach certain people. Meeting and visiting someone still adds more value to the kind of contact established, mutual respect and knowledge about each other.

From this 'phone-as-a-research-assistant' example it follows that the upfront implication of mobile phones as new methodological tools for doing research is likely to generate new forms of bias. Phone users are in the category of the 'haves' and conducting research with phone users alone risks bias and little contact with the phoneless who are barely benefiting from the coming of the 'phone age'.[22] These so-called 'mobile losers' are finding themselves even more excluded than before. If the phone is to be considered as a (digital) research assistant, it definitely excludes the people not accessed.[23] Conducting research in an urban environment I caught myself postponing appointments with those who did not have a phone and I stayed in touch more frequently with those who had a phone. As phone owners became brokers for the phoneless, they put their stamp on my network of informants. This bias illustrates the importance of a conscious evaluation of the shaping effects of the mobile phone on research methodology.

The mobile phone shapes the researcher as a research assistant would: it is through differences in social appropriations of the mobile phone that the researcher and his/her work are continuously being moulded, resulting in paradoxes of availability and expectations of intrusion. The phone can be seen as an irritating intruder in face-to-face communication once an appointment has been made and an interview has started because subjects discussed before a call are not likely to be picked up on again later. Nevertheless, these intrusions can also turn into an asset as particular topics may arise as a result of the intrusive call. Intrusions can be advantageous because they can result in unexpected data about (intimate) relations between friends and sometimes result in new informants.[24] Lastly, in an interview setting, the

---

[21] Even then, a minimum of trust is required to be given a phone number.

[22] Only 200 million people on the African continent are connected and this leaves 700 million potential African users still to be connected.[22] This so-called 'digital divide' (e.g. Miller (forthcoming) is central in the ICT for Development) discussion.

[23] This bias could also work the other way around. There are researchers who cannot use a mobile phone due to lack of coverage, others consciously do not use a mobile phone when in the field because they stick to a romantic notion about fieldwork. A colleague explained how a local contact convinced him of the importance of the mobile phone, which he used for the first time in Africa and only then started using at home. 'My local contact person asked for my mobile phone number, only to find out that I didn't have one. He convinced me that one cannot be in Africa without having a mobile phone because "if you don't have a phone here some people might consider you unreliable (as a researcher)."'

[24] For example, I got to know some of my informants because of a phone conversation I witnessed between him and his friends. Boubacar lived in Paris from 2005 to 2007 when he was in his twenties. In 2006 I was present at a phone conversation in Bamako between him (in Paris) and his Malian friends. As the phone was connected to speakers, everyone in the vicinity was able to participate in their conversation. Boubacar sounded depressed and told his friends that he had decided to return to Mali. In 2007 when I was in Mali,

phone can be a convenient medium to check information or discuss what is happening in different locations at the same time. Absence-presence and intrusion are shaping effects of the phone on the content and direction of interview settings.

The mobile phone and other digital media have increased the options and possibilities of obtaining information. Through these technologies, initiative has become more within the reach of local informants. It is no longer the researcher deciding who, why and where to phone. Locals can get back to the researcher more easily (and for free by flashing), so feedback, sudden events, ideas, suggestions and questions about the research topic can be added by local informants. This opens up a whole field of related questions such as when, why and how people can be or feel disconnected. Who has the final or main authority over the data? And does the local initiative of 'speaking back' significantly affect the dialectical quality of our information?

New clusters of information are readily available on the phone as an information source in itself. Recorded (voice) archives in phones can be used to obtain on-the-spot interpretations and reactions to (sensitive) issues. Data about people's networks and social ties are now more easily accessible than ever before by resorting to their address book. Discussing who is in it, why, and the frequency and purpose of contact with this or that person can offer insight into many aspects of a person's social life.[25] Here it is essential for the researcher to pause and reflect on the ethics of the issue: can and should we inquire about private information?

Another point that comes up is the volatility of oral communication. As opposed to the advantages the mobile phone offers for archiving SMS messages and pictures or voice recordings, the oral information exchanged during phone calls is extremely volatile and is hardly ever recorded literally. One might worry about the current non-reproduction of state archives since enormous amounts of information that policy makers are currently discussing by phone will never be traceable again and will render 'slimmer' archives. Personally I regret not having kept all my SMS messages and even a complete list of calls so that I could have quantified some of my impressions for this chapter.

Concentration in face-to-face settings is more likely to be reshaped by phone presence. People may seemingly be at an event or socially engaged but their attention is elsewhere. Gergen (2002) labelled the intermediate form between not and fully communicating with the phone in the presence of others (e.g. checking an SMS or scrolling the menu, or playing a game) as 'absence presence'. An informant and/or interpreter checking or writing text messages will obviously be concentrating less on the contents of an interview.

I met up with Boubacar, who in the meantime had returned to Mali and decided not to go back to France anymore, despite pressure from his peers, as I had witnessed during their call.

25 For a concrete ethnographic example of this technique, see Horst & Miller (2006: 89-101).

Finally, the supervision and management of students conducting face-to-face interviews in the field by a supervising researcher in another location has become easier thanks to the mobile phone. The supervising researcher in Europe can guide and teach local people in the field by giving tips, hints and advice from a distance. However, here again, problems relating to anonymity and the difficulty of framing the context on the other side of the line should not be underestimated. The need for concrete face-to-face in addition to oral phone contact often seems to remain for optimizing contextual understanding.

Shaping the authority of the message: Challenges faced by phone information exchange

> ... the one concept that often remains outside the debates on anthropological knowledge: information. (...) What has not been given sufficient consideration is that about large areas and important aspects of culture no one, not even the native, has information that can simply be called up and expressed in discursive statements. This sort of knowledge can be represented – made present – only through action, enactment, or performance. (Fabian 1990: 6)

What would happen if information was solely obtained through online communication? Can we do without the face-to-face exchange of information so essential to the anthropological encounter and participant observation in the field? What is lost and what is gained in terms of the quality of information received from online communication? Because the road to information production-in-context is so central to the anthropological endeavour, it is crucial to map the effect of the mobile phone on the reshaping of authority of information as precisely as possible.

> Travel has played an important part in the construction of an ethnographic authority. (...) The concept of travel still plays an important part in distinguishing ethnography from other analytic approaches. (Hine 2000: 44)

Increasingly research is taking place exclusively online, thus reducing researchers' mobility and the need for travel. The change from real-time and long-time engagement with informants to online engagement at specific (short) moments demands a conscious evaluation of what the minimal requirements are for anthropological fieldwork. Hine (2000: 21) describes how the application of the ethnographic approach to an online setting is challenging the classis ethos of long-term anthropological engagement. 'The selectivity of these approaches [in online settings] goes against the ethnographic ethos of engagement with events as they happen in the field, and of a holistic attention to all practices as constitutive of a distinct culture.' The advantage that these new forms of online communication offer for doing research when used in addition to classical fieldwork are obvious: '... the use of different ways of observing and communicating with participants provides a kind of triangulation through which observations can be cross-checked' (*Ibid.*: 21).

Online communication mediated by phone necessarily reduces information to purely oral statements, which inevitably entails a loss of social cues.[26] One of the main methods and differences of anthropological methods compared to those employed in the other social sciences is the emphasis on participant observation as it enables inclusion of visual and performative aspects of communication. If three-quarters of all human communication is non-verbal, it is clear that visual, gestural and behavioural features are highly valued in anthropology as providing complementary information. The artificial separation that is created between the verbal and the visual in phone communication is the price one pays for the speed and availability of information. Most of the researchers surveyed were not convinced that information obtained by phone was viable.[27] For reasons mentioned above, they prefer face-to-face instead of phone-to-phone contact. As a colleague[28] said, 'I am very old-fashioned. I never phone to obtain additional information. I want to be there myself: seeing is believing.'

Besides the loss of social cues that generate a kind of distrust of phone-mediated information, there seems to be a more general fear of technology. In their evaluation of phone communication, most of the researchers I interviewed stressed the inappropriateness or even negative impact of the phone as a mediator in such a complex domain as intercultural communication. Whether such fears are grounded remains to be seen and mainly depends on one's position regarding what the basic qualities and requirements for understanding are thought to be and what is deemed good anthropological research.

Paradoxically, the loss of social cues that comes with face-to-face contact[29] makes online phone communication more interesting when some degree of anonymity is required to discuss sensitive issues and private matters. Another advantage of anonymity is that it helps avoid socially desirable answers. Online (phone) conversation can convey a greater sense of security when discussing personal matters, sometimes even more so than face-to-face interaction. Information exchanged online might thus become more personal and less socially desirable. A Malian journalist-researcher told me that since the arrival of the mobile phone, he has had many more reactions (both positive and negative) to his articles

---

[26] Horst (2004: 153) discusses the advantages of not knowing the class, gender, age, etc. of the people participating in her research on transnational communities.

[27] There is indeed the possibility of role playing, which can work two ways: fooling or being fooled by the researcher.

[28] Man, 46, social scientist/agronomist, West Africa.

[29] In a path-breaking study of the social reception of the telephone in the United States, Carolyn Marvin (1988) demonstrated that Victorian-era Americans believed, justifiably, that the telephone reduced social cues ordinarily conveyed in the richer channels of face-to-face interaction and written correspondence. By masking cues, such as the location and social status of the caller, the telephone denied important cues that assist in making judgments about the interlocutor. It is thus easier to violate social and legal codes. These concerns remain valid even after a century of telephone use and have arisen again with contemporary communication technology such as the mobile phone and the Internet.

on controversial issues. The phone offered his critics the chance to remain anonymous (sometimes distorting their voice) but nevertheless to have their say. For them, the information provided could only be given on condition of anonymity, which is guaranteed by the option of phoning privately.

Yet another advantage for the quality of information conveyed is that while using a mobile phone, unlike public phones in public places (in a shop, on the street), one can avoid intrusive background noise, so intimacy during phone calls is generally likely to increase. Discussing intimate issues is less difficult when using a mobile phone compared to a public phone. On a mobile phone, a user can separate him/-herself from the social context s/he is in and be on his/her own.[30] In Mali until a few years ago one had to discuss issues with people living in the same city on a land-line phone in a phone booth with the manager sitting right there. The mobile phone has rendered private conversations in relative privacy more feasible.

A central aspect that either facilitates or constrains (the quality of) information sharing, is language. Language is often a barrier for researchers in foreign countries. Language skills and literacy are important technologies themselves in, for example, the ability to make use of SMS texting facilities. In countries with low literacy rates, the use of text messages is low (Hahn & Kibora 2008: 92). On the phone, high-level skills in language proficiency probably result in higher social capital mobilization by phone. Weak language skills are more noticeable and make communication even more difficult if solely mediated by phone.

There is a clear difference in the information obtained through written SMS or mobile phone conversations: messages differ not only in content (length) and form (language) but also in the emotions they trigger. Voice contact has a greater capacity to articulate personal emotions and the relevance of phone contact is especially high when connecting with absent family members and close friends (Sawhney & Gomez 2000 in Geser 2004). SMS in general allows for more audacity. Plant (2000) also points to fewer risks of embarrassment through the use of SMS. As with email and other written sources, SMS can also lead to (interpretative) misunderstandings.

As far as costs go, oral phone conversations tend to be expensive but are in most cases cheaper than a few years ago. Do the costs affect the speed at which these conversations are held and might this result in oversimplified information being given? Some anthropologists[31] believe the opposite to be true: 'Conversations are much more to the point on the phone because people don't want to waste credit. The information therefore becomes much more structured. Of course, you miss all the non-verbal signals. I myself have never done interviews over the phone but I have used it for updates and additional information.' On the other hand, other phone applications can significantly reduce costs. Filming, photographing and re-

---

[30] With the exception of mobile phones that are offered as a service in a kind of public (mobile) phone box.
[31] Man, age 27, cultural anthropologist, Anglophone West Africa.

cording with a mobile phone have made it possible for local African researchers and journalists to become mobile reporters.[32] The fact that they are on the spot and can obtain information digitally allows them to be the first to deliver to media centres and contribute to reporting from remote areas. This in turn makes more varied information available to researchers who cooperate with local informants and journalists.

Once again, it is important to stress that while the quality of information obtained by phone is not necessarily less, one needs to re-contextualize it more consciously. For the purpose of mutual understanding, the value of understanding the social appropriation and shaping effects of the phone on social interaction cannot be underestimated. According to a colleague: [33]

> The researcher should be consciously asking himself questions such as: 'Who sent the message and under what circumstances? How much can s/he show of him/herself in an SMS message and at what social and financial cost? What is the local culture of text messaging about (or not about) and where does this particular message fit in? What were the person's emotions at the moment of sending the SMS? Why did s/he send it at this particular moment or was it coincidence? ... Thus a whole new ethic is emerging. Students who go on fieldwork ask me whether or not they can phone someone to establish a first contact or whether an SMS would be more appropriate. And when using SMS: what should they write and what are the opening words they should use? These kinds of questions definitely demand a new methodology that depends on the cultural context in which an anthropologist is conducting research.

Indeed, new questions arise about what is ethical when using a phone as a research assistant and as a gateway to information. Accessing the archives of someone else's mobile phone might be interesting but what is acceptable and ethical? In other words, how close is your contact with a person allowed to be? What is private and what is not? Can researchers use data by buying used prepaid cards from companies? What about SMS messages that are sent to TV programmes? Is their content valuable and can it be considered public information that scientists can use without additional consent? Is it ethical to ask people to show their contacts in address books and ask them to display their SMS messages? These questions can only be answered if the anthropologist is aware of and sensitive to local socio-cultural ideas about information exchange when attempting to obtain informed consent.[34]

---

[32] cf. http://www.africanews.com/site/list_messages/10175

[33] Male colleague, aged 38, cultural anthropologist, South-East Asia.

[34] In Mali local friends used to show me their text messages (mostly about love). I did not feel comfortable sharing this intimate information with them because it created expectations that I felt unable to reciprocate. In my opinion, a text message contains private information that one might consider reading out in exceptional cases but actually showing such a message to others feels excessive. These are perhaps subtle differences in culture which nevertheless impact on social interaction and interpretations of meaning.

Connecting through space and time:
From the stone age to the phone age? [35]

> *However, the field can never be just a physical site. It is in the head, whole body and beyond*
> *one designated locality. Too often the construction of the field as time and space bounded is the*
> *invention of those who would declassify anthropological fieldwork conducted in the West or in*
> *the anthropologists own country.*
>
> (Okely in Marcus & Okely 2007: 360)

In addition to the changes in fieldwork practices described above, we should consider changes in the epistemology of anthropological theory as a result of phone use.
The production of anthropological knowledge is doubly relational: it attaches itself
to relations between people and objects and it emerges from a dialogical field (cf.
Hastrup 2004).[36] Since anthropological knowledge (theory) is fundamentally embedded in its epistemology[37] rather than in its object,[38] the need to analyze its
shaping through tools such as the mobile phone becomes all the more pertinent. In
other words, if our knowledge production is relational (an encounter of subjectivities), then analyzing the channelling of related subjectivities through ICT, such as
the mobile phone, is crucial. Mobile phone use in research inevitably demands re-
visiting moral ideas about what constitutes good ethnographic knowledge.

The rise of ICT may be making this issue more important but with an additional
twist. Besides self-reflection on interaction between the researcher and the informant and methods of information gathering, it seems equally, if not more,
important to pay attention to the research tools that mediate our (self-)reflections
since these tools are agents (shapers) in themselves. The question is whether the
increasing simultaneity of time and space created by using mobile phones[39] is
contributing to the increased inclusion of the Other in anthropological writings
(ethnography). Or are we, on the contrary, at risk of becoming armchair anthropologists, no longer travelling because we maintain contact by phone instead of

---

[35] 'From the Stone Age to the Phone Age' is the title of Sadie Plant's study in the 'On the Mobile' project
conducted for Motorola.

[36] 'If in fieldwork the anthropologist gets to know by way of social relations, this relational aspect has more
general bearing on the processes by which facts are established as relevant in the first place. Ontology and
epistemology converge in anthropology' (Hastrup 2005: 143).

[37] Following Fabian (1990: 5), I propose defining epistemology as 'conditions that enable us to know (...)
ways of accounting for the production of knowledge. ... If in fieldwork the anthropologist gets to know by
way of social relations, this relational aspect has more general bearing on the processes by which facts are
established as relevant in the first place. Ontology and epistemology converge in anthropology' (Hastrup
2005: 143).

[38] The anthropological object is emergent: 'the social relation to the object is already installed as part of the
object when anthropologists begin to understand it' (Hastrup 2005: 143). Exactly because of this emergence, anthropological fields are constantly shifting and being redefined.

[39] And ICTs more generally.

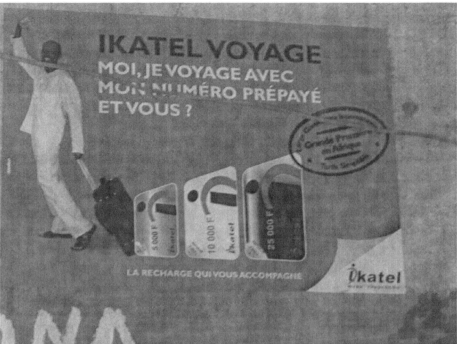

Photo 2.2   The mobile phone facilitating contact over distance (travel and migration)

face-to-face contact? Changes in the emergence of anthropological knowledge are related to shifts in experiences in both time and place.

Timing interactions anytime

In a debate in *Social Anthropology* (vol. 16, no. 2) about how short fieldwork can be, Okely (2007: 358) suggested that there is no one answer because criteria for what is deemed good field research have been stretched in both directions and are entirely dependent on context, goals and method. There are 'anthropologists who have demonstrated the power of long term and continuing involvement over decades' (Howell & Talle 2007). Others are exploiting cheap travel for repeated but shorter visits that are now supplemented by email and the mobile phone in what Wulff (2002) has called 'yo-yo fieldwork'.

Hannerz (2003: 201-202) describes Evans-Pritchard's moral evaluations about what being an accomplished fieldworker in social anthropology in the 1950s was all about. Evans-Pritchard stressed the longevity of the researcher's stay (two consecutive years in the field) and the longevity of his/her completion of the monograph (a ten- year project), ideally to be complemented with another ten years in another area for the sake of comparison. Evans-Pritchard's ideas about time and ethno-

graphic research are clearly old-fashioned today and t there is no funding to stimu-
late such longitudinal research. On the contrary, the saying 'publish or perish' and
the increasing time pressure on researchers' professional time management would
mercilessly condemn longevity as 'worst practice' in funding and policy circles.
Many researchers would agree that this is a problematic development because it
risks stimulating superficial and 'trendy' research, leaning much more on journalistic
than ethnographic methodologies and traditions.[40]

A general paradox of the information revolution, which also applies to the
mobile phone, is that saving time by using ICT actually makes us feel as though we
have less instead of more time. Instead of gaining time, we actually experience a loss
of time. The anthropologist Eriksen[41] suggests that the acceleration of time is a fundamental aspect of modern times that can be countered by attention to more 'down
time' in our daily existence. He does not consider boredom an evil but a virtue that
we should cherish. All the same, intensive phone use seems likely to make us lose
the positive aspects of 'down' or 'empty' time. As Fortunati (2000 in Geser 2004)
puts it:

> These moments of non-connection were very precious, because they structured the web of rela-
> tions inside the rhythm of presence/absence. At the same time, these moments could also fill up
> with reflection, possible adventures, observing events, reducing the uniformity of our existence,
> and so on. The possibility of perpetual contact that the mobile offers, risk shaping time into a
> container that is potentially always open, on the model of connecting times guaranteed by the
> world of information, which tend to be 24 hours out of 24.

When discussing his use of the mobile phone for contacting family and friends, a
colleague[42] concluded: 'I have a lot more contact with home, especially through
SMS. During my first fieldwork (in 2002), I contacted home once a month, last year
it was everyday. Personally I think this is a great advantage, also for doing research,
as it makes you feel less lonely and therefore it is possible to stay in the field for
longer periods.' Of course more contact with family and friends is possible but does
the mobile phone make researchers stay longer in the field? The opposite could just
as well be argued: that the presence of ICT might result in shorter stays as more can
be done now in a shorter time span.

---

[40] I am aware that discussing the history of fieldwork and ethnography is crucial to embedding my argument
more profoundly. However, it does not seem possible within the scope of this chapter to do so. For a
general overview of the several ideological 'turns' that anthropology took during the 20th century (from
the biological to the linguistic and the literate to the current topographic turn), see Hastrup (2005: 133-
50).

[41] *NRC Handelsblad*, 16 December 2006.

[42] Man, 38, cultural anthropologist, South-East Asia.

Researchers as high-tech nomads:[43] *From places to spaces?*

This picture shows nomadic fisherman on a small temporary island in the River Niger charging their mobile phones from a big, old motor producing lots of smoke and noise. In this remote area of Mali, fishermen's phones were ringing as if they were birds singing, turning silence into an increasingly precious commodity.

Photo 2.3   Charging mobile phones

Katz (2006: 116) remarks that: '… even domains that were formerly free of phones, or had their access to them sharply restricted, have become part of the broad fabric of telephonic communication. Once inviolable, beaches and mountain-tops are now part of the "chatter sphere."' Much in the same vein, anthropological notions of 'abroad', 'place' and 'field' have become part of this chatter sphere of the all-terrain mobile phones.

Will the frequency of field visits decrease in the near future? This can be contested on various grounds related to broader discussions about ICTs immobilizing rather than mobilizing people. Rietveld & Vickerman (2004: 246-47) concluded that: 'Indeed, the partial adoption of new technologies has changed our way of doing things, not by reducing transport and the need for movement, but by actually in-

[43] I borrow this term from Garreau (2000) as quoted in Geser (2004: 22): 'In fact, modern mobile technologies may facilitate the emergence of new segments of "high tech nomads" (e.g. venture capitalists, global traders, business consultants, itinerant journalists, etc.) who feel sufficiently integrated into society without possessing fixed addresses and any stationary resources.'

creasing it. ICT thus proves to be a complement to physical transport rather than its substitute.'

Hardung (2005: 145) describes how the most recent 'topographic turn' in ethnographic writing came as a result of 'place' being put back on the map as a unit of analysis that impacts on people's imaginations and embeds concrete interactions. She suggests that in ethnography there is an increased awareness, celebration even of the necessity of being there, of face-to-face contact and immediacy as integral ways of obtaining knowledge. Garreau (2000 in Geser 2004) on the contrary argues that many reasons for researchers' nomadic activities and travel have evaporated because 'they can communicate from anywhere, why do they bother moving around at all?'.

There seems to be a paradox here. While the mobile phone is a nomadic tool, instead of increasing researchers' mobility, it sometimes seems to decrease it. One would expect the importance of place-boundness would diminish by the day for so-called high-tech nomads. Nevertheless, people themselves often re-establish place as an important category from the first sentence of their online conversation. Asking where someone is is often part and parcel of an introduction in phone conversations. This same paradox also applies to migrants and expats: the further away they are, feeling place-less, the more they become obsessed with place-bound images and the customs of home. Such ideas of flow and closure (Meyer & Geschiere 1999) also apply to the research context. On the one hand, the phone has the potential to render researchers nomadic and placeless (e.g. travelling with informants from here to there), while on the other hand, there are trends that suggest that long-term immersion in certain places is no longer necessary to obtaining information (cf. Wulff 2002).

Ethnography is now practised in all kinds of settings – think of the emergence of transnationalism, of multiple field sites, of combining the here-and-there of people into one single analysis. This flow of localities has its closure: a non-compliance to rely on mere online communication for fieldwork. A fieldwork setting consisting exclusively of online communication seems increasingly inappropriate in the current moral landscape of anthropology as it lacks the face-to-face advantages (performative social cues) that are part of the discipline's epistemology. It is impossible to replace fieldwork. Indeed, what has changed is not that fieldwork has become placeless but that the spaces of interaction of fieldwork have multiplied. In short, the places of our field encounter are no longer place- but space-related. The spaces of encounter are becoming related to individual networks (of the researcher and informant alike) in multiple places.

So one of the challenges to traditional fieldwork is the increased access to what happens between sites through so-called multi-site research. Hannerz (1998) observed that it is not sufficient to study transnational communities or networks in multiple localities but that it is essential to use research methods that are able to grasp what happens between sites. In this vein, Horst (2002) describes the advantages of the Internet and email for conducting research in the diaspora that is neither here nor there and thus is an 'in-between site'. The transnational dialogues she has with these moving communities by email offer insight into this community and 'a new perspective on her ethnographic fieldwork in Somali refugee camps in Kenya'. Although the added value of grasping the contents of mobile phone conversations for doing transnational research is yet to be analyzed in depth, its potential is clearly there.

Maintaining contact with home has become easier, and difficult situations can be overcome by contacting a friend or family members when one feels the need to do so. Even simple unpleasant moments can be filled by phoning someone or being phoned. 'Woman on their own now use their mobiles as "barrier" signals in the way that they used to hold up a newspaper or magazine to indicate to predatory males or other intruders that they were unavailable' (Fox 2001 in Geser 2004: 9). Of course some of the issues discussed were also true for landline phones but its intensity, speed and quantitative presence give the mobile phone era its proper dynamics and have resulted in the increased connectedness of researchers in both their professional and private lives. In a way, field options and research topics have become more accessible and the action radius of the researcher has potentially expanded: formerly dangerous areas or groups no longer seem so threatening as the past isolation is now being broken by the mobile phone.

Definitions of public and private differ between cultural contexts. Foreigners often feel their privacy is threatened in developing countries. The mobile phone has however generated more options for opting out and fencing oneself off in intrusive situations such as in the hassle of a busy African market place. Places have thus become more easily evadable and the ethnographic device of simply 'being there' and 'participant observation' is severely interrupted by these kinds of private evasions. Anywhere and at any time it is possible to create a personal mini-private sphere, which Geser (2004: 10) calls 'virtual emigration' and Fortunati (2000)[44] labels 'nomadic intimacy'.

As Geser (2004: 10) remarks: 'observing 5 million people migrating to a huge city may not allow any conclusions about the likely emergence of any kind of "urban mentality" and "urban culture", when it is known that most of these new inhabitants remain firmly embedded in their original ethnic setting by daily phone contact with their relatives left behind in rural regions.' Of course there is more contact with family and friends but one wonders whether this results in fewer engagements in the field and in less 'being there'. The use of the mobile phone for all the researchers in the survey resulted in more contact with family and friends. However all of them

---

[44] Quoted in Geser (2004: 10).

agreed that not only 'home' became easier to reach and therefore nearer, but also colleagues, informants and 'work' more generally came closer and was more reachable.

The mobile phone has definitely had an impact on the shifting boundaries between work and family life and on the blurring of the public and the private.[45] Generally, the mobile phone has created greater expectations of availability, productivity and access (to family, informants and work). This might add to new pressures on one's professional life and reduce the romance of going 'out there', to the field, when compared to a few decades ago when it was still 'virgin, isolated and impermeable'. As a colleague said:[46]

> .... contact with family and friends back home becomes easier, but also more compelling. Not phoning for a week has become impossible because everyone would be very worried. And just as well, once back home, people from abroad phone, send an SMS and ask for money. To be honest, the arrival of mobile phones has cost me a lot of extra money because refusing to help or to give is rather impossible if informants/assistants tell you they don't have anything to eat.

Some researchers, however, stress the advantage of this blurring of work and private life to obtain access to officials (e.g. ministers) with fewer unnecessary and tiring visits.[47] According to another colleague and anthropologist:[48] 'Planning of interviews (even while not in the field) and the direct accessibility of "big men" (ministers, MPs, directors of NGOs, etc) became a lot easier and faster. Being sometimes unable to talk to or get to a minister with whom I attended the same meeting because he was surrounded by others, I simply decided to phone him (being physically separated 10 metres) and was directly connected and thus able to make an appointment.'

The borders between institutional spheres (work and home) are likely to change in three ways: by becoming: more permeable (components of one sphere can more easily enter the other); by being more flexible so that the extension of different spheres can be varied according to current situations and needs; and by interpenetration (blending), i.e. activities belonging to different domains coming together at the same time (Geisler *et al.* 2001 in Geser 2004: 35). The mobile phone has empowered individuals to decide on their own about the segregation or permeability of different institutional settings, social systems, inter-individual relationships and individual roles. The boundaries between these are much more fluid, modifiable and

---

[45] Wajcman (2007) is conducting a study on the impact of the mobile phone on working time and the work/life balance, focusing on Australia and the UK.

[46] Man, aged 45, West Africa.

[47] This often turns out to be a double advantage for journalists or researchers in conflict settings: Not only is it easier to reach top persons in obscure organizations (as exchanging phone numbers becomes common) but it also renders negotiations about meeting in safer, neutral places easier, to the relief of journalists (e.g. those reporting on LRA activities in Uganda and Sudan).

[48] Man, aged 28, West Africa.

unpredictable than before and all this has resulted in an increasing emphasis on choice, control and intention.

Othering anytime? Phoning anthropology's epistemology

Since the 1950s, ICT has contributed to shifting understandings of time and place, making it possible to save time, money and energy. The new technology demands 'experiential rather than physical displacement (...) The lack of physical travel does not mean, however, that the relationship between ethnographer and reader has collapsed' (Hine 2000: 45). 'The popularity of the ethnographic approach to online phenomena probably owes something to the accessibility of the field site to increasingly desk-bound academics. In the current academic climate, time for long time immersion in a physically located ethnographic field site is hard to come by' (*Ibid.*: 22).

What is the impact of the shift from fieldwork time to any time on the contents of one's ethnography and how does mobile phone use contribute to different ethnographic representations of the Other in time and distance? In *Time and the Other*, Fabian (1983) criticized the discrepancy in the discipline of anthropology between the interactive fieldwork period and the objectifying process of writing about it afterwards (ethnography). Fabian was one of the first to highlight the need for self-reflexivity in ethnography. From then onwards, the interaction between researchers and their Others[49] has been given more weight in ethnography in the form of dialogues and self-reflexivity.[50]

We can mourn what is lost but should focus on what has been gained when the online approach is added to existing techniques: doing research in different field settings (face-to-face, online, multi-local) is generating new forms of interaction, relating and knowledge that were impossible, and even unthinkable, in the Evans-Pritchard era. Acknowledging the centrality of the researcher in these new forms of interaction and knowledge generation seems inevitable because s/he is the only constant element – and therefore point of reference as a source of attribution of meaning – in these multiple settings. Anthropological research is no longer bound to place but more to the social networks and temporary spaces researchers surround themselves with.

> Reflecting on the influence of these changes on ethnographic writing is important. Sir Evans-Pritchard's proposals for a two-year fieldwork period have evaporated: fieldwork-time has become any time. The boundaries between now and then and here and there are increasingly blurred. This makes it impossible to shut the Other out of the written ethnography, as interaction and communication is ongoing, also during the writing process. Hastrup (2005: 133-50) described how anthropological knowledge production in the 20th century shifted in what she labels different 'turns' from a preoccupation with the biological to the linguistic and the literate

---

[49] 'Others' here is used in the way Fabian (1983) applies the concept.
[50] Probably the best example of this line of thought is J. Clifford & E. Marcus (1986) *Writing Culture: The Poetics & Politics of Ethnography*, University of California Press.

to the topographic turn. The epistemological challenges that mobile communication brings about might arguably add up to a new turn in 21st century anthropology, that is the 'ICT-mediated turn'.

To phone or not to phone in anthropology

Before the widespread availability of CMC,[51] mediated forms
of communication simply did not seem sufficiently interactive
to allow the ethnographer to test ideas through immersion
(Hine 2000: 44)

This chapter has argued that not only computer-mediated communication but also mobile phone communication is sufficiently interactive for ethnographic immersion and is worth looking into to trace changes in ethnographic projects. Although the heart of the anthropological venture (i.e. performative knowledge generation through participant observation during fieldwork) has not disappeared, it is suggested that the places, times, tools and forms in which oral communication takes place have profoundly altered research in the so-called 'phone age'.

The first section entitled 'absent relating' dealt with changes in relatedness through the use of the mobile phone as a communication channel. Since the mobile phone shapes all social interaction more generally, it necessarily also shapes that between researcher and informant. Ideologies of phone use are embedded in the prevailing social norms of the society under study (social appropriation). 'Flashing' practices were discussed as an example of the local reproduction of power relations through phone-shaped communication. For the anthropologist, the mobile phone poses new challenges of cultural adaptation to different social embeddings of this technology. Learning how to interact with local people through this medium should not be underestimated as a social skill that assists mutual understanding.

The impact of phone use on anthropological practice was central in the discussion on the new methodological options of the phone as a multiple tool (visual, archiving, recording, broadcasting) and its potential as a research assistant in the way it brokers but is also biased towards certain relations and informants. Finally, the implications of mobile phone use for the exchange of face-to-face versus phone-to-phone communication were analyzed, resulting in renewed questions about what gives authority to information. While face-to-face contact will always remain crucial for participant observation, it was concluded that additional ways of absent relating through phone communication is celebrated by some (e.g. because of its advantageous anonymity) and rejected by those who fear technology in general. The importance of sensitivity surrounding ethical questions about what kind of information one is allowed to use in the context of online information was stressed.

---

[51] CMC= computer-mediated communication.

Mental travel seems to be superseding physical travel as the realities being studied are increasingly less 'external' in place and time. This has resulted in an increased blurring of people's professional and private lives in and outside of 'the field', whatever that may be. The mobile phone (like other ICTs) has generated relative emancipation from local settings in place and time, which has resulted in increased access to promising new research fields, such as the transnational and what happens 'between sites'. Social appropriation of the mobile phone has lessened the degree to which anthropological encounters are anchored in specific places at restricted times. Instead, these encounters are increasingly being situated in networks stripped of restricted timing and emplacement (of the interaction). The continuing shift from location-based to personal-based social networks can be witnessed here.

And finally, the impact of mobile phone use on research practice necessarily impacts on the writing process and shifting ideas about epistemology more generally. The formerly separate processes of writing and conducting fieldwork are increasingly merging and becoming simultaneous practices in themselves. Whether this results in an increased inclusion of the Other in our ethnography remains to be seen. Nevertheless, the reshaping of current anthropological epistemology and morality is definitely challenging. We seem to be witnessing an ICT-mediated epistemological 'turn' in 21st century anthropology.

Anthropology is an empirical discipline whose database now increasingly covers the whole world. Due to various processes, such as the worldwide introduction of ICT, anthropologists have gained access to new fields that have multiplied complexity and blurred experiences and practices of time, place and relatedness. ICTs, such as the mobile phone that is a tool independent of physical travel and place, are thus constitutive of but also constituted by these new multiple fields and the resulting theory and practice. Considering phone-to-phone research as a valid method for replacing participative fieldwork appears impossible since relating through face-to-face encounters remains crucial to anthropological epistemology. In short, while face-to-face contact remains a basic requirement for the performative relating that is so central to the anthropological endeavour, phone-to-phone contact and online research certainly have advantages and have generated new forms of access. To phone or not to phone is not the question, the challenge is to acknowledge and reflect on the shaping capacities of mobile phones when relating online in the absence of 'the field'.

References

APPADURAI, A., ed., (1986), *The social life of things: Commodities in cultural perspective*, Cambridge: Cambridge University Press.

CHARPY, M. & S. HASSANE (2004), *Lettres d'émigres: Africains d'ici et d'ailleurs*, Paris: Editions Nicolas Philippe.

CLIFFORD, J. & E. MARCUS (1986), *Writing culture: The poetics & politics of ethnography*. London, Los Angeles, Berkeley: University of California Press.

CUMISKEY, K.M. (2007), 'Hidden meanings: Understanding the social-psychological impact of mobile phone use through story telling', Paper presented at the Mobile Media Conference 2007, University of Sydney, 2-4 July.
http://www.mobilemedia2007.net/12_proceed.html

DE BRUIJN, M.E., R. VAN DIJK & J-B. GEWALD, eds, (2007), *Strength beyond structure: Social and historical trajectories of agency in Africa*, Leiden: Brill.

DE LAET, M. & A. MOL (2000), 'The Zimbabwe bush pump: Mechanics of a fluid technology', *Social Studies of Science* 30(2): 225-63.

DIOME, F. (2003), *Le ventre de l'Atlantique*, Paris: Anne Carrière.

FABIAN, J. (1990), *Power and performance. Ethnographic explorations through proverbial wisdom and theatre in Shaba, Zaire*, Madison: University of Wisconsin Press.

FABIAN, J. (1983), *Time and the other; How anthropology makes its object*, New York: Colombia University Press.

FISHER, C. (1992), *America calling: A social history of the telephone to 1940*, Berkeley, Ca.: University of California Press.

GERGEN, K. (2002), 'The challenge of absent presence'. In: J.E. Katz & M.A. Aakhus, eds, *Perpetual contact: Mobile communication, private talk, public performance*, New York: Cambridge University Press, pp. 222-241.

GESCHIERE, P. & B. MEYER (1999), *Globalisation and identity: Dialectics of flow and closure*, New Jersey: Blackwell.

GESER, H. (2004), Towards a sociological theory of the mobile phone.
http://socio.ch/mobile/t_geser1.htm

HAHN, H.P. & L. KIBORA (2008), 'The domestication of the mobile phone: Oral society and new ICT in Burkina Faso', *Journal of Modern African Studies* 46(1): 87-109.

HANNERZ, U. (2003), 'Being there ... and there ... and there! Reflections on multi-site ethnography', *Ethnography* 4(2): 201-16.

HANNERZ, U. (1998), *Transnational connections: Culture, people and places*, New York: Routledge.

HASTRUP, K. (2005), 'Social anthropology: Towards a pragmatic enlightenment?', *Social Anthropology* 13(2): 133-50.

HASTRUP, K. (2004), 'Getting it right. Knowledge and evidence in anthropology', *Anthropological Theory* 3: 309-323.

HEAVENS, A. (2007), 'Digital Africa: The 3G Generation', *BBC Focus on Africa*, April-June.

HINE, C. (2000), *Virtual ethnography*. New Delhi & London: SAGE Publications Thousand Oaks.

HORST, C. (2002), 'Transnational dialogues; Developing ways to do research in a diasporic community', Working paper WPTC 02-13.
http://www.transcomm.ox.ac.uk/working%20papers/horst1.pdf

HORST, H.A. & D. MILLER (2006), *The cell phone: An anthropology of communication*, London & New York: Berg Publishers.

HORST, H.A. & D. MILLER (2005), 'From kinship to link-up', *Current Anthropology* 46: 755-78.

KATZ, J.E. (2006), *Magic in the air: Mobile communication and the transformation of social life*, New Brunswick & London: Transaction Publishers.

KLINE, R. & T. PINCH (1996), 'Users as agents of technological change: The social construction of the automobile in the rural United States', *Technology and Culture* 37(4): 763-795.

MARCUS, G.E. (1995), 'Ethnography of the world system: The emergence of multi-sited ethnography', *Annual Reviews Anthropology* 24: 95-117.

MARCUS, G.E. & J. OKELY (2007), 'How short can fieldwork be?', *Social Anthropology* 15(3): 353-367.

MAURY, F. (2007), 'Le dossier Télécoms', *Jeune Afrique* 2422: 55.

MULAMA, J. (2007), 'Africa at large; A rural-urban digital divide challenges women', IPS (14/02/2007). http://ipsnews.net/news.asp/idnews=36563

MILLER, D. & D. SLATER (2000), *The internet; An ethnographic approach*, Oxford: Berg Publishers.

NYAMNJOH, F.B. (2005), 'Images of Nyongo amongst Bamenda grassfielders in Whiteman Kontri', *Citizenship Studies* 9(3): 241-269.

ONG, W.J. (1992), *Orality and literacy: The technologizing of the word*, New York: Methuen.

PLANT, S. (2000), 'On the mobile. The rffects of mobile yelephones on docial and individual life'. http://www.motorola.com/mot/documents/0,1028,33,00.pdf

RIETVELD, P. & R. VICKERMAN (2004), 'Transport in regional science: The death of distance is premature', *Papers in Regional Science* 83: 229-248.

SINHA, C. (2005), 'Effect of mobile telephony on empowering rural communities in developing countries', Paper presented at the IRFD Conference 'Digital Divide, Global Development and the Information Society', 14-16 November.

SLATER, D. & J. KWAMI (2005), *Embeddedness and escape: Internet and mobile use as poverty reduction strategies in Ghana*, London: Routledge, pp. 15-31.

SÖKEFELD, M. & J-P. WARNIER (2008), 'Changing generations in anthropology-so what?', *Social Anthropology* 16(2): 221-228.

TALL, S.M. (2004), 'Senegalese emigrés: New Information & Communication Technologies', *Review of African Political Economy* 31(99): 31-49.

WAJCMAN, J. (2007), 'Intimate connections: The impact of the mobile phone on work life boundaries', Paper presented at the Mobile Media Conference 2007, University of Sydney, 2-4 July.

3

From the elitist to the commonality of voice communication: The history of the telephone in Buea, Cameroon

Walter Gam Nkwi

Introduction: Staking the landscape

This chapter considers how developments in telephone communication have changed the social landscape in an urban area, namely the university town of Buea in Cameroon. The historical development of voice communication and the use of the telephone in the colonial era and its post-colonial development have recently culminated in the rapid introduction of the mobile phone. The revolution of the mobile phone has been hailed as an important element in present-day developments in countries in the South and is generally considered positive. This study assesses this development in relation to urban society in Cameroon and its economies of insecurity and inequality.

As point of departure, we follow the line of reasoning already introduced by other scholars researching the mobile phone in societies in the South. For instance, Horst & Miller (2006) have shown in their study in Jamaica how the mobile phone is culturally and socially appropriated and, in turn, shapes society. In this process, the social and economic landscape also changes. Similar observations of this process of appropriation have been made by Pertierra(2005) for the Philippines and Smith (2006) for political life in Nigeria. Nyamnjoh (2005), who has written extensively on Cameroon in general and the Grassfields of that North west Cameroon, emphasizes the intensification of the cell phone helping to linking with people faraway and how this creates new forms of fear and anxiety in society. These studies discuss how society and technologies are dialectically related and how society shapes the technology as much as the technology shapes society. The way in which the phone has been integrated into society cannot be separated from the specific culture, economy and history of a society.

In this study we concentrate on the phone as a particular form of communication technology, a direct means of (almost instant) exchange that differs from radio, television or other media. And it is this direct or instant voice exchange that makes the mobile phone so attractive. Although it is true that an exchange in the form of letters was also available in colonial times to large groups of people, access to voice communication has only developed into a common form of communication in the recent period of mobile phones. The effects of the popularization of voice communication and the reasons for this development are central to this chapter.

Our interest in the inter-relatedness of society and voice technology was raised when we arrived in Buea town in April 2007 and noted the presence of so many phone booths (in daily parlance 'call boxes') even when there were no visible boxes in the strict sense of the word, on the street. These boxes were used for business purposes and it appeared that young people in particular were involved in this kind of enterprise. We decided to do a survey among the call boxes and systematically went up and down the larger streets making an inventory of them. We also did open interviews with the people in these call boxes, as we were interested in the stories behind them and the changes they have brought about. To better situate this 'booming' call box and mobile phone industry, we tried to understand voice communication as it appeared in Buea in the twentieth century. For this, we mainly relied on archival research carried out in Buea town's archives.

This chapter follows the development of phone technology in Buea town and, more specifically in Molyko, the town's university quarter. Our focus was informed by the novelty of the ubiquitous 'phone boxes' in this city, and by the fact that the mobile phone revolution is rapidly changing the geographical space in this sub-region. We will first attempt a history of voice communication and see how it evolved in Buea from about 1922 when the British Colonial administration was taking over that part of the country and the phone was a luxury to 2005 when the phone appears to be a necessity. We are also interested in how phone technology was linked to social relations and differences in society. Has the phone developed

Photo 3.1   This is a typical call box. They are normally about 60x60 cm, 190 cm high and are made of timber with plywood around the lower half. They have four 'windows' that open outwards and look like wings when open. When standing inside the telephone box, only a person's top half can be seen. The roof slants and the call box can be green, brown or yellow but they are often yellow as MTN, the main mobile telephone company, has yellow as its trademark colour. These boxes are ubiquitous, omnipresent and pervasive and are rapidly changing the region's landscape/socio-scape.

from an elitist means of communication to a means of communication for every-one? And how does this type of communication technology fit into the economy of the society under study? The expansion of phone communication takes us into colo-nial history and specific social relations that were created in that period, and to the present mobile phone revolution that appears to be democratizing an authoritarian African state.

To understand the specific form the phone revolution has taken we should also consider changes in economic and social relations in Cameroonian society. Today the economy is depicted as one of uncertainty (Mbembe 2000); as it is an economy structured around the uncertainties in daily life where people never know what will happen tomorrow and their lives are being shaped around the social and economic insecurities they face (see de Bruijn & van Dijk 1995). This specific economic form appeared during the economic downturn in Cameroon in the mid 1990s when the currency was devalued, salaries were slashed three times and the Structural Adjust-ment Programme (SAP) aggravated the situation by laying off thousands of civil servants. Consequently thousands of dependents were left to grapple with the awk-ward socio-economic situation and nobody knew what would happen the next day. People started to live 'without a tomorrow'. To eke out a living, they have had to find ways to survive in times of continuing uncertainty. We question here how the emerging economy of the phone, i.e. a form of appropriation of the mobile phone, can be explained in these dynamics of uncertainty. Reference to the colonial period shows a totally different picture, as will become clear. Since the introduction of the phone, some parallels can be drawn with what is happening today.

The early history of the telephone in Buea

This section traces the introduction and use of the telephone in Buea from an his-torical perspective. The Cameroons were officially colonized by the Germans in July 1884 and by 1888 the need for telegraphic communication with Europe became a *sine qua non* for Governor Von Soden. To justify the colony's need for voice com-munication, Soden cited the death of the Kaiser, news of which only reached the colony twenty-seven days after he had died. In that justification he said *inter alia*: 'This long delay made the governor wonder about the possible difficulties the colony might get into if current rumours of war should result in actual hostilities involving Germany, and the Cameroons should learn of it too late' (Rudin 1938: 217). After much debate among the authorities in Germany, it was decided that a cable connection beyond Bonny, the present day Benin Republic in West Africa, to the Cameroons via the Spanish island of Fernando Po would be a good idea. An English company would lay the connection but it depended on whether the Spanish authorities on the island allowed them to land there. The discussions came to nothing although after further talks, a contract was signed in 1892 with the English company which was going to provide a direct cable between Bonny and Douala. The company received a twenty-year subsidy from Germany. Work began and in February 1893 the colony's first message was sent directly to Germany in the form of a congratulatory cablegram from the Governor to William 11 (Rudin 1938: 217). The completion of that telegraphic link with the outside world led to demands for an extension of similar services within the colony. However, it was not until 1898 that telephonic and telegraphic connections were made with Buea and Victoria (Rudin 1938: 217). Some of the local people were trained as telegraphers and after 1900 lines were extended into the interior depending on the demands of the planters or the missionaries there.[1]

The First World War saw the Germans leave Cameroon and the country was partitioned between France and Britain, with Britain taking one fifth while France took the remaining four-fifths. The British section was christened the British Southern Cameroons and later the Cameroons Province and Bamenda Province and then just the Cameroons. These nomenclatures are used interchangeably here.

The telephone service in the Cameroons was formerly the property of the German Imperial Posts and Telegraphs Department (*Reichspostamt*). During the First World War, telephone poles, wires and other equipments were considerably damaged and when the Peace Treaty of Versailles, which dealt specifically with Germany and her allies, was signed, the Posts and Telegraphs Department of Nigeria (to which Southern Cameroons was attached), acting on the instructions of the Governor-General of Nigeria, took over all the telegraphs and telephones in the British sphere of the Cameroons.

Buea, the capital of German Kamerun, came into the limelight of the telephony system during the German administration.[2] The city became the hub of the telephone system during the German/British periods and from there lines radiated out to Victoria; through Kumba to Tinto, and then on to Ossidinge on the one hand and to Bamenda on the other. It only arrived in Bamenda in 1949. This system was connected to the main Nigerian system via Ossidinge and Obubra on the Cross River in Nigeria's Calabar Province.[3] There were improvements in communication in 1930 when a wireless telephone line was installed in May in Buea to link up with Nigeria. It was even suggested that it would hook up with stations in Bamenda and

---

[1]   See also Post und Telegraphensachen 2c.Acten betreffend die Einrichtung einer Postverwaltung and Post und Telegraphensachen 7c.Acten betreffend das Telegraphenwesen in Kamerun cf. H, Rudin (Yale: Yale University Press, 1938: 217).

[2]   Letter No. T662/322/18 from Posts and Telegraphs, Director of Government Telegraphs, Lagos, Southern Nigeria, 12 August 1918, National Archives Buea (henceforth cited as NAB).

[3]   File No. 474/1921 Ba (1922) 2 Report for the League of Nations 1922; Report on the Victoria Division, Cameroons Province written for the League of Nations by A.R. Whitman, District Officer, 30 September 1921, NAB.

Mamfe with Buea being at the centre.[4] In 1937 some seventeen new telephone installations were made, and five trunk lines were connected to the telephone exchanges in Victoria and Tiko, with the main centre being Buea. The three wireless stations based in Buea remained in service and that year there was no major breakdown in communications with Lagos.[5]

These telephones were most frequently used by the senior management of the various plantations during the German period and, under the British colonial administration from 1946, by the Cameroon Development Corporation (CDC). The main communication was for business and political transactions and the telephone remained, therefore, a tool of the colonial elite. It was very expensive and never came down to a level that the ordinary people could afford. Part of the explanation for this is that keeping telephone communications up and running was not an easy task, as letters, correspondence and memoranda show. From the beginning, Rudin (1938: 217) noted that:

> … maintaining poles and lines for telephone and telegraphic services involved problems peculiar to the tropics. Poles were often tumbled to the ground by elephants who robbed [sic] against them to relieve itching backs. Tropical storms accompanied by violent winds also caused harm. Copper wire was always exposed to theft because native vanity could use a good deal of it for ornament on necks, arms and legs.

The in-tray of the Director of Posts and Telegraphs, who was based in Lagos, was flooded with complaints about the unreliability of the telephone service. Letters capture the story more clearly. For example, in 1920 the manager of the Tiko Plantations complained about the telephone service to the Supervisor of Plantations who forwarded his letter to the Director of Posts and Telegraphs:

> Sir, I have to complain of the inefficiency of the telephone system between Tiko and other places especially Buea. The working is quite unsatisfactory when working at all the 'speaker' cannot be heard with any degree of clearness. Tiko is an important port being the landing place from Douala it is essential that the line should be in good working order for the purpose of receiving and transmitting important messages. I have also to complain of much inattention and sometime recklessness on the part of the native operators at the central telephone exchange service at Buea. On several occasions I have been unable to get any other reply than a laugh from the operator or someone at his end. It is difficult to catch the offender but I think the above should be brought to the notice of those in authority.[6]

In another instance, the Manager of Ekona Estate wrote to the Supervisor of Plantations in Bota on 9 September 1921 saying that:

> It was impossible to carry on our conversation on the telephone this morning owing to interruptions on the line by someone trying to listen. I endeavored to get you but ten minutes after I

---

[4] File No. 121/1931, Notes on Cameroons Province for the League of Nations Report, 1931, Ba, (1931) 6, NAB.

[5] File No. SP.920, Notes for the League of Nations Report, 1937, NAB.

[6] Letter No. 199/21, Manager Tiko Plantation to the Supervisor of Plantations, Ekona, 20 September 1920, NAB.

was informed by the Molyko office boy, that the Buea operator whose name was Burnley would not answer the telephone. I am reporting the matter to the Inspector of Telegraphs.[7]

In addition to general difficulties with service, these letters also show the role Buea had in the first telephones. With hindsight, it can be deduced that the indigenous telephone clerks were seen in a rather derogatory light by the CDC colonial administrators whenever they could not get through on the phone. For instance, on 16 September 1919 the Manager of Ekona Estate, Mr A.J. Findlay, wrote to the Director of Posts and Telegraphs, Lagos, as follows:

> I regret that I have again to complain of inattention and incivility on the part of the Telephone exchange clerks at Buea. My clerk at Molyko has under my instructions been trying to, all day to get through to Bota to ask for an engine to be sent to cacao (sic) from Molyko to Bota, and has failed, the answer from Buea always being that 'Victoria is engage'…. The Molyko clerk has as yet, 5 p.m. failed to get through further than Buea, and now Buea refuses to answer repeated calls either from Molyko or Ekona.[8]

It would seem the fixed-line phone remained a colonial means of communication but Africans appropriated it at most for making ornaments. The fixed-line phone served the colonial state and the settler economy but not the politics, social life and economics of the ordinary African citizen.[9] It also defined relations between those who made up the colonial state and its servants.

The Plantations Department wrote to the Director of Posts and Telephone in 1921 and laid the blame for the frequent failure of the system on the 'Native Staff'.

> I regret to report that since your departure telephone communication as far as plantations are concerned, are practically useless. Am strongly of the opinion that your local native staffs are deliberately and maliciously obstructing the lines especially Buea. Cannot they all be transferred to a district where they will be under direct competent supervision? Present position in plantations paying considerable sum annually for practically non-existent service.[10]

These and other complaints point to the fact that the telephone was an elitist tool during the colonial period. They portray the master and servant relationship in which the servant received the blame for all phone calls that failed. In a way, it also shows how the indigenous population used the voice communication medium to resist colonialism. The so-called telephone operators were employed by the European colonial administration. This was ironic because the colonial masters claimed that they were out to spread civilization to the heathens who were drawers of water and hewers of wood. Secondly, their employment in the colonial administration was because the administration lacked staff. Unfortunately, the indigenous staff received the blame for everything that went wrong with the telephone system. The reasons

---

[7] File No. 58/16 Telephone Service Et/1921, 11 August 1921, NAB.
[8] File No. 132/1920, Telephone Service Complaints Re, 11 September 1920, NAB.
[9] It could also be argued that the Cameroons had various other types of communication during the colonial period but they never had an immediate impact on the colonial administration.
[10] Letter No. M.P. No. 791/262/1921 from Plantations Department to Director Posts and Telegraphs, Wolley, Lagos, 17 March 1921, NAB.

for this are not very clear. It could however be speculated that the indigenous population or the telephone operators never received adequate training regarding the operation of land telephones. This remains a point of speculation.

Voice communication from independence until the present

The political whirlwind that swept African colonial states south of the Sahara in the 1940s and culminated in independence and the birth of new states both in French and British Africa also hit Cameroon. On 1 January 1960 the French part of Cameroon gained independence and on 1 October 1961 the British Southern Cameroons gained independence by reunification with French Cameroon. The new state was known as the Federal Republic of Cameroon, with Buea falling under the Federal State of West Cameroon and French Cameroon known as the Federal State of East Cameroon. In 1972 the state underwent a political metamorphosis and became known as the United Republic of Cameroon (see Ngoh 2004). Buea continued to play an important role following the post-independence period with the opening of a post and telecommunications school in the early 1970s. The telephone land lines were still appropriated by the elite and telephone boxes or booths were unheard of and remained so until the late 1980s.

With the introduction of the Structural Adjustment Plan in Cameroon as a palliative to cure its ailing economy, some of the telecommunication structures were privatized in the late 1980s and later. For instance, in 1998, the Cameroon Telecommunication Company (Camtel) was established by bringing together Intelcam and the Department of Telecommunications at the Ministry of Post and Telecommunications. The Cameroon Telecommunication Mobile Company (Camtel Mobile) was set up with the specific task of installing and exploiting mobile phones across the whole country and, according to Nyamnjoh (2005: 209), with this initiative:

> ... private investors such as Mobilis or (Orange) and MTN-Cameroon have since extended and improved upon the telecommunications services. From a fixed telephone network of around 87,000 subscribers since independence, Cameroon now boasts more than 200,000 cell phone subscribers for MTN Cameroon alone.

In Anglophone Cameroon in general and Buea in particular owning a mobile phone has become a given and people take their cell phones wherever they go, attached to their belts, in their hands and or in their handbag. It is indeed a paradox that when structural adjustment was introduced and many people were rendered poor, citizens could still on the whole afford to purchase mobile phones. As if that was not enough, they displayed them prominently so everybody could see they had one. Mobile phones have led to the birth of call boxes that have changed the urban landscape of most towns. Within eight years of the introduction of the mobile phone in Buea and just seven years after the first telephone box was opened, Buea now boasts at least 550 call boxes honeycombed all over the town, with Molyko being the most congested area. The next section investigates the phenomenon of the call box in Buea.

New landscapes: Boxes and the people in them

The people who use telephone boxes come from different social backgrounds and share various ambitions. In discussions it became clear that the boxes are like safety valves or a panacea for their problems. Of the two hundred people interviewed, 55 were between the ages of 13 and 25 and were either working for people and had ambitions of going back to school or wanted to learn a trade. They had dropped out of school for reasons ranging from a lack of money to the death of sponsors. The other 145 people owned the call boxes and sustained their livelihoods in this way. Below are a few examples of the people working in the call boxes from dependents to those who own the boxes themselves.

The young people we talked to were often school drop-outs who maintained they were only working temporarily in call boxes. Their main aim was to raise money and continue their education. Dropping out of school had not been of their own making but often either their sponsors or parents had died or through an accident they had become incapacitated or been laid off with no social security benefits forthcoming. Ayeh Justine is a young girl of 23 who had dropped out of school after the death of both her parents. She had come to Buea from Bamenda to be with her married sister and initially had worked for three years in somebody's call box for FCFA 15,000. After that she decided to open her own call box. 'Everyday I make a profit of at least FCFA 5,000 and play my *njangi* while planning to go back to school. I really want to go back to school.'[11]

Thirteen-year-old Yvette Fon shares her aspirations of going back to school. She captured her disillusion and aspirations as follows:

> After my elementary school my parents retired from the Tole tea estate.[12] I could not go back to school because they were not paid their pension. The woman who owns this call box came and took me from our house to help her in this box and after a year she will send me back to school. Apart from working in this box, I also help her in the house by cleaning it; washing clothes and cooking. I do not make much profit because as you can see there are many boxes here and each is open everyday.[13]

She does not earn a fixed wage but has the illusion that the owner of her call box will send her back to school. Whether this will be a reality in September when the schools reopen is anybody's guess.

---

[11] Interview with Justin, 9 May 2007. *Njangi* means to save money as a group with the aim of helping each other in turn.

[12] Until the 1990s this was a state-owned tea estate but since then it has been privatized although this did not improve workers' working conditions (for more on the plantation economy in Cameroon see Konings 1993).

[13] Interview, 30 April 2007.

The last example in this category is Oliver who is twenty-five years old. He starts his story in Pidgin English and then continues in Standard English.

> I don work for this booth since 2005' (I have worked in this call box since 2005). It is owned by my older brother who works in the Paramount Hotel. He does not really pay me but does provide for my daily needs. This is because he plans to send me to a welding workshop as an apprentice. I make at least FCFA 5,000 profit everyday.'

These three cases are examples of young people who have ambitions of future careers after working in telephone call boxes. These young people come from poor backgrounds and depend on the owner of their box for their daily needs and their future. Whether their dreams will come true or not remains unclear.

The second category of people are those we could call the 'responsible' because they use their call box to increase their standard of living and at the same time consider themselves as self-employed. Monica is a history graduate from the University of Buea and owns a telephone call box at the motor park at Mile 17 in Buea. She was introduced to the call-box business by her friend, Adeline, who had been in the business for six years and was about to go to Denmark with the money she had made from it. Monica is not married and has a daughter in the Presbyterian Girls' School in Limbe, one of the prestigious secondary schools in the Southwest Province. According to her, the call-box business is very profitable. Looking very serious, she said:

> … that is why you see many boxes cropping up everywhere around Buea. In a single day I make a profit of FCFA 7,000 and I am not working under any stress from anybody. If I am tired, I stay at home. With the money from this box I have been able to sponsor my child in secondary school who will be writing her final exams this June. With the profit I get I also pay the rent of my apartment and can afford to send some money to my parents in the village.[14]

Monica is not only self-employed but can also help her daughter and her parents. The rent on her apartment is also paid thanks to her telephone call box.

People working in call boxes can earn a decent salary from them. One such case is Jonathan who is married and has one child. At first he was working as a bar attendant before finding employment as a worker in a call box that belongs to a university student. Jonathan's remuneration used to be FCFA 20,000 per month but at peak times of the year he is paid FCFA 30,000. From his salary he sponsors his son at school and his wife at a tailoring workshop. Jonathan feels that the call-box business is not as profitable as it used to be because of the competition. All the people we talked to who work for others in call boxes, they are paid at least FCFA 20,000 per month. If according to the Cameroon Labour Code the national minimum wage is FCFA 20,000, then those who are working in these boxes are not badly off because most, if not all, the informants claimed to be earning at least FCFA 20,000.

---

14 Interview, 17 May 2007, Buea.

The call-box economy

The key player in the call-box economy is the Mobile Telephone Network, fondly known by its acronym MTN. Once the owner has appropriated space for a call box, the next step is to negotiate with a carpenter who makes the box and the owner goes ahead with registering it with Buea Urban Council. After this, s/he can contact MTN or a Super Dealer. A Super Dealer is an MTN agent who liaises with the public and MTN by providing services to the public. The call-box owner then purchases his/her EVD (Electronic Voucher Distribution) and the air time that will be used by customers to make calls and transfer credit. In this sense MTN effectively provides credit to people who can afford to buy it and then these people distribute air time to other distributors, finally ending up at the lowest level which is the owners of the boxes who in turn distribute it to people according to what they have in their wallets and their financial standing in the economy. This MTN distribution system has led to a highly competitive call-box economy in which people have to participate and indeed gamble for a living on a daily basis. The call boxes themselves are not all the same. Some are better off than others depending on how much capital there is at the disposal of those opening the boxes and how many customers are attracted to a call box on a daily basis.

From our discussions and interviews it appeared that the call-box economy is not very stable and fluctuates according to the number of people working in it but also in relation to the competition. Mary is in her mid-forties, a widow with three children and the owner of a telephone call box. According to her:

> … the business of a call box in relation to profit has been fluctuating. … When the business was just introduced in Buea in 1999 I saw from my big sister that it was quite profitable. When she left for America, I took it over. Many people have entered the business and everybody now is doing whatever he likes. If you just see this box near me (pointing at a box) you will realize that instead of making a call for 40 seconds per FCFA 100 it is 59 seconds per hundred. How then do you think that I will make any profit? Even look at the transfer of credit. It reads differently from all what is obtained around us. I however thank my God because with the little that I have, I can pay my children's school fees, pay my rent, buy food and clothes for myself and the children.[15]

What Miss Mary is suggesting is that call boxes have homogeneous characteristics regardless of the language in front of them. This is the language of credit transfer and sales of MTN cards. At each call box the following information is on display:

Call Box here or Make your calls here. 0-40 seconds = 100 FRS.
There is also credit transfer orange and MTN.
500 FRS = 500 FRS
1000 FRS = 1000 FRS
2000 FRS = 2000 FRS
5000 FRS = 5000 FRS, etc.

---

[15]   Interview, 23 May 2007, Buea.

There are, however, two exceptions to the rule which we need to revisit in detail. These show that competition is high and the phone-box market is tough. Increasingly, bigger boxes are competing in the market and people with capital are investing in the phone business. One example is Elvis's box. We spoke to him between 11 and 15 May 2007. In front of the box there is a notice board with the following message:

> *Make your calls here, 0-59 secs = 100 and also transfer your credit for free.*
> *The credit transfer is as follows:*
>   *500 = 525 FRS*
>   *1000 = 1,100 FRS*
>   *1500 = 1,650 FRS*
>   *2000 = 2,200 FRS*
>   *2500 = 2,700 FRS*
>   *5000 = 5,500 FRS*
>   *10,000 = 11,000 FRS*
>   *11,000=12,000 FRS*
>
> *MTN cards available also for:*
>   *5000 FRS*
>   *1000 FRS*
>   *2000 FRS*
>   *10000 FRS*

He explained as follows (translated from Pidgin English):

(He starts by sighing). This business these days is not moving as it used to be. I was introduced to this call box business by a friend after my small business collapsed. He was a worker with the MTN Company. I can tell you that it is a lucrative business and if somebody wants to employ me on a salary of 80,000 FRS per month I cannot accept. I swear to God. This is because this work has a lot of gain. I have a friend who works with the MTN and occupies a good position; he is the one that used to send me the credit at any time that I want it. When I buy credit for 24,000 FRS I gain 15,000 FRS bonus. This total is 39,000 FRS. We have a specific SIM card which we call EVD. This amount will be automatically divided in this SIM card into two – the one for making calls by my customers and the one to transfer credit for a bonus. When I want to check the amount of money remaining for my money transfer bonus, I use star 159 star 1 star and press OK. When I want to check my normal credit I use the code, star 155 hash and press OK. (At this juncture somebody interrupts the discussion to ask him to beg his business partner in Douala to send to him credit worth 24,000 FRS and within two minutes the credit signals in the phone.) I tell you that there is money in this call box business. When I have credit worth 24,000 FRS it takes me a day to finish or two and I will make a profit of 13,000 FRS out of it. There are some people that do not give this type of credit because they do not have the money to operate so. I think I am simply lucky and there is no stress in the business. The only small stress in it is that I pay the council tax of 31,000 FRS per annum and this small place where you see this small box standing I pay 4,000 FRS to the landlord. As you can see for yourself all these people about eight have given me a nickname and they call me their master. This is simply because I help them when they need to have credit of a particular amount. When they are in need I just dial my man in Douala and within a short time the credit comes. They will then give me the money and I will hand it over to my friend over the weekend when he comes to Buea. However, I cannot tell them the secret of my own business of how I transfer 1,000 = 1,100; 2,000 = 2,300; 10,000 = 11,000 FRS etc. I first of all transfer 0-59 seconds for 100 FRS for two reasons. First, most people do not call up to 30 seconds and pay 100 FRS and because of this I make my 100 FRS. Secondly, the person who goes over 59 seconds by 1 second must pay 200 FRS. This again brings in a lot of money for me.'

By saying that the business is not what it ought to be the informant was not comfortable with the competition of other call boxes which were entering the town in a way that he felt was not regulated.

Photo 3.2   A board announcing cheap transfers in a street of Buea

However, several issues Elvis raised need further explanation and cannot be taken at face value. The first is that everybody in society seemingly stands to make a profit from their call box and MTN, although it will differ with the typology of the call box. The first is that those in the boxes benefit by always trying to win over more customers. In an attempt to woo new customers for their services, they offer services below cost. Offering services below cost increases demand and is in itself a gamble because MTN taxes any transfer of credit, any small or insignificant amount of money and if somebody is instead transferring funds with a bonus, then there is more to it. This is borne out by the fact that the more one purchases and transfers credit, the more incentives – in the form of more credit – are given by MTN. This can only hold true if the owner of the call box is 'rich'. This has been demonstrated by Elvis because he has enough capital. But those who do not have sufficient capital obviously have to grumble, as was evidenced by the replies of more than fifty respondents.

The council and landlords also stand to gain from telephone call boxes as they charge rent on the small piece of land on which the box stands. Secondly, it shows that society has developed a different language. SIM is an acronym meaning Security Identity Memory and EVD means Electronic Voucher Distribution, a business SIM card that costs twice the normal price of an ordinary card. Thirdly, MTN appears to have lost control over what is going on. When we approached some MTN workers, they accepted that the company was aware of what was happening but unfortunately could not stop it and called it an act of 'dumping'. MTN is interested in selling their cards and the company is not responsible for anything else that may be going on in telephone call boxes. The higher the amount you purchase the cards for, the higher your bonus. Fourthly, it could be realized that not all those working in call boxes are in agreement. Those who do not have enough capital to attract more customers express disgust about those who do have the capital and can raise profits on a daily basis. They feel marginalized in the business. The final point is that this man is working complicity with influential people within MTN.

The boxes' customers

Call boxes like those represented above have similar features but there is another type that has the same qualities but in the superlative. Situated a few metres from University Junction, it is called 'C-13 call box'. This section considers the behaviour of the people who make calls; the customers; and looks at how they benefit from the cheap boxes. I have taken this big box, situated at the entrance to the University of Buea where I observed customer behaviour over several days, as an example. I decided to call it 'the mother of call boxes' because of its unique qualities. The box attracts probably the highest number of ordinary people, although my observations also showed that there were some rich men who visit the box from time to time, but infrequently. It is really a call box in a room whose walls are covered with information aimed at customers. The behaviour of these customers tells one a lot about the call box economy from the users' side. Because of its intensity of use, the importance of this box cannot be overemphasized. It attracts the largest number of ordinary customers that I had observed in the field so far. The box also does what MTN could not perfectly understand and transfers credit from up to FCFA1000 for FCFA1150. The more credit you transfer the more bonuses you get. The information that appears in this call box is shown below (p. 64).

Of all the call boxes we visited in the field this one appeared to be an exception in terms of organization and structure and was by far the cheapest. One could make a call for FCFA75 a minute or FCFA150 for an international call to any country in

C-13 Call Box UB Junction
National Calls, MTN, Orange and fixed phones = 75/60 seconds
International calls all countries = 150/60 seconds

Amount Paid	Easy Transfer Amount Gained	Extra Gain
1,000 FRS	1,150FRS	1 free call
2,000 FRS	2,300FRS	1 free call
2,500FRS	2,900FRS	1 free call
5,000FRS	6,000FRS	1 free call
10,000FRS	12,000FRS	1 free call
20,000FRS	24,000FRS	1 free call

1-minute call = 75 FRS
2-minute call = 150 FRS
3-mnute call = 225 FRS
4-minute call = 300 FRS

EVD Supplier
Tel: 7789.71.90

Money paid	Credit EVD Side	Credit Transfer Bonus
9,300 FRS	10,000 FRS	8,000 PLUS 4,000 FRS
18,600 FRS	20,000FRS	16,000 PLUS 8,000 FRS
27,900 FRS	30,000 FRS	24,000 PLUS 15,000 FRS
46,000 FRS	50,000 FRS	40,000 PLUS 20,000 FRS

Credit Transfer Notice to Customers
1) The customer is responsible for the number which he/she writes inside the transferring phone.
2) The customer listens or waits for the message to know if the transfer is successful or not.
3) After 15 minutes we are not responsible for the reimbursement.
4) For transfers above 5,000 FRS you are entitled to free calls.
5) In case of any problem, call 7180405 or 73134 85.

Credit Transfer Notice
1) Write your number and give it to the operator.
2) The operator will call you if the call is successful or not.
3) If your call is successful, he gives you the phone automatically to answer the call.
4) After the phone is headed (sic) to you, the operator puts on the meter which identifies your call.
5) You are to answer or make only your call.
6) When your call is ended, hand over the phone to the operator. He will then stop the meter.
7) If your call does not go through, tell the operators to insist.
8) In case of a problem, contact 7718.04.05.

the world that would have been FCFA 100 or FCFA 500 respectively. Those who run telephone call boxes depend heavily on the C-13 call box for their credit transfer and bonuses because of the particularly attractive bonuses they offer. The call box has 'Thirteen Commandments' (see above) which are divided into two parts: five for credit transfer customers and eight for those who want to make calls. Our observations indicated that between 8 a.m. when this call box opens and 10 p.m. when it closes more than eighty people make calls on a daily basis. Of these eighty, thirty-five make international calls. This was a far higher number than at the ordinary call boxes around town. After going through the call registers of most of our respondents other than this one, it was evident that only twenty to forty people make calls daily at other call boxes. Most people who came to make calls from either the C-13 call box or other call boxes came with their phones and scrolled the numbers directly from their own phones. Asked why they prefer to make calls from call boxes, the answer was that it was cheap to call from the booth. Those at the C-13 call box claimed that it was cheaper there. This logically answered our question and again revealed that people own mobile phones for reasons of prestige or for incoming calls as most prefer to *make* their calls from call boxes. It is therefore common to access phones through call boxes because they are cheap. Again the fact that there are many boxes tells us how many people do not have phones in the strict sense of having a phone and preferring to call via boxes.

New hierarchies? Call-box owners, workers and customers

Most of the owners of the boxes work in them but a minority of the owners have other duties. A case in point is the call box run by Jonathan but which is owned by a university student who cannot be at the box and at the same time effectively attend lectures at the university. Another box is owned by a pastor who is always busy with his pastoral duties. Yvette's call box is owned by a woman who works for an NGO. The C-13 call box is owned by a business magnate who lives and works in Douala and employs six people who work shifts in his call box. The C-13 call box could be seen as the pinnacle of the boxes in terms of the capital that has been pumped into business and customer operations. The owner has invested capital worth FCFA5 million in it. The fact that people work and own call boxes gives an indication of the history of the economy in general. MTN Buea used to own some of the boxes but had to discontinue ownership. In an interview (name withheld), one of their staff claimed it was because they only used them to promote their business interests.

At a time when Cameroon's economy is going through an economic blizzard as a result of a second reduction of 80% in workers' salaries and a devaluation of the currency by 100%, the economic and social situation of most Cameroonians is being accentuated and aggravated by unemployment. It is because of this that many are opting to employ themselves to operate telephone calls boxes and remain self-employed as palliative measures. Others, whose salaries are very low, prefer to open telephone call boxes and employ others, thus raising additional income. The bottom line is that call boxes generate income for both the owners and those working in them. What do these boxes then symbolize for society? It has rapidly changed in outlook and new competition has emerged that is leading to further inequalities although creating employment at the same time.

Since the introduction of the Structural Adjustment Programme, the Cameroon economy has experienced difficult times. Those who have not lost their jobs now earn very low salaries and in order to increase them have been quick to open call boxes since the arrival of cell phones on the scene. They now own call boxes and employ people to work for them. Those who have remained unemployed after graduating from university or who dropped out of school for whatever reason have found employment in these boxes. Some now even own their own call boxes. The popularization of the cell phone by MTN led to many people purchasing their own phones, not necessarily in order to make calls but to store numbers and then call from call boxes. Owning a phone was for prestige and status. Amongst all these owners, workers and customers, MTN is the key player in the business field in Cameroon in general, and Buea in particular, fulfilling the needs of an uncertain economy.

For Buea Rural Council, telephone call boxes symbolize a new form of revenue and so a new column has been added to their *Ledger*. All our respondents maintained that they pay the council FCFA 30,000 per annum in compulsory business tax. If we assume that there are 550 call boxes in Buea and each pays FCFA 30,000, then the council is making FCFA 16,500,000 (approx. € 21,000) a year. The actual figure may be higher given that new boxes are opening on a daily basis. For the landlords, telephone call boxes come with new forms of revenue. A call box stands on 60 cm² of land that is rented by the box owner. According to our informants, they pay a fixed rent of FCFA 5,000 and a few rents their boxes from the owners for FCFA 5,000. Out of the forty-five call boxes at the Mile 17 motor park, thirty pay rent to those who own the boxes. This is, of course, the minority.

Conclusion

Cameroon was colonized by the Germans in 1884 and by 1888 the need for telegraphic communication was under discussion. However it was not until 1898 that telephone cables reached Buea and by 1900 the lines were being extended to the country's interior. Telephone communication was continued by the British for business and political transactions but the phone remained a tool for the rich and was beyond the reach of ordinary Cameroonians. The introduction of the mobile phone in Buea in the early 21st century has offered a new dimension to communication. The geography of communication and the social landscape have been transformed. What was fundamental was the uncertainty in the economy and this was accompanied by the arrival of telephone call boxes or booths that never existed during the colonial era or in the first three decades after independence. These boxes appear to symbolize new hierarchies in society and we could talk, in general, of the hierarchy of the boxes. There are those who own boxes; those who sell telephone cards; and those who are employees. These inequalities also open up new opportunities for access to wealth. Elvis's call box comes in the next of hierarchy and then the others follow. Closely related to this is the social inequality that these boxes accentuate in society. There is inequality between those who work in them for others and those who own boxes and thus work for themselves. Hierarchies have either been created or reinforced through the voice of communication and in today's uncertain economy, the model thus fits. This is different to the plantation economy that dominated the littoral quadrant of Cameroon in the first decades of the 20th century and when people were certain of what they could earn depending on where they worked.

These boxes symbolize the gender inequality in society. Following our demographic statistics of a total of 200 boxes, 150 were occupied by women and only 50 by men. These women represented a different position in society. Most were not married and ranged in age from about thirty to their mid-forties. Others were school dropouts. For both men and women, the boxes were, above all, an avenue to employment. Most respondents saw working in the call boxes as the only way to be self-employed.

From the discussion above on council revenues from call boxes, it could be concluded that the State, in the form of the council, is making a profit. MTN is doing the same for the benefit of the state and not so much for its customers who have to deal with uncertainties in their daily lives by gambling on finding the best opportunities available.

And last but not least, these telephone boxes offer a new landscape in the Buea municipality. Yellow is the omnipresent colour of communication and air time as promoted in MTN's adverts and cannot be avoided. MTN may even be writing a new chapter in the history, ethnography and social sciences in Buea, and perhaps also in other African towns and cities.

References

National Archives, Buea

File No. 474/1921 Ba (1922) 2 Report for the League of Nations 1922; Report on the Victoria
    Division, Cameroons Province written for the League of Nations by A.R. Whitman, District
    Officer, 30 September 1921.
File No. 121/1931, Notes on Cameroons Province for the League of Nations Report, 1931, Ba
    (1931) 6. NAB.
File No. SP. 920, Notes for the League of Nations Report, 1937.NAB.
File No. 132/1920, Telephone Service Complaints Re, 11 September 1920, NAB.
Letter No. M.P. No. 791/262/1921 from Plantations Department to Director Posts and
    Telegraphs, Wolley, Lagos, 17 March 1921, NAB.
Letter No. T662/322/18 from Posts and Telegraphs, Director of Government Telegraphs, Lagos,
    Southern Nigeria, 12 August 1918, National Archives Buea (henceforth NAB).
Letter No. 199/21, Manager Tiko Plantation to the Supervisor of Plantations, Ekona, 20 September
    1920, NAB.

Other references

DE BRUIJN, M. & H. VAN DIJK (1995), *Arid Ways, Cultural understandings in Fulbe Society, Central Mali*,
    Amsterdam: Thela publishers.
HORST, A. & D. MILLER (2006), *The cell phone: An anthropology of communication*, Oxford: Oxford
    University Press.
KONINGS, P. (1993), *Labour resistance in Cameroon: Managerial strategies and labour resistance in the agro-
    industrial plantations of the Cameroon Development Corporation*, London: James Currey/Heinemann.
NGOH, V.J., ed. (2004), *Cameroon: From a federal to a Unitary State, 1961-1972: A critical study*, Limbe:
    Design House.
MBEMBE, A. (2000), 'Everything can be negotiated: Ambiguities and challenges in a time of
    uncertainty'. In: B. Brenner & P. Trulson, eds., *Manoeuvring in an environment of uncertainty:
    Structural change and social action in Sub-Saharan Africa*, pp. 265-275.
NYAMNJOH, F.B. (2005), *Africa's Media: Democracy and the politics of belonging*, London: ZED Press.
PERTIERRA, R. (2005), 'Mobile phones, identity and discursive intimacy', *An Interdisciplinary Journal of
    Humans in ICT Environments* 1: 23-44.
RUDIN, H. (1938), *Germans in the Cameroons, 1884-1914: A case study in modern imperialism*, Yale: Yale
    University Press.
SMITH, D.J. (2006), 'Cell phones, social inequality and contemporary culture in Nigeria', *Canadian
    Journal of African Studies* 40(3): 497-523.

4

The mobile phone, 'modernity' and change in Khartoum, Sudan

Inge Brinkman, Mirjam de Bruijn & Hisham Bilal

Introduction

This chapter considers the impact and appropriation of the mobile phone in Khartoum, the capital of Sudan, by focusing on the social and cultural processes that accompany it. Central to our argument are local interpretations and meanings attributed to the mobile phone. These new dynamics and debates involve topics as diverse as morality and landscape, family ties and linguistic puns. Through this wide variety of themes we gather not only the hopes and aspirations but also the fears and critique that people in Khartoum may have in connection with the mobile phone.

During its short history, the socio-economic meaning and effect of the mobile phone in Khartoum have undergone vast changes. As the mobile phone was first introduced in Khartoum in 1997, its initial glamour has started to wear off and people are now assessing not only their positive experiences with mobile phones but also the problems related to mobile telephony. People in Khartoum describe the impact of the introduction of the mobile as a combination of benefits and disadvantages, of opportunities and restrictions. Many have come to appreciate the possibilities offered by mobile telephony but are wary of the risks and social problems involved.

The focus during the team's fieldwork was, although not exclusively, on university circles and networks related to the educated. Students are known to form an important group of mobile telephone users despite their sometimes limited financial means. And quite a number of university graduates have found employment in the mobile telephone business. For this case-study, some eighteen people working in the sector were interviewed. Except for one, all of them were men. Although a number of women are active in the mobile telephone business, the great majority are male. Interviews were held with people from the highest level in the sector to credit sellers in the market, and they all talked about their activities in the business as well as of their experiences with mobile telephony as end-users. In addition, eight end-users, four of them women, and one non-user were interviewed. The interviews were conducted in various parts of Greater Khartoum.

This chapter is based on research carried out as a pilot study in the framework of collaboration between the telecom company Zain and the African Studies Centre in Leiden that started in July 2007. The study aimed to interpret the interaction between new ICT and social relations, especially with regards to mobility patterns. It consisted of three case-studies: one in Karima, a small town in the north, one focusing on the recent developments in communication technologies in Juba in Southern Sudan and the case-study presented here in Khartoum. The term 'interaction' was crucial in our focus: we explicitly view ICT not only as shaping societies but also as societies shaping new ICT (de Bruijn & Brinkman 2008).

Such interaction can only be studied meaningfully with a qualitative methodology. Qualitative research engenders a better understanding of people's evaluations of the mobile phone and the meanings attributed to new communication technologies. The study was inspired by other studies on mobile telephony based on observations in Latin America, the US and Europe. In their approach towards 'communication anthropology', Horst & Miller (2006) studied the social relations that are created by the use of the mobile phone. Goggin (2006) and Katz (2006) offer an interpretation of aspects of mobile phone culture in which the issue of identity is central. In these approaches, new communication technologies are not seen in deterministic terms: the introduction of the mobile phone does not automatically dictate changes in society. On the contrary, technology and society are defined in a relationship of mutual appropriation. This has also informed our approach and we argue against the thesis of technological determinism that presumes a causal relationship between technology and society. Processes of such mutual appropriation in the past may be instructive, and since such appropriation is likely to be related to particular historical, socio-cultural, economic and political contexts, we

seek to combine the anthropological qualitative approach with historical interpretation.

The project in Sudan was a pilot study. It was conducted over a five-month
period and included a literature study, fieldwork, the transcription of interviews and
observations, the writing of a report and the production of a short film. The
findings presented here must therefore be regarded as preliminary, and should be
read as an invitation to more extensive research into this interesting and important
theme.

Photo 4.1   Zain Street in Khartoum

Khartoum: The hub

Although the area where Khartoum is located today had been a settlement for a
very long time, the city as such was only established as a small garrison town after
Ottoman-Egyptian rule was extended into Sudan in the 1820s. The Ottoman Vice-
roy of Egypt, Muhammad Ali, saw the expansion into the Sudan as a chance to gain
access to local wealth resources based on land, cattle, gold and the slave trade.
Situated strategically near the junction of the White Nile and the Blue Nile, the town
soon grew, became an important trading centre in the region and was established as
the national capital. The Ottoman-Egyptian Empire included many regions of to-

day's Sudan, although in the south their control was minimal, and their rule was contested in other areas too.

The Mahdist Revolt that started in the 1880s has often been presented as the most successful attempt to resist government by the Ottoman-Egyptians but it was also a movement that focused on religious purity in a politically insecure situation (Holt & Daly 2000). They managed to take large parts of Sudan, and shifted the capital from Khartoum proper to Omdurman, the town on the opposite bank of the White Nile. For many Sudanese, Omdurman is still the historical capital of Sudan, partly because it is larger and more densely populated. After the Mahdists lost the crucial Battle of Omdurman in 1898, the British returned the capital to Khartoum and General Kitchener planned the city so that its neighbourhoods were in the pattern of the Union Jack (Hamdan 1960). It attracted a growing number of in-habitants and became important as the country's political and administrative centre. A store house and arsenal were built on the other side of the Blue Nile and this area came to be known as Khartoum North (Bahri). It became the major industrial area, although its population also grew over the years from 700,887 at the time of the last population census in 1993 to an estimated 1,725,570 in 2007.

These three towns came to form a conglomerate called Greater Khartoum. Omdurman is by far the largest of the three, having over three million residents. In 1956 the Greater Khartoum area had some 98,000 inhabitants, in 1983 there were well over 1.3 million inhabitants, the total population was approaching 3 million by 1993, and today the figure is over 7 million (Hamdan nd). This growth has been due to natural causes, to international refugees coming from neighbouring countries in the 1970s, and to a large influx of internally displaced persons (IDPs) from the war zones in the south and Darfur from the 1980s onwards.

Khartoum's markets
Markets are a central feature of this tripartite city. In many cases, markets are linked to transportation facilities and are located near bus stations or large traffic inter-sections. The important markets include the well-known *el Suq el Arabi* (Arabian Market) in Khartoum's city centre, *Suq Omdurman* and *Suq Bahri*, but also the *Suq Libya* (Libyan Market in Omdurman), the popular *el Suq el Shaabi*, *Suq el Wihda* (Unity Market in Khartoum North), *Suq el Leffa* (Turn Market in Khartoum) and *el Suq el Mahali* (the Market of the Place). Many people in Khartoum visit one of these markets every day. While road transport is generally sparse in Sudan as a whole, Khartoum's city centre is plagued by long traffic jams and high levels of air pol-lution as a result. Public transport comes in the form of shared taxis, buses and, within neighbourhoods, rickshaws.

Markets are usually organized by product, with each street offering its own product. Obviously such connections between location and product are subject to change. For example, a street in Foreigners' Market in the centre of Khartoum where clothes used to be sold later changed to being a 'mobile telephone street'.[1] However, in less extensive markets, people have to diversify as much as they can. Thus a businessman may have a licence for a photo shop but at the same time offer credit transfers and repair services in mobile telephony.[2]

The relatively new business of mobile telephony is highly visible in the markets: mobile telephones and accessories are on display and businesses have elaborately decorated shop windows. Street vendors, however, may have no more than a suitcase, three mobile phones (so as to include the Zain, Sudani and MTN networks) and a placard announcing their activities. Survival is precarious for such street vendors: the police may appear at any time, confiscate their wares and demand payment before their possessions are returned to them.[3]

Many of the businessmen are part of extensive international trading networks. One man the research team met had received his education in business and technology in Egypt and now, as a trader, regularly travelled to Dubai to buy products to

Photo 4.2   A luxury mobile phone shop in Khartoum

---

[1]   Interview with a shopkeeper in Khartoum's Foreigners' Market, 22/09/07 & 23/09/07.
[2]   Interview with a shop owner (photography/mobile phones), Omdurman, 19/08/07.
[3]   Interview with a mobile phone shop owner in Khartoum's Arabian Market, 10/08/07.

sell in Sudan.[4] The economic chains involved are extensive and, at the multinational level, incredible sums of money are being earned. Some of this is being reinvested in modern, upmarket shops.

The sector also consists of chains of distribution from local shops to market stalls and, like the multinational companies, these are often tied to economic trading networks in Egypt, Saudi Arabia, Dubai, Uganda and elsewhere.

Morality and socio-economic meanings

Economic opportunities and restrictions

The mobile phone is opening up a wide range of new economic possibilities for many people. Handsets have their seasons and prices rise sharply round special occasions such as Ramadan and Eid al-Fitr, and during the Hajj pilgrimage period. At this time people import brand new models from the countries they visit and these new phones can fetch up to double the price originally paid for them. It is a risky business, however, as prices can also drop spectacularly soon afterwards.

Economic possibilities are also growing for some merchants not directly involved in mobile telephony. Through their mobile phones, traders can attract new customers and people active in petty trading and small businesses have their mobile phone numbers clearly displayed so that they can be reached by prospective clients.

The advantages of having a mobile phone are especially relevant for women in business. As they are not always allowed to walk outside on the streets and may not be able to travel at all times of the day, making appointments by phone can help them to plan their lives and allow them to operate within the imposed limits of 'respectable' behaviour. The mobile phone can also help to limit the number of fruitless visits they make. For Fatima, a henna painter, the mobile phone constitutes an important income-generating tool. All her customers reach her by phone and she used the first income she ever had (in 2002) to invest in a mobile phone. When asked the reason, she answered: 'I heard that the mobile phone would bring work and that was exactly what has happened.'[5] Many business people testify that the mobile phone offers new possibilities to fix up business appointments, arrange for wares to be delivered and develop clear time schedules. In short, business organization is greatly enhanced by the mobile phone.

Economics is not only important for those in business. End-users also try to use the mobile phone for their own benefit and as economically as possible. Credit transfer has become an important way of sending money between relatives and between lovers. End-users agree on a 'sign language' so they can place orders with petty traders. Tea sellers, for example, may be reached through a 'missed call' system

---

[4]   Interview as above.
[5]   Interview with a female henna painter at her house in Khartoum North, 23/09/07.

that costs nothing at all.[6] The initial purchase of a mobile phone is a financial burden for many people so, to deal with this, students at one of the colleges in Khartoum established a credit association through which they saved money to buy a mobile phone for each member in turn.[7]

Many people have more than one SIM card and, if they can afford it, several handsets. In Khartoum this is predominantly to ensure the best rate: calling contacts with the same operator is usually cheaper and some companies have special rates at night or offer other incentives or promotional packages. Other people use different phones for different aspects of their lives and have separate phones for work and private use. These strategies indicate the lengths people go to in order to reduce costs and gain maximum benefit from their mobile phone.

Concerns were regularly raised during the team's interviews about the risks of spending too much on calling. Some people mentioned a local saying: '*Mobile yakul israb*' (the mobile phone eats and drinks with you), implying that a large percentage of a household budget can be spent on a mobile phone.[8] People who, for whatever reason, do not have access to or can only make limited use of a mobile phone are excluded from the economic networks and chains mentioned above. For some, this is a choice; they may be against the mobile phone in principle or feel that they do not need one. Even so, economic considerations play a role in many of these cases. One non-user indicated that he saw no need to have a mobile phone and mentioned a number of disadvantages related to it, but he also held that mobile phones were too expensive: 'In the past I had one but I stopped it due to the high running costs. The normal telephone is cheaper and it does the same thing that a mobile phone does.'[9] This man saw no need to have a mobile phone as he felt his fixed line was serving him well, but there are also large numbers of people in Khartoum who simply cannot afford a mobile phone.

Social bonds and privacy
The mobile phone is not only relevant for the economic sector in Sudan. Social bonds are perceived as extremely important in Sudanese society and people are using modern communication technologies to forge, re-establish or reinforce these bonds. In many cases, people use the mobile phone exclusively to create and/or maintain social connections. These may involve existing networks of family and friends but also new networks of mobile phone users. This (re)production of social

---

[6]   Interview with the Deputy Directory General, NTC, at NTC's office in Khartoum, 1/08/07.
[7]   Interview with a male college graduate working at the International Center for Peace Culture in Khartoum, 7/08/07.
[8]   Informal conversation with a university teacher and interview with a male trader at his shop in Khartoum North, 9//08/07.
[9]   Interview as above.

Photo 4.3: 'Credit Hiba'

Hiba is a 26-year-old graduate student at the University of Khartoum who has just begun her practical specialization year at the Ministry of Irrigation. She started university in 2002 and was immediately given a mobile phone by an uncle who lives in the US: 'Uncle Seddig was refusing the idea of a mobile phone but he bought it for me to keep in touch with my family.' As Hiba is from Kordofan and has many relatives in Bahrain and the US, it is difficult for her to reach her relatives other than by mobile phone. Soon her bills reached 25,000 Sudanese pounds every quarter, and, although her family helped her to settle the bills, she felt the financial burden had become too high.

That is why she started a credit service a year ago: 'I thought: if I use the mobile phone to transfer credit on a commercial basis, I can use the money to run my own mobile phone. I use the profit from the credit calls to communicate with my family (my mother, my father and so on). Instead of being a financial burden, my mobile phone covers itself financially.'

Initially she had only a few customers but as her network started to grow her income increased and she no longer spends extra money on her telephone bill. Hiba knows her customers well; most of them are relatives or female friends from university. She experienced problems with some of them as they did not pay her and would try to postpone clearing their financial debt with her indefinitely. That is why she no longer accepts customers who want to pay later. Despite the income she gets from the credit transfer, she stated that she will stop the business as soon as she has a job. Hiba's nickname is 'Hiba Rasiid': 'Credit Hiba'.

For this young woman, the mobile phone constitutes an important way of keeping in touch with her family: 'The mobile phone is one of the technologies which is very effective and we benefit from it. For example, you can use it to communicate with those you cannot reach physically, especially in emergencies, wherever they are.' Once Hiba had to sit an exam but was mistaken about the time. The teacher called her on her mobile phone and, as she was able to appear within ten minutes, allowed her to participate. This way she did not miss her exam, which would have cost her an extra year of study: 'Think about it, if I had not had a mobile phone, how would he have been able to find me?'

Yet Hiba is sharply aware of the negatives side of the mobile phone and feels that it should be used 'rationally', not in a 'bad' way such as for 'immoral relations' in which people 'spend their time chatting on the mobile phone all night'. 'There are many advantages. It is a means of communication and people use it in their businesses. It can help people to win millions but at the same time, through it, they can also lose millions in meaningless conversations against God's will!'

bonds redirects the function of mobile telephony. While designed for communication and information exchange, people in Sudan are also using it as a form of technology to maintain, create and/or expand their networks *per se*. This explains why some interviewees talked about the 'wrong way' of using the mobile phone.

> Sudanese people like to talk very much! That is Sudanese. In Europe it is: 'Hello … goodbye'. Only a small subject is discussed and then: 'Bye bye'. In Sudan, however: 'How is your family? How is your brother? How are your friends? How are you since the last time I saw you? and so on. Talking very much! That is Sudanese.[10]

In terms of privacy, opinions about the mobile phone vary. Some people appreciate the possibility of talking in private on their mobile phone; in stark contrast to fixed lines in houses and shops. Amr, a young university graduate who deals in credit transfer, explained that privacy was the most important reason for him to buy a mobile phone: 'I think the most important motivation for me to buy a mobile phone is the privacy; that you can be sure that any phone call for you comes to you directly.'[11] Others, however, find it tiring and annoying that they can be reached day and night by everyone and they consider it a breach of their privacy. People can switch off their mobile phone if they feel tired or depressed, or if they can no longer tolerate the indirect form of contact that the phone establishes.[12] Some people indicated that they cannot survive without their mobile phone and feel anxious without it: 'It is like a drug. After one month you cannot do without it,' one man commented. Obviously such cases of 'mobile phone addiction' are adversely related to the issue of over-expenditure.[13]

Generations and the family

For many Sudanese, relations within the family are the most intimate and intense ties in terms of social contact. Such ties are not restricted to the nuclear family but may include ever-widening circles of relatives. A number of Sudanese of working age, especially men, have moved away from home to earn an income and this migration may involve moving from the rural areas to a regional town, further afield from one region to another or to Khartoum. International migration, especially to the Arab world – Saudi Arabia, Egypt and other countries – is also common. Many families from war zones have been separated: some members have continued living in the South or Darfur, others have fled as IDPs to Khartoum, and yet others may have ended up in Uganda, Chad or elsewhere. For these families, the mobile phone provides a welcome opportunity to restore or maintain kinship bonds.

---

[10] Interview with a shop owner in Khartoum city centre, 21/07/07.

[11] Interview with a male student and credit transferer, Omdurman, 17/08/07.

[12] Interview with a male college graduate working at the International Center for Peace Culture in Khartoum, 7/08/07. Interview with a male end-user and journalist at his sister's house in Khartoum, 28/08/07.

[13] Interview with the male manager of Mobitel's Arkaweet shop in Khartoum, 30/07/07.

Family news can be passed on much more rapidly than before. If there is conflict or a problem in the family, decisions can also include absent family members if required, whereas in the past it was usually impossible to reach all the family members who might need to be involved in a discussion. In cases of bereavement, for example, it was often difficult to reach relatives to pass on the news. The mobile phone now offers almost instant access to all family members.[14]

A handset and SIM card have become important presents and remittances that children offer their parents when they work elsewhere. The elderly in most cases do not buy telephones themselves and it is usually those who have an income who buy mobiles both for themselves and for family members. Sons in particular tend to send their parents a mobile telephone so that they can remain in close contact. For many elderly people, their telephone is their 'life line' to the outside world. A 63-year-old woman from Sinja who had moved to Khartoum explained in an interview that at first she felt that people with mobile telephones were 'acting crazy'. She regarded the loud and intrusive presence of the mobile phone negatively and was 'shy' about becoming a mobile phone user herself. Now however, she is convinced of the advantages of the mobile phone as it is the only way her sons, who are living abroad, can contact her.

> Once when I had been in Sinja my sons were trying to call me and they didn't find me at home. Then they tried at my father's house and they told them that I had gone to my sister's place but when they called me there, I had left already. When I heard that, I decided to get a mobile phone to make it easier for them to find me wherever I am.[15]

The mobile phone intensifies links between the town and the countryside as people working in urban areas can call their relatives and friends 'at home' in the rural areas more frequently.

It is also argued that the mobile phone allows people to lie more easily. When asked what changes the mobile phone had brought to Sudanese culture, a businessman argued:

> It changed matters, it really did: everything is different. Before the mobile phone, Sudanese people they would not talk so much but all they said was true, but when this mobile phone came, everybody is just telling falsities on the cell phone. They will always say matters like:

> 'Where are you?' 'Just near you!' But he is not near me at all, he is maybe two hours away from me![16]

Many people take a highly balanced view of the relationship between the mobile phone and social interaction:

---

[14] Informal conversation with a university graduate.
[15] Interview with an elderly female housewife and end-user at her house in Khartoum, 22/0807.
[16] Interview with a male shop owner in Khartoum city centre, 21/07/07; iinterview with a male worker at a credit transfer shop in Khartoum North, 9/08/07; iinterview with a male mobile phone shop owner in Khartoum's Arabian Market, 10/08/07.

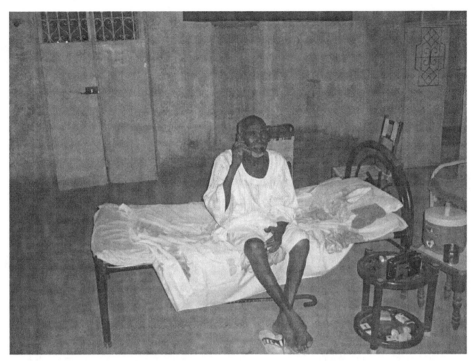

Photo 4.4   Grandfather in the village calling his son in Khartoum

> The mobile phone decreases visits between people and this is a disadvantage. Face-to-face interaction between people is more comfortable and people feel free to take their time with this. The mobile phone does not offer this possibility. At the same time, however, it has intensified my relationship with relatives abroad and connects Sudan and its various parts.[17]

Even within the household, informants argue, the mobile phone can lead to increasing distance between family members. Sons and daughters may quickly switch off their mobile phone when parents appear and they then wonder what their children are hiding from them.[18] Secret conversations tend to be held in their bedrooms where parental control is less. In most cases, these 'secrets' concern relations between the sexes.

Gender and morality

In line with stereotypical representations of gender relations in Islamic societies, it is often assumed that Islamic women are subordinated and confined to the private sphere, while men dominate the public space and are in charge of the political and economic arena. The reality is infinitely more complex (Nageeb 2004: 1-2). Under

---

[17]   Interview with a male electronics engineer in a maintenance shop in Khartoum North, 9/08/07; interview with a male student and credit transferer, Omdurman, 17/08/07.

[18]   Informal conversation with a university teacher.

Islamic law, women in Khartoum are subjected to several dress restrictions and, at least in the public space, the sexes have to be kept separate as far as possible. In Khartoum, there is sharp controversy about the nature of respectful Islamic behaviour. In the view of those defending Islamist policies, traditions kept women submissive, while islamization allows women to actively participate in public life. The women interviewed by Salma Nageeb, however, were negative about 'the attacks that claimed traditional norms of gender segregation were not Islamic enough'. They felt that in the past men and women each had their social space and respected each other's activities. In their view, the new Islamist policies have led to a disintegration of this system and, albeit under a veneer of Islamic appearance, disrespectful behaviour.

> I see them from my house when they come out of university. They wear their black cloth [referring to the Islamic dress] and cover their heads, but their laughter breaks the ears – walking with men and eating in the street. Where is modesty? (*Ibid.*: 21-24)

Similar debates about gender relations and morality have also surrounded the introduction of the mobile phone. During fieldwork, it was the issue that was most frequently brought up when discussing the advantages and disadvantages of mobile phone behaviour. Issues of respectful behaviour and sexual morals have become closely tied to the introduction of the mobile phone. Some people hold that the mobile phone directly contributes to immorality and the increasing divorce rate. Appointments can now even be made from the house and keeping a wife confined to her home is no longer enough to 'control' her activities.[19]

Especially for young people, the mobile phone has become a central strategic device in courtship. In the new dynamics of relations between men and women, 'love' is a central theme. Given the financial aspects involved, it is astonishing how many youngsters of high-school age and especially university students have a mobile phone. They regard it as a necessary tool for social networking and will do everything possible to become a subscriber.

Parents may give their daughters a mobile phone in order to be able to exert closer control over their whereabouts but young women overcome these restrictions and use their mobile phones to reach and be reached by admirers. The mobile phone gives, especially women, new opportunities to establish contacts and be masters of their own networking. As one young man explained: 'Communication technology has made it easier to be in touch with a girl. In the past it was difficult because of our traditional society but today they can't control it if a girl has a mobile phone.'[20]

Obviously this comes with risks involved. Stories circulate of young women being contacted by mobile phone and lured on a date only to be robbed of their

---

[19] Informal conversation with a university teacher.
[20] Interview with a male worker at a credit transfer shop in Khartoum North, 9/08/07.

handset and their jewellery.[21] This is a general complaint: the mobile phone does not only make social and business contact easier, it also facilitates crime. The mobile phone can be crucial in emergencies and many see it also as a form of security to be able to reach the police or the emergency services straightaway but many Khartoum residents also see the mobile phone as encouraging theft and offering increased opportunities for criminals.[22]

A number of young people regard the increased possibilities of communicating with age-mates of the opposite sex as one of the most important features of the mobile phone. 'In the past it was very difficult to communicate with the opposite sex on fixed telephones, especially in the evenings given the social norms. But the arrival of the mobile phone broke down all these borders.'[23] However, many people fear that this is leading to an increase in indecency and immorality. They refer to the exchange of pornographic pictures via mobile phones and to young people speaking at length to one another behind their parents' backs: 'On the negative side the mobile phone makes it more difficult for the family to follow their sons and daughters. You may find a girl talking to a boy [on the phone] in her room for the whole night.'[24]

Young men are sometimes pestered by women who ask them to send credit,[25] while women complain of strangers calling them. Fatima, who gives her number to many women who may want to call her to make an appointment for a henna painting appointment, is sometimes harassed by male callers who she does not know.

Q: You give out your number to your customers. Have you faced any problems as a result?
A: I am annoyed by some men who call to harass me. Actually they don't even know my name and call me to speak foul language, they shock me!
Q: Could you tell me how that happened to you?
A: Once someone called me here…
Q: After you had got married?
A: Yes. He said 'Hello' to greet me. I asked him: 'Who are you?' He told me that he wanted to speak to the owner of the mobile phone. I asked him: 'Did you call this number [mentions her number]?' He said: 'Yes.' I said: 'So in that case you should actually know whose mobile phone this is.' He said: 'No, I don't know. I don't know her.' I said: 'Well, if you don't know her, then why are you calling? What do you want?' He said: 'I want a … [refrains from mentioning the word].' So I insulted him and scolded him, insulting him and his mother and his sister; he drove me mad!

Another time somebody called me and told me that he had found my number in his mobile phone. Well, he annoyed me very much and I turned the phone off in his ear. I explained to my husband that I did not know that person. My husband was present when that person

21 Interview with a male shop worker in Khartoum city centre, 21/07/07.
22 Interview as in note 21.
23 Interview with a male student and credit transferer, Omdurman, 17/08/07.
24 Interview with a male trader at his shop in Khartoum North, 9/08/07; interview (quote) with a male credit seller on a street in Khartoum North, 10/08/07; interview with a male mobile phone shop owner in Khartoum's Arabian Market, 10/08/07.
25 Interview as in note 24.

called me. … My husband ordered me to end the call and not to talk to strangers any-more![26]

Mobile phone culture

Modernity and social status

The mobile phone is not only influencing patterns of social and economic inter-action but is also changing notions of time, privacy and prestige. The mobile phone is becoming a part of the environment, the language and the body and, in this sense, we can talk about a 'mobile phone culture'.

The mobile phone has changed patterns of social interaction in that people may start a telephone conversation in the middle of a meeting or face-to-face conversa-tions. Hierarchical social contact has thus come into being, whereby mobile-phone conversations take precedence over face-to-face contact. As these phone conver-sations may be between lovers, spouses or relatives, the boundaries of public and private space are being redesigned in the process. Conversely, people complain of being called for business purposes at most inconvenient hours, when they are re-laxing or enjoying leisure activities.[27]

The mobile phone is seen as constituting a breach with the past: letter writing is on the decline and, as indicated above, people fear that face-to-face contact is also decreasing. The mobile phone is associated with modern life, with new dimensions of speed and immediacy. 'I depend on SMS to organize my day,' one man said.[28] The mobile phone is perceived as something new and revolutionary: 'This is the age of speed and globalization.'[29]

In its early phase, all Mobitel services were post-paid lines and customers would receive their bill afterwards. Only people with a certain income had access to this system and mobile phones were thus only available to Khartoum's well-to-do. Pre-paid accounts were introduced in 1999 but customers still had to pay to receive calls. When this barrier was removed, competition started between companies to offer the best rates for their customers and the network expanded to areas outside Khartoum. Mobile telephony became more widespread and attracted customers from the mid-dle classes and the poorer strata of society.

These two phases in the history of mobile telephony in Khartoum clearly had a bearing on the patterns of prestige related to the industry. As initially only a few people could afford a mobile phone, it was considered a sign of great wealth to pos-sess one. 'Mobile phones invaded Khartoum recently, particularly thanks to busi-nessmen, and rapidly became significant items of status presentation' (Nageeb 2004:

---

[26]   Interview with a female henna painter at her house in Khartoum North, 23/09/07.

[27]   Interview with a male shop owner in Khartoum city centre, 21/07/07.

[28]   Interview with a male college graduate working at the International Center for Peace Culture in Khar-toum, 7/08/07.

[29]   Interview as above; interview with a male credit seller on a street in Khartoum North, 10/08/07.

26, note 3). During the first five years of mobile telephony in Sudan, having a mobile phone was regarded as an indication of prestige and riches.

With the mobile phone's increased popularity, the upper classes have felt less need to show off their cell phones and they have just become an integral part of their lives, their culture, and even their body. They always carry their phone switched on and, with money not a consideration, they use the models that give them access to all the amenities they might ever need. However, while the mobile phone has become so self-evident for them, it has become less of a mark of prestige than it used to be.

The function of status marker related to the mobile phone has shifted to middle-class residents and even to those on low incomes. They save up to buy the latest model, decorate it with lights and other accessories, equip it with fancy ring tones and wear their phone conspicuously on their belt.[30] A statement from a young man who received his mobile phone as a present from a friend back in 2001 is indicative of its changing prestige:

> Maybe in the past it was somewhat strange to exchange a mobile phone as a gift amongst people. It gave rise to many reactions that shows how unusual it was because of the rarity and costs of a mobile phone. So giving it as a present was the highest limit and only for closest relatives. But recently this has changed. You may remember that time when people told tales of people who presented their fiancées with a mobile phone. It was regarded as a source of pride and indicated that they were rich. But nowadays I think buying a mobile phone as a present may be less expensive than other items that can be used as a gift. Taken from a financial perspective, a great number of relatives and contacts may be given a mobile phone. As for me, I gave one as a present to my fiancée and there is another one I gave away as a present. This is a normal thing to do.[31]

In its brief history, the mobile phone has had consequences for the way in which social differentiation is conceptualized. Some people in Khartoum regard it as an 'equalizing' force: 'It is lessening the gap between the rich and the poor.'[32] Yet although some hold that the mobile phone has changed from being a luxury to a necessity,[33] many mobile phone users still try to buy a 'good' model or attempt to turn their phone into an exclusive and special item through ring tones or accessories. Although many people from poor backgrounds cannot afford a mobile phone at all, attempts at 'distinction' through models and features counter the mobile phone's 'equalizing' tendencies.

---

[30] Interview with a male Sudani engineer at his house in Buri, Khartoum, 20/07/07; interview with a male shop owner, Khartoum city centre, 21/07/07; interview with a male credit seller on a street in Khartoum North, 10/08/07; interview with a male student and credit transferer, Omdurman, 17/08/07.

[31] Interview with a male end-user and journalist at his siter's house in Khartoum, 28/08/07.

[32] Interview with a male worker at a credit transfer shop, Khartoum North, 9/08/07; interview with a male credit seller on a street in Khartoum North, 10/08/07.

[33] Interview as above.

Language, numbers and popular culture

In the context of new communication technologies, different linguistic patterns are developing. During colonial times for example, Italian, Maltese, Greek, Syrian, Turkish, Egyptian, British and Sudanese workers were all involved in the railway sector in the sprawling town of Atbara. The railway jargon used in Atbara reflected the cosmopolitan nature of these early Atbara railway workers: *wardiya* was used to indicate a guard or a change of duty (from the Italian *guardia*), *wabur* was used for any steamer, motor vessel or locomotive (from the French *vapeur*) and many English words also entered the Atbara language (Hill 1965; Sikainga 2004).

The introduction of mobile telephony likewise has been accompanied by a new vocabulary and forms of literacy. People are learning the alphabet to be able to do SMS text messaging, whereas those already using SMS may use the codes and abbreviations applied in their network. Such coded linguistic forms are particularly important for youth cultures.[34]

New concepts related to mobile telephony are widely used, many being borrowed from English: the word 'mobile' itself is a case in point. The various models have received nicknames. Thus the name Nokia 3310 was turned into a pun: *talatain ashara* (3310) shifted to *hasharteen hashara* (2 insects, 1 insect). The first Nokia model that could have its cover changed was called *Hirboya* (chameleon) but as it is now considered old-fashioned, big and heavy, its name has changed to *Toba* (brick). Ring tones can be associated with the insects they sound like (e.g. grasshoppers).

Most models are given a local name in addition to their official name. One Samsung model was called after the popular Syrian singer Asalah (Nasri), while another was given the name of a song (*A'ashiqa*) by the Lebanese female pop star Najwa Karam. As is often the case in popular culture, politics has joined the new linguistic patterns; one model is called *janjaweed*, another Rebecca (the name of John Garang's widow) and yet another Salva Kiir (now President of the GOSS).

Mobile telephone numbers came onto the market in a fixed order. As people associated these numbers with the specific groups that were most likely to buy a mobile phone at that time, the numbers are in line with that group. Thus numbers starting with 129 are known as *Sit el shay* (tea sellers), while all those that came next are identified as *El talaba* (students).

In the first few years of mobile phones, the numbers all started with the digits 121, 122 and 123. These numbers are now highly sought after as they are linked to the wealth and prestige of the initial phone buyers. Huge sums of money can be

---

[34] On literacy: interview with a male Mobitel regulator and government affairs consultant at Mobitel headquarters, Mograin, Khartoum, 25/07/07. On youth culture: this is not restricted to Khartoum. The relationship between youth cultures and the new literacy of the Internet and mobile phones has been discussed elsewhere. See, for example, Wang (2005: 185-201).

asked for numbers starting with these digits. A man who trades in handsets and SIM cards was asked whether he was interested in such numbers:

Q: Are you one of those who like special numbers and special models of mobile phone?
A: Yes, I am forced to care about this. I care about special numbers and expensive models because the number of the mobile phone has become a tool for evaluating a person. So I have found myself forced to deal with this, and I have become one of those looking for special numbers even though I have thus had to change my number many times [as a consequence].[35]

Some people go out of their way to buy such a number. One of the researchers involved in the project observed how girls started laughing at a young man who had no money to call but still used an early, and hence expensive, number (Bilal 2007).

In the meantime, the mobile phone has also entered others parts of Sudanese popular culture. It has become a theme in popular songs and the phone companies sponsor television programmes. Advertisements are placed on YouTube and recently the logos used by the mobile phone companies have started to be used as henna tattoos.

Landscape and reach

For those who do not have a mobile phone, the mobile phone can seem to be omnipresent and very conspicuous. There are so many phone shops that people are confronted with the presence of the mobile phone wherever they go and there are the sometimes aggressive advertising campaigns that have come to dominate the city landscape. Entire streets are now filled with huge billboards, buildings are painted in the colours of company logos and companies take out whole-page advertisements in newspapers.

In these campaigns, the companies are trying to appeal to Sudanese sensitivities and play on issues of social bonding, relations with relatives and gender sensitivities. For example, one ad presents a mother who is told that she need not worry when her daughter leaves home to get married because with a mobile phone she will not go 'missing' as she would have in the past. The campaigns do not always fit the Sudanese context perfectly. For example, some people associate the MTN yellow (in their advertisements, MTN uses the concept 'yello') with the madness of the pink palace, called 'yellow palace' in Arabic and now a mental institution. And the word *zain* (Arabic for goodness or beauty) is apparently not used in colloquial language in Sudan.[36]

The mobile phone companies are heavily involved in social work and development projects. This is not only an international trend among multinational companies but is also related to business traditions in the Islamic world. However, quite

---

[35] Interview with a male college graduate working at the International Center for Peace Culture in Khartoum, 7/08/07; interview with a male student and credit transferer, Omdurman, 17/08/07.

[36] Informal conversation with a university teacher.

a lot of people are suspicious of the motives for these activities. 'Sometimes I feel that the social projects in which these companies are involved serve no other purpose than self-promotion,' one informant stated. [37] The same informants also complained that people are lured into becoming subscribers but get very little in return:

> I think competition has led to good results both for the companies and the users. Yet I believe the communication companies should shift from the quantity concept to one of quality because they have already cheated a large number of customers. They focus on how to attract an ever-larger number of customers but don't care about improving their services.

Some campaigns are considered misleading as the conditions are only stipulated in small letters, while the advertisement itself may be gigantic.[38] Customers discuss the (dis)advantages of the promotions offered in the ad campaigns at great length and attempt to benefit as much as they can from the offers presented by the different companies. Complaints that ads do not match end-users' expectations are widespread and intensive debates may follow about the 'cheating' by this or that company.

The conspicuous presence of the mobile phone and companies' ad campaigns have transformed Khartoum's urban landscape. The mobile phone has entered daily conversation as a fully-fledged subject. In this sense, it is also very present for those who do not even possess one. The phone's impact goes far beyond its level of usage alone and has both a material and an immaterial presence in many spheres of life.

In conclusion

The mobile phone in Khartoum: Changes and continuities
The mobile phone has indeed become part and parcel of people's lives, not only in the urban landscape, in people's daily activities and in keeping in touch with family, relatives and business partners, but also in terms of identity construction and the moral debate. Over the ten years that the mobile phone has been around in Khartoum, there has been a shift from it being a status symbol for the well-to-do to it being used by the middle-classes and even poorer people. Aspects of mobile phone culture show not only in the new discourses on numbers but also in the names given to mobile phones and the ways in which people discuss 'modernity' in relation to the mobile phone. It is important to realize that in the other case studies carried out in Sudan (in Juba and Karima), the mobile phone is little used as a gadget for self-identification. The same holds for the new linguistic categories and forms of popular culture. The Khartoum case revealed many examples of puns, nicknames and sayings related to the mobile phone. This may be explained by the phone's relatively long history in Khartoum, although another explanation could be the city's urban

---

[37]   Interview with a male end-user and journalist at his sister's house in Khartoum, 28/08/07.
[38]   Interview as above; informal conversation with a university graduate; interview with Deputy Director General, NTC, Khartoum, 1/08/07.

culture where people have a different attitude to life. All over Sudan, the mobile phone is associated with youth (although in practice many elderly people also use it) but in Khartoum there is concern about the changing practices of courtship, women's mobility and social interaction.

The Khartoum case study also shows that the mobile phone's presence has led to the development of a totally new economic sector. It provides many people with an income through direct involvement in the business, or the mobile phone is used to develop economic activities, also by the poorer strata in society. This economy has introduced new linkages, for example, strong links with the commercial centre of Dubai, and between Khartoum as a distribution point and other parts of Sudan. Older long-distance economic ties are being reinforced; such as relations with Egypt and Saudi Arabia.

In addition, the mobile phone is regarded as an important device for existing businesses to reach new markets and set up different ways of organizing trade. These economic possibilities only form part of the story of the positive factors associated with the mobile phone. Social contact and personal exchange feature highly in people's evaluations of the mobile phone. As a result of the current wars and also due to economic reasons, the Sudanese context has seen a great deal of internal movement and now has a diaspora in many parts of the world. The mobile phone is seen as offering new chances to restore and/or maintain social networks with relatives and friends. As end-users, Sudanese people try to use their mobile phones in the most economic manner, trying to keep, and also enlarge, their social networks as cheaply as possible. The mobile phone has entered the system of gift exchange/remittances that is important in these networks too.

Social networks do not only include close kin. Youngsters, especially students, keep in touch with age-mates by phone, women are using the mobile phone to create new patterns of exchange with other women, and it has also come to play a crucial role in courtship and love affairs. For people whose possibilities for social exchange had previously been limited, the mobile phone constitutes a new form of freedom, offering a sense of privacy, combined with more leverage over the conditions of social interaction. This is not to say that the mobile phone has contributed to more equality in Sudanese society. On the contrary, the mobile phone reinforces, and may even have enlarged, existing social hierarchies as it functions in a complex set of meanings about modernity, trends and display. This is also reflected in popular culture; with the meanings attributed to the oldest mobile phone numbers being a case in point.

In this sense, the mobile phone is not a 'revolutionary' factor in Sudanese society: it largely confirms existing inequalities, both in terms of social status at large and within the family. However it is significant that people regard the mobile phone as 'revolutionary' and an icon of 'modernity'. The notion of modernity is prominent in the positive as well as in the negative evaluations of the mobile phone. Many of what are seen as the phone's advantages are at the same time evaluated as potential risks. An intense debate is being waging about sexual immorality in Islamic culture, increased opportunities for theft and organized crime, addiction to the mobile phone in a context of poverty, secretive behaviour disrupting the relationship between parents and children or husbands and wives, and people 'acting crazy' in contrast to the value placed on 'respectable behaviour'. In addition to these concerns, people are also discussing the scrupulousness of the phone companies, their unbridled campaigning that is transforming the urban landscape and the lack of control over prices and services for customers. The debates on the mobile phone in Khartoum thus include fears and concerns about morality and modernity as well as a positive evaluation of the newly gained freedoms, increased possibilities for economic enterprise, and new ways of creating and maintaining links within social networks.

New media and appropriation

The debate and usage that surround the mobile phone in Khartoum clearly flout a simple dichotomous acceptance/resistance model. In much of the literature on technology in Africa this opposition underlies the interpretation. This is not to say that a consensus exists on the effects of newly introduced communication technologies: views range from interpreting new ICTs as Western hegemony and capitalist exploitation ruinous to African 'traditions' to automatically lauding new technologies as beneficial for the development and progress of the African continent. What binds these two opposite views is that little attention is paid to local evaluations of the mobile phone, or to local interpretations of 'exploitation' and 'development' for that matter. In the final analysis, both views boil down to technological determinism. The introduction of new technologies is interpreted exclusively in terms of 'impact', 'effects' and 'consequences' on the societies concerned, be they positive or negative. The concept of appropriation points to a multi-directional approach: transformations do not only take place in the societies into which the new technologies are launched, the technologies are also transformed under the influence of local creative usages and the process of becoming embedded in a historical, cultural context. The meanings attributed to the mobile phone do not adhere to schemes of 'exploitation' or 'development' and render superfluous the discussion on new technologies being external to Africa. The functioning of the mobile phone in courtship, gift-exchange practices, popular culture and phone business in the Khartoum context has rendered it a new tool, one entirely unforeseen by its designers.

A thesis that presupposes Western tools and technology as a colonizing force misses the point of appropriation and reduces the contradictory meanings of new media to technology to a simple hegemonizing force. In an article on vampire firemen stories in the East African colonial context, White also argued against an interpretation of externally introduced technologies as a purely imperial device designed to serve Western interests:

> Tools and technology have recently been studied as one of the ways Europeans dominated the colonized world; they were supposed to overpower Africans or to mystify them. But the contradictory meanings of tools in these stories is too complex, and too layered, to be explained in any single way. The tools in these stories have already been assimilated; to some extent they were already familiar objects, whatever their origin. What made them fearsome was how and why they were used. (White 1993: 38-41)

The debates surrounding mobile phones in Khartoum show similar concerns. The interviews reveal how mobile telephones are made to fit into local history, how they are creatively used and what strategies have been developed to get the maximum benefit possible from this new device. At the same time, people are expressing anxiety about the ways in which this new technology is being put to use. These worries do not reflect baffled Africans confronted with externally imposed modernity that they are unable to handle nor do the positive evaluations offer proof of the development potential of new communication technologies in Africa. It might be more fruitful to view the mobile phone in Africa in terms of a process of familiarization than as a hegemonizing or developing force *per se*. New media have always posed new risks and offered new possibilities. This is as true in Africa as it is elsewhere. As Gitelman & Pingree (2003: xii) put it in the introduction to *New Media, 1740-1915*: 'There is a moment, before the material means and the conceptual modes of new media have become fixed, when such media are not yet accepted as natural, when their own meanings are in flux'. At such moments, when the meanings and usages of emergent media are still unfixed, the interplay between technological innovation as a factor of change in society and users as agents in shaping technology is sharply apparent (Kline & Pinch 1996: 763-95). The case of the mobile phone in Khartoum amply demonstrates the complex interplay between tools and people.

Future alleys for research

Some of the findings on mobile phone usage in Khartoum are not dissimilar to those described in other African contexts. In the Nigerian as well as in the Burkina Faso context, new dimensions in economic networks and a historical pattern from elite status symbol to more common usage can also be perceived (Smith 2006: 496-523; Hahn & Kabora 2008: 87-109). All the same, the particularities of moral debate and the in-depth nuances of the perceived (dis)advantages of the mobile phone as described above relate to the specific context of Khartoum. The civil wars, long-standing migration patterns, the debate about Islam and respectful behaviour and an urban culture are all important factors in people's understanding of mobile phone usage in Khartoum.

In future research on mobile telephony in Khartoum these concerns and debates need specification, especially in terms of gender, generation and identity. This requires an in-depth study of the relationship between the mobile phone and older communication technologies in Sudanese history. Such historical linking would involve the relationship between older and more recent patterns of mobility as well as past and present policies and politics with regards to the new media. The latter aspect may lead to greater insight into the political economy of mobile phone technology. Much more research is still necessary into the political tensions, national policies and the relationship between the mobile phone companies and political circles in Sudan. A final issue that warrants more attention is the issue of development: how is 'development' defined and how do people view its relationship with the new communication technologies such as the mobile phone?

This contribution has proposed several alleys for future research into the study of communication technologies in Sudan. It is based not so much on theoretical considerations as on conversations held with people living in Khartoum who voiced their understandings and evaluations of the mobile phone. This descriptive framework enabled us to study local processes of appropriation and to move beyond a theoretical debate on new communication technologies as a fixed force either in 'development' or as 'hegemony'.

References

AHMAD, A.S. (2001), *'City of steel and fire': A social history of Atbara, Sudan's Railway Town, 1906-1984*, Oxford: James Currey.

BILAL, H. (2007), 'The study of the social effects of the mobile phone in Northern Sudan: The cases of Khartoum and Karima', unpublished report.

DE BRUIJN, M. & I. BRINKMAN WITH H. BILAL & P. TABAN WANI (2008), *The Nile connection: Effects and meaning of the mobile phone in a (post)war economy in Karima, Khartoum and Juba, Sudan*. Leiden: African Studies Centre, unpublished report.

GITELMAN, L.B. & G.B. PINGREE, eds (2003), *New media, 1740–1915*, Cambridge: MIT Press.

GOGGIN, G. (2006), *Cell phone culture, mobile technology in everyday life*, London: Routledge.

HAHN, H.P. & L. KABORA (2008), 'The domestication of the mobile phone: Oral society and new ICT in Burkina Faso', *Journal of Modern African Studies* 46(1): 87-109.

HILL, R. (1965), *Sudan transport: A history of railway, marine and river Services in the Republic of the Sudan*, London.

HOLT, P.M. & M.W. DALY (2000), *A history of the Sudan. From the coming of Islam to the Present Day*, Harlow: Longman.

HORST, H.A. & D.L MILLER (2006), *The cell phone. An anthropology of communication*, Oxford: Berg.

HAMDAN, G. (1960), 'The growth and functional structure of Khartoum', *Geographical Review* 50(1): 24.

HAMDAN, G. (1960), 'The growth and functional structure of Khartoum', World Gazetteer website: http://www.world-gazetteer.com/wg.php?x=&lng=de&dat=32&geo=-188&srt=pnan&col=aohdq&men=gcis&lng=en (accessed January 2008)

KATZ, J.E. (2006), *Magic in the air: Mobile communication and the transformation of social life*, New Brunswick & London: Transaction Publishers.

KLINE, R. & T. PINCH (1996), 'Users as agents of technological change: The social construction of the automobile in the rural United States', *Technology and Culture* 37(4): 763-95.

NAGEEB, S.A. (2004), *New spaces and old frontiers. Women, social space, and Islamization in Sudan,* Lanham: Lexington Books.

SMITH, D.J. (2006), 'Cell phones, social inequality and contemporary culture in Nigeria', *Canadian Journal of African Studies* 40(3): 496-523.

SPAULDING, J. (1993), 'The birth of an African private Epistolography, Echo Island 1862-1901', *Journal of African History* 34(1): 115-141.

WANG, J. (2005), 'Youth culture, music, and cell phone branding in China', *Global Media and Communication* 1(2): 185-201.

WHITE, L. (1993), 'Cars out of place. Vampires, technology and labor in East and Central Africa', *Representations* 43: 38-41.

5

Trading places in Tanzania: Mobility and marginalization at a time of travel-saving technologies

Thomas Molony

Introduction

This chapter explores everyday socio-economic interaction at a time of travel-saving technologies and looks at the use of mobile phones among workers in Tanzania's domestic tomato and potato trade. The business communication of Kamwene Sanga, a trader based at Dar es Salaam's Kariakoo municipal market, is used as a case study. However, as a wholesaler, he is unusual because he does not have a mobile phone. The emphasis in this chapter is on the centrality of mobility in dealings between farmers in isolated rural communities and wholesale buyers like Kamwene, and it is suggested that mobile phones play a minor role in sustaining a working relationship between the two. For some of the most successful and respected wholesale buyers, interactions with their rural suppliers are as much social as they are economic and this type of interaction appears to rely more on face-to-face communication that cannot be substituted for by distance technologies such as the mobile phone. The chapter also shows how others on the 'mobile margins', who potentially seek to benefit tremendously from easier communication with their urban buyers, are in little position but to maintain their old, pre-mobile-phone methods of interaction.

The chapter starts by explaining the importance of agriculture to many Tanzanians and states the case for looking at perishable foodstuffs in this context. The methods of data collection are then briefly outlined and this is followed by a short sketch of the typographies of the market actors, along with a summary of the advantages mobile phones bring to agricultural trading. The reactions of some people on these mobile margins to their infrastructural marginality and constraints on market access are discussed using what are termed here as 'network reception spots'. The analysis then turns to Kamwene, the successful buyer at Tanzania's trading (and communications) epicentre who travels widely and has gained notoriety for his refusal to use a mobile phone.

Agriculture and mobile phones in Tanzania

Agriculture is Tanzania's most important economic activity and is the country's largest employer of labour, providing a livelihood for some 80% of the economically active population and making the largest contribution (45.3%) of any sector to GDP in 2006 (World Bank 2007). The country's economy is thus predominantly based in the rural areas where about 70% of the Tanzanian population lives (World Bank 2004) and where the extent and severity of poverty is greatest. Tanzania's rural population is however growing more slowly at 1.33% than the 5.06% growth rate among the urban population (UN-Habitat 2002). Urban residents buy most of the remaining half of the total agricultural output that is not consumed by subsistence farming at domestic urban food markets, where the urban poor spend well over two-thirds of their income (World Bank 1999). Added to this growth is the massive influx of migrants to cities such as Dar es Salaam, which is growing at an annual rate of 5.4% (UN-Habitat 2004) and is placing pressure on food supplies. This further calls for a greater understanding of the role of the new information and communication technologies (ICTs) in the marketing systems that direct the production and distribute output to the main points of consumption to ensure that Tanzania's burgeoning urban population, which accounts for 25% of the country's total population (UNFPA 2007)), can buy affordable food. An understanding of domestic food-marketing systems is important here because of agriculture's role in feeding into the industrial and commercial sectors that rely upon agriculture as a source of raw materials and as a market for manufactured goods (Crawford 1997). The functioning of food-marketing systems therefore has considerable impact on both the livelihoods of rural producers and, at a time of rapid urbanization and increasing levels of urban poverty, is also a serious issue in urban development. Despite this, research on agro-food systems has mainly concentrated on exports of produce (Lyon 2003: 12), which runs the risk of ignoring the politically strategic importance of basic food entitlements at the domestic level as 'part and parcel of every Tanzania's birthright' (Bryceson 1993: 4).

Locating the mobile

Perishables were chosen over more staple grains such as rice and maize as the focus in this chapter because they deteriorate more quickly and the delivery process over huge distances relies on fast decision-making lest the crop rots.[1] This necessitates efficient and prompt communication in trading, and ICT has frequently been praised for having the potential to facilitate this in developing countries (DOI 2001; Grace *et al.* 2004; UNDP 2001; World Bank 1998). Any praise of ICT in business, however, is often directed at the Internet which, despite the overwhelming enthusiasm among the poor for mobile phones, still seems to be favoured by multilateral development agencies (Qiang *et al.* 2006). The ICT for Development (ICT4D) community has been aware of this preference for some time (Donner 2006; Duncombe & Heeks 2001; Esselaar *et al.* 2007) and, as Horst & Miller (2007: 157) note in their study of mobile phones in Jamaica, this has also been recognized by *The Economist* which, in a 2005 edition entitled 'The Real Digital Divide' (12-18 March 2005), noted that the Internet requires too many skills and too much knowledge to be the force that can actually bring people out of poverty in the first place. Subsequent editions of the influential magazine, including one with the appropriate title of 'Does Not Compute' (*The Economist*, 8 November 2007), have continued to devote much coverage to the prominence of mobile phones as the key ICT in developing countries.

In contrast to the predictably market-oriented reports of *The Economist*, Horst & Miller's study provides a rich investigation into why mobile phones are so popular among low-income communities and how technology facilitates a wide range of networking strategies beyond simply the accumulation of capital. The process of the establishment of the networks they describe is identified by their Jamaican informants as 'link-up', a practice with kinship and genealogical roots that includes the creation of spiritual and church communities, the search for sexual partners, and coping strategies adopted by low-income households. 'Link-up', argue Horst & Miller (2005), can also account for the rapid adoption of mobile phones and their patterns of use by low-income Jamaicans, and highlights the importance of understanding the local incorporation of these technologies in local forms of networking.

The nuances of 'link-up' are uncovered through ethnography, a method that the authors devote some time to defending, and which they believe can help illuminate

---

[1]   Staples are the most closely documented food crop in terms of government and academic studies because they dominate production and consumption. Ponte's major work on fast crops is one exception.

the connectedness between the different genres (i.e. economic, social, communicative) that observers of ICT in developing countries tend to reduce observations to. As anthropologists, they see link-up as representing their discipline's 'sense of holism as the ordinary experience of individuals who have no reason to compartmentalize their own desires and interests into conventional academic categories' (Horst & Miller 2007: 170). At the same time, they wish to translate their considerable understanding of the context of their informants' experiences, gained through ethnography, and to marry this to a wider international audience of evaluators whose academic or developmental interests they are also familiar with. While this contribution from Tanzania attempts to engage with aspects of the academic literature that relate to social networking, I would concur with Horst and Miller that the in-depth methods that helped to highlight the social appropriation of mobile phones and their use in these networks are not always easily reconciled with evaluative concerns, especially in the field of 'development' (Molony 2008).

Much of the early observation for this study was conducted through observation while 'hanging out', a crude definition of ethnography that was given more academic rigour by a series of semi-structured interviews, which mostly took place in March, April and September 2003. Some follow-up questions were then posed during social visits to Dar es Salaam in subsequent years. I was able to penetrate the network of a small number of wholesalers (madalali; sing., dalali; literally 'auctioneers', but in effect wholesale buyers) with the help of Eliab Chijoriga, a director and foodstuffs marketing expert at the Tanzania Commission for Science and Technology (COSTECH).[2] I visited tomato and potato farmers for initial meetings and was able to establish a complete marketing chain of suppliers and traders whose business dealings I could follow in order to track their use of mobile phones. These farmers are geographically marginal within Tanzania's fertile Southern Highlands and some 500 kilometres from the main wholesale market that many of them supply in Dar es Salaam.

A series of detailed semi-structured interviews were conducted with a sample of fifteen tomato and potato farmers, ranging from subsistence small-scale farmers to large-scale farmers who hire labourers and have land to farm in various locations throughout the year. Four intermediary traders were also interviewed, as were various other key informants involved in the trade. Two further wholesalers were interviewed to cross check some of the findings of the ethnographic work. Informants were restricted to those working in this chain and, much like other studies of traders in Tanzania (see Bryceson 1993: 120; Sebastiani-Kuoko 1998: 58), all the

---

[2] Chijoriga introduced me to wholesalers in Kariakoo, Dar es Salaam's municipal market, and urged the wholesalers to give me the contacts of the farmers who supplied them. They did so once I had gained their friendship and trust during our preliminary meetings. Bartholomeo Sanga, Festo Mkilama and Kamwene Sanga were also most helpful.

farmers and traders in this sample happened to be male. An advantage of this method was that I was able to both chart the stages of the business relationship between the farmer and the wholesale buyer, and show that, for many farmers, the wholesaler to whom they sold played an important role in supplying credit to cover purchased input use.[3]

Brief typographies of market actors

Farmers

Based on personal observation and the categorization of traders and the farmers themselves, the broad categories of farmer seem to reflect their access to capital. Small-scale farmers (*wakulima wadogo*) are often risk averse (Thomson & Terpend 1993: 4), barely existing above subsistence level and, with the help of labour from members of the immediate family, they rely on farming as their main source of income to cover their basic needs. At the other end of the spectrum is a smaller group of large-scale farmers (*wakulima wakubwa*) who, because their assets and annual turnover are greater than most MSEs, can be categorized as medium-scale entrepreneurs. Large-scale farmers oversee the farming of larger areas of land than small- and medium-scale farmers (the group that comes between small- and large-scale farmers). Large farmers usually own their land themselves and, in addition, farm land that they rent locally from smaller farmers in different geographical areas across the country.

Perishable foodstuffs can either be sold by a farmer at a nearby market or to one of two types of middlemen: he can either sell locally to a mobile intermediary trader (*mfanyabiashara*; pl., *wafanyabiashara*) or send the products to a wholesaler (*dalali*) in a larger city market such as the Kariakoo wholesale market in the Kariakoo market complex in Dar es Salaam.

Lorry drivers

The most itinerant group in the sample are the lorry drivers who physically deliver the perishable foodstuffs. Of the eleven drivers at the Dar es Salaam end of the Iringa/Mbeya run, about half have mobile phones that they use for work, having either purchased them themselves or been issued them by the owner of the lorry. One large farmer now issues all his lorry drivers with mobile phones in case of

---

[3]   This study forms part of a research project investigating how, why and to what affect ICT is being adopted for use in micro and small enterprises (MSEs) across different sectors of the Tanzanian economy. It cautions that, despite the huge uptake of mobile phones, some traditional pre-ICT aspects of the African business culture look set to remain for some time. Trust and the need for direct, personal interaction through face-to-face contact – one of the most pervasive features of African MSE economies – emerges as a common theme across the case study industries and is likely to remain a crucial aspect of the way most MSE business is conducted. See Molony (2007).

Photo 5.1   The building of the Kariakoo Market Corporation, Dar es Salaam, where many of the perishable foodstuffs from Tanzania's Southern Highlands are sent to.

breakdown.[4] Despite this, however, and depending on his relationship with the lorry owner, a farmer may still wish to travel with the lorry. This may simply be because he needs to go to Dar es Salaam anyway to see his wholesale buyer or for other business, but it may also be because the farmer is wary that the crops he depends on for his livelihood may not reach their destination safely. Yet while lorry drivers are increasingly being given mobile phones, a driver will usually first call his boss (i.e. not the owner of the perishable foodstuffs) if his lorry breaks down.

In this event, both the drivers and farmers believe that the lorry owner tends to care more about fixing his lorry than the state of somebody else's perishable cargo. Although drivers with close ties to a large farmer will act with more urgency (by calling a nearby town for spare parts if the problem can be repaired, or informing the waiting wholesaler to send new transport from Dar es Salaam if it cannot), some farmers still prefer to be with their crops and to make decisions themselves rather than rely on the ability of others to arrange new sources of transport.[5]

---

[4]   Interview with Samwel Kiando, Uyole, 24/05/03.
[5]   Interview with lorry drivers, Kidongochekundu, Dar es Salaam, 14/04/03 and Angelo Kilave, Mtitu, Iringa Region, 07/05/03.

Wholesalers

The wholesaler is usually an auctioneer stationed at Kariakoo where he receives farmers' produce via an intermediary trader (*kiunganishi*, literally 'connector'). Acting as the farmer's agent, the wholesaler handles the crop and sells it on to buyers who can be owners of, or distributors to, smaller sub-market stalls throughout the city as well as to hotels and traders delivering to Zanzibar and Comoros. In relation to their role as credit suppliers, the most competitive wholesalers are supplied by a large pool of farmers and have multiple selling channels that enable them to oversee the efficient receipt and sale of consignments at even the busiest times.

While it is uncertain why some successful farmers move into trading instead of progressing as cultivators, the testimony of the sampled wholesalers indicates that the decision to enter their trade is not financially motivated.[6] What is also clear from the biography of wholesalers is that being an intermediary trader is an essential prerequisite to becoming a wholesaler. In doing so, those intermediary traders who have the confidence to break away from only collecting produce from their original home locality take a series of high risks, not least because of the uncertainty of transport arrangements in rural areas and the availability of supplies and destination markets. This requires having good relations in multiple new locales with suppliers and other traders in order to be able to gather market and transport information which, as Bryceson (1993: 141) notes, demands a character that is both resilient and gregarious. 'Resilient' and 'gregarious' are appropriate words to describe successful traders, such as Bartholomeo Sanga and Kamwene Sanga in this sample, who, many other traders point out, tend also to be socially popular at the same time as being respected by fellow traders and farmers as resourceful businessmen. Referring specifically to wholesalers, Bryceson (1993: 130) judges well the qualifications needed to progress in trading:

> ... the main prerequisite is 'being known'. Several traders confirmed the importance of being popular. A wholesaler has to have 'nous' (*akili*) and a reputation for having many clients, being well-liked, respected and trustworthy. An outgoing personality, shrewdness and an aura of invincibility as 'Mr Fix-it' combine to form the mystique of the successful wholesaler.

The successful trader applies these traits when operating in the markets where he gains the experience, contacts and reputation that attract new suppliers to his pool who can then learn from his trading experience and, later on in their relationship, gain access to credit. To have the chance of reaping these benefits, an emerging farmer new to the market must first position himself with a wholesaler because, as

---

[6] According to Bryceson (1993: 130), access to large amounts of capital is not vital to becoming a *dalali*. This is disputed by van Donge (1992b: 183, 198) who sees that capital requirements increase as traders rise up through the hierarchy and notes their option of continuing to operate at a lower level when capital increases can make them richer than someone else at a higher level.

one informant puts it, 'farmers fail when they are unable to penetrate the network of wholesalers'.[7]

Advantages of mobile phones in agricultural trading

The business relationship between a farmer and a wholesaler is initially built on personal, face-to-face interaction. Once the relationship has been established, farmers and traders alike report that most of the communication between the two is conducted at a distance. This chiefly involves the exchange of information about supply and demand between the wholesaler in the commercial capital and the rural-based farmer. It is here that, for those who can access them, mobile phones hold the most benefit because they allow first-hand exchanges of information while it is still up-to-date and can be acted on. Along with a better knowledge of demand and improved coordination of supply that mobile phones bring, traders report the advantage of having to spend less time and money on travel. Using mobile phones better enables farmers to keep track of consignments in transit and on their arrival at market. They also regard mobile phones as being a far more reliable and faster means of sending information than the previous method of using a messenger, a bus or the postal service to deliver a letter. Nevertheless, many farmers deep in the 'mobile margins' of Tanzania's Southern Highlands are still infrastructurally marginalized from their buyers in Dar es Salaam.

Some reactions to infrastructural marginality and constraints on market access

In terms of infrastructure, roads in the Southern Highlands – other than the well-maintained Dar es Salaam-Zambia TANZAM highway – are still in very poor shape. Farmers far from the main road are not only marginalized because they have difficulty in reaching market but are becoming even more so because private traders avoid farmers in areas off the main road, where transport costs are too high, in favour of areas with a good transport infrastructure (Bryceson 2002: 728). They shun those locations where information is more uncertain (Thomson & Terpend 1993: 8). With an ageing and limited fixed-line infrastructure, and despite ongoing efforts by mobile phone operators to expand their network coverage, the problem of marginality that comes with distance from the TANZAM highway transfers largely to the availability of telecommunications. Faced with the difficulty of contacting traders in local towns, farmers and others seeking to communicate by mobile phone have started to apply a series of innovative methods to take maximum

---

[7] Interview with Gerald Mgaya, VECO offices, Mbeya, 21/05/03.

advantage of what coverage is on offer, and ways of paying for it when they cannot afford to purchase the equipment themselves.

Local network coverage and network reception spots

When network coverage does not immediately serve a location where a farmer requires reception, they and others needing to contact towns and cities have managed to locate the nearest point of reception emitted from transmission towers (base stations) adjacent to and designed to serve the Dar es Salaam-Zambia TANZAM highway. This practice was witnessed in every settlement visited where potatoes and tomatoes were being grown, and which was within range of the signal given by the roadside base stations (about 30 km from the station in each direction), and where no natural features disturb the straight line of transmission. These I call 'network reception spots', a term that suitably emphasizes that it is a location where mobile phone reception can be obtained only in certain areas and as a consequence of more blanket coverage intended primarily to serve other areas (in this case, the main road). The locations of the spots were first identified by villagers and *wafanyabiashara* who were travelling with mobile phones from the country's main towns (where coverage was first made available by mobile phone operators) and trying out reception areas by roaming around the countryside, starting with the areas nearest to their settlements and then branching out to areas of higher altitude and locations with a greater obvious chance of a clean line of transmission. Three types of network reception spots were observed and are being used by farmers and traders in Tanzania's Southern Highlands:

1) 'Opportunistic physical'

This is the simplest and commonest type of network reception spot, and most closely fits the above description where mobile phone reception is obtained as a consequence of more blanket coverage intended primarily to serve other areas. It is opportunistic in that most of the sample indicated that they were not actively searching for coverage when they first realized it was available. It loses its 'opportunistic' label, of course, as word spreads about where coverage can be obtained by this method, or where physical features such as trees can be climbed to gain reception. It is physical when users rely on physical features, often hills, to obtain reception. Ntokela (Rungwe District) at an elevation of around 8,500 feet (5 km) and five km from the main road to Malawi is an example of an area where potato farmers have found a location on a rise on a track where coverage (both Vodacom and Celtel) can be picked up near to their farms. Ukumbi (Kilolo District, Iringa Region) is another area where reception is intermittently picked up at around 6,000 feet above sea level in a few square feet of a maize plot (there is a clear path

Photo 5.2 An opportunistic human network reception spot outside Mtitu
village, Iringa region, Tanzania. The sign above Angelo Kilave,
a farmer, reads 'Danger/Hatari 220,000 volts'.

through the crops leading to the best area) and where more reliable coverage is
received on parts of a bare hill some half an hour's walk away.

2) 'Opportunistic human'

A second type of network reception spot can be found in areas where there is no
obvious line of transmission but where human (as opposed to natural) physical
objects are exploited to receive reception. One such spot was found in Mtitu village
(also Kilolo District, Iringa Region) 30 km from the nearest known base station at
Ihemi on the TANZAM highway, where Angelo Kilave led the author to a swamp
in a valley with no obvious line of transmission. Here he used a line of electricity

cables two km from his house to serve as a spot from where he could contact his wholesale buyer in Kariakoo.

3) 'Manufactured human'

Using a principle similar to the opportunistic human network reception spot, entrepreneurs (who are often farmers themselves) in Kidamali (Iringa District) have now taken the further step of creating what I term 'manufactured human network reception spots'. These are phone kiosks (*huduma ya simu*) set on stilts to obtain reception. The entrepreneurs stated that they oversaw the construction of the raised kiosks, although the design of all four of the structures along the road was similar and each had placards nailed to them advertising Celtel (the only operator whose reception could be obtained using this method).

The network reception spot can be anything up to two hours away on foot for farmers in Iringa and Mbeya who are especially marginalized from infrastructural services. In this situation, it is not unknown for a busy farmer wishing to contact a buyer in Dar es Salaam to send others (usually a male youth, though sometimes women) with a mobile phone to the nearest *known* network reception spot so that a message he has written can be sent. This method can only be used when sending information that does not require an immediate response, since even if a phone call were received in reply straightaway the youth would not be able to make decisions on the spot himself on the farmer's behalf.

To deal with this problem, a few farmers have arranged for their buyer in Dar es Salaam or a relation to call them at a certain time on specific days. They are then able to make sure that they are at the network reception spot when the call is due. The disadvantage here is that if the spot is far from where the farmer lives then he is away from his farm for most of the day. He also has to rely on his city contact remembering to call at the agreed time. Francis Mbegalo, one of the tomato farmers who receives weekly calls at the network reception spot from his Dar es Salaam-based buyer, added that through this arrangement he can lose a little of the advantage of having up-to-date knowledge of market demand. Early morning is the time that the market and therefore Francis's buyer are most active. It is also the time when Francis does most of his farming. For this reason, Francis is reluctant to leave the farm in the morning and so can only reach the network reception spot by mid-afternoon. Doing so means that Francis receives demand information later than those who are not as constrained by their marginality from network reception, and he loses a day's preparation time when sending his perishable foodstuffs to the distant market.[8]

---

[8]   Interview with Francis Mbegalo, Ukumbi, Iringa, 06/05/03.

Photo 5.3   Exoni Manitu, a tomato farmer, at a manufactured human network reception spot in Kidamali village, Iringa region, Tanzania.

In general, those farmers who own mobile phones are large- and medium-scale smallholder farmers or, as the senior statistician at Kariakoo market put it, 'the educated: businessmen and emerging businessmen, not mere peasants. The peasant-businessman uses them.'[9] These farmers are a minority who, in addition to being able to afford the cost of a mobile phone and credit, may also be linked to the national electricity grid or, in rural areas, own a generator with which to charge their

---

[9]   Interview with Nicanor Omolo, Kariakoo market, Dar es Salaam, 27/08/03.

handset.[10] When asked about what influenced them to buy a mobile phone, most farmers replied that they saw the popularity of mobile phones when in Dar es Salaam and thought they would help their business. This idea seems to have spread rapidly, probably because others saw the advantages that the first farmers to own a mobile phone gained. By 2003, the majority of farmers in this sample had some sort of access to mobile phones. As might be expected, their popularity is a more recent phenomenon in rural areas, spreading roughly with available coverage, with most owners in 2003-2004 having obtained their handsets and SIM cards in 2003, as opposed to 2001-2002 among those sampled in Dar es Salaam. In the small village of Kidamali, for example, four farmers purchased mobile phones over the space of two months in mid-2003, bringing the total number of tomato farmers owning mobile phones in the settlement to six.[11] A follow-up study is planned to find out present mobile phone ownership and usage to help chart changes over time.

For some smallholder farmers with meagre incomes, the financial costs of mobile phone access, let alone the purchase price, are so prohibitive that any type of regular use is simply not feasible. This can be because there is no (known) network reception spot and the nearest point of access is a phone kiosk in a nearby town and travel and being away from the farm are deemed too costly to justify the journey. In tandem with this, though not exclusively, a couple of farmers and a wholesaler said that they do not use a telephone *per se* (i.e. they did not expressly state a 'mobile phone') because they do not see its advantages:[12]

> People talk much about the telephone these days, but personally I don't see how it can help me. It is expensive to be told to bring my few tomatoes to Dar es Salaam for very little profit. I don't need to be told by somebody in the city that I am making little money here farming tomatoes.[13]

Personal relationships and success without a mobile phone

That the mobile phone appears to have only one significant benefit in the trading of perishable foodstuffs – facilitating the flow of supply and demand information – raises a final question, and one that farmers are increasingly asking themselves as mobile phone coverage grows and the cost of using the technology drops: Is it still possible to operate successfully without a mobile phone?

---

[10] In the most recent survey of Iringa Region, only 2% of houses had electricity (URT. 1997. *Iringa Region Socio-economic Profile*, Dar es Salaam: Planning Commission and Regional Commissioner's Office, Government of the United Republic of Tanzania). Samuel *et al.* reveal a positive correlation between mobile phone ownership and access to electricity See J. Samuel, N. Shah & W. Hadingham 2005. 'Mobile Communications in South Africa, Tanzania and Egypt: Results from Community and Business Surveys' in D. Coyle (ed.). *Africa: The Impact of Mobile Phones*, Newbury: Vodafone, pp. 44-52).

[11] Interview with Exoni Manitu, Mangalali, Iringa, 06/09/03.

[12] Interviews with Petro Lyelu (Tosamaganga Jnction, Iringa, 06/09/03), Lukelo Mahenge (Mangalali, Iringa, 20/03/03) and Kamwene Sanga (Kariakoo, Dar es Salaam, 17/04/03).

[13] Interview with Lukelo Mahenge, Mangalali, Iringa, 20/03/03.

For the farmer, the answer is probably 'yes' as long as he is not tied into a credit relationship with a wholesaler and is prepared to accompany his crops to Dar es Salaam and travel around the city finding better prices if the price offered to him in Kariakoo is not attractive. This costs time and money that could be saved by ng a mobile phone to contact the market beforehand.

For a wholesaler, travelling would be more difficult. One wholesaler, however, does manage to do so successfully, if at times precariously, in the seemingly frantic trading he conducts in Kariakoo and the countryside. Kamwene Sanga, a prominent and very popular Kariakoo-based potato wholesaler, is (at least was in 2004) notorious for his refusal to use a mobile phone and was mocked for this reason by his fellow wholesalers as being a 'peasant' (*mshamba*). Kamwene explains his reasons for his personal rejection of the telephone in terms of how information he offers over the telephone can spread so much that it becomes counterproductive to all and in fact reduces prices:

> I don't trust the telephone; it always lies. I can tell a farmer to bring potatoes because the price is high, but then when the potatoes are delivered to me he [the farmer] complains that the price has dropped. I receive calls at my office but I never call the farmers back... They ask if they should pack, but when I answer and say 'Yes, send me potatoes', then many of farmers send me them, which lowers the price and the farmers then complain.[14]

In contrast to wholesalers who during the early stages of a relationship will use the mobile phone to coordinate supplies, Kamwene chooses not to use a telephone and – through a combination of having many contacts to sell to in Dar es Salaam and disappointing some farmers when he cannot sell their potatoes at a good price – still manages to deal with whatever quantities of potatoes are sent to him in Kariakoo, and to sell them quickly. Ordinarily, this would make a wholesaler unpopular among those who send to him and do not get their crops sold for a fair price, but something about this particularly charismatic wholesaler enables him to get away with it and still receive a steady supply of potatoes. This, Kamwene hints, lies in his genial relationship with suppliers and buyers and in being selective about who one tells, if anyone at all, about the need for crops in Dar es Salaam, which is where the demand is.

In a departure from the broadly correct observation that wholesalers 'are stationed at the Kariakoo wholesale market and are only involved in receiving farmers who bring their produce to the market' (Chijoriga 1992: 7) and will only travel when supplies are low, Kamwene takes the time to visit his farmers in the farming areas even when he has no shortage of supply. By drinking with them and discussing farming, trading and anything else the farmers wish to talk about, Kamwene applies his social skills to meetings with farmers that are little different to those in the market place, but on their home turf. That the big man who they supply potatoes to

---

[14]   Interview with Kamwene Sanga, Kariakoo market, Dar es Salaam, 17/04/03.

comes to meet and drink with them was not lost on the farmers, whose appreciation was expressed by one smallholder farmer of a (rather drunk) group who had congregated around him:

> Kamwene comes to the farming areas because he is a good *dalali* and he likes to drink home-brew with us. Other *madalali* come to farmers when they want something, like a politician when it is time to vote. Kamwene comes many times and stays with us for a long time.[15]

These empirical findings from Tanzania have a close parallel to those that have influenced the conceptual literature on trust, and in particular the work in Ghana of Fergus Lyon (2000), who regards what he terms 'customer friendship' as one of the key mechanisms of trust in the relationship between farmers and traders. Here the division between social and economic activities is unclear, with farmers and traders visiting their customers when passing, and gift-giving and reciprocity (on village visits or when the farmer visits the customer) serving different purposes for the different actors at different times. According to Lyon's analysis of such a relationship, customer friendship can be seen to be economically functional. It is based on the same information and sanctions as working relationships but also draws on shared concepts of morality and altruism based on culturally specific norms (Lyon 2000: 672). It would seem that by visiting the farmers as a wholesaler, Kamwene is able to adopt the 'outwardly-directed social lifestyle' of the mobile intermediary trader as described by Bryceson (1993: 141) and cited above.

This is a role that Kamwene appears to be comfortable with, and one that has helped him to become well known throughout Kariakoo and among many farmers in his area. So while not having a mobile phone may make his job hectic and he may lose some friends along the way when he is unable to sell farmers' consignments to his many contacts in Dar es Salaam, his visits to farmers ensure that he is known locally and, crucially, recommended to emerging farmers (who may also have attended or heard of his meeting-cum-drinking sessions in their local area). All farmers in the area that he is from send their produce to him, which ensures him a constant supply of potatoes with which to supply the smaller markets of Dar es Salaam and further afield, and allows him to make a good profit in the process.

The point worth emphasizing about this wholesaler's ability to operate without a telephone and yet still have a steady supply of crops to sell is that he has managed to build up relationships with farmers and buyers so that they seem only to consider supplying to and buying from him. It appears that this is not because his suppliers know of no alternative buyer or seller, but because he takes the time to do business with them face to face, even when farmers are unable to come to him. One large tomato farmer explains that, irrespective of the location, meeting people physically is still important.

---

[15]   Interview with Geoffrey Sanga, Ntokela village, Mbeya Region, 23/05/03.

For us Africans often an explanation over the phone is not enough even when you've greeted one another. When you see each other again you start afresh, greeting each other again. Likewise in business even if you've talked on the phone a businessman feels like he's not satisfied so he likes to meet face to face so you talk and this satisfies him. That's a way to build faith in business. You know nowadays there's so much competition in this business, so we get customers through information. It's imperative to see each other.[16]

Conclusion

The evidence from this case study on perishable foodstuffs trading supports Trulsson's (1997) study of entrepreneurship in Tanzania, where he noted that the telephone may be considered relatively unimportant because personal relationships are formed during meetings conducted in person. He offers an example of dealing with government administration where, 'if one does not appear in their offices in person, the case will not be dealt with. Using a phone call or sending a letter rarely generates the desired response. It is the personal encounter that matters most' (Trulsson 1997: 133). The evidence of this case study suggests that this is certainly the case for Kamwene. His success, it seems, is attributed more to his personal mobility than to any advantage he might gain from having a telephone that would allow him to stay in touch with his suppliers. Incidentally, this study also shows that those farmers on the 'mobile margins' who are assumed to benefit drastically from new information and technologies are often caught in a credit dilemma whereby they have little choice but to accept the price they are given by their creditor.

Many poor people in developing countries are embedded in similar systems of power that are more intricate than much of the pro-ICT community seems to acknowledge. These relationships need to be understood and applied to the new ICT context in developing countries so that donor development policies and the expansion plans of the ICT industry can better serve those on the mobile margins. The ethnographic approach employed in the collection of the data presented here goes some way towards revealing these complexities.

---

[16] Interview with Berod Mhanga, Ilula Mazomba village, Iringa Region, 04/09/03.

References

BRYCESON, D.F. (1993), *Liberalizing Tanzania's Food Trade*, Oxford: James Currey.

BRYCESON, D.F. (2002), 'The scramble in Africa: Reorienting rural livelihoods', *World Development* 30(5): 725-39.

CHIJORIGA, E.S.M. (1992), 'The role of middlemen in the marketing of staples: The case of Kariakoo wholesale market'. MA Thesis, University of Dar es Salaam.

CRAWFORD, I.M. (1997), *Agricultural and food marketing management*, Rome: FAO.

DE HAAN, L.J. & P. QUARLES VAN UFFORD (2002), 'About trade and trust: The question of livelihood and social capital in rural-urban interactions'. In: I.S.A. Baud & J. Post, eds, *Re-Aligning Actors in an Urbanizing World*, London: Ashgate, pp. 243-264.

DOI (2001), Creating a development dynamic: Final report of the digital opportunity initiative, New York: UNDP.

DONNER, J. (2006), 'The use of mobile phones by micro-entrepreneurs in Kigali, Rwanda: Changes to social and business networks', *Information Technologies and International Development* 3(2): 3-19.

DUNCOMBE, R. & R. HEEKS (2001), *ICTs and small enterprises in Africa: Lessons from Botswana*, Manchester: IDPM University of Manchester.

ESSELAAR, S., C. STORK, A. NDIWALANA & M. DEEN-SWARRAY (2007), 'ICT usage and its impact on profitability of SMEs in 13 African Countries', *Information Technologies and International Development* 4(1): 87-100.

GRACE, J., C. KENNY & C. QIANG (2004), *Information and communication technologies and broad-based development: A partial review of the evidence*, Washington, DC: World Bank.

HORST, H. & D. MILLER (2005), 'From kinship to link-up: The cell phone and social networking in Jamaica', *Current Anthropology* 46(5): 755-78.

HORST, H. & D. MILLER (2007), *The cell phone: An anthropology of communication*, Oxford/New York: Berg.

LYON, F. (2000), 'Trust, networks and norms: The creation of social capital in agricultural economies in Ghana', *World Development* 28(4): 663-81.

LYON, F. (2003), 'Trader associations and urban food systems in Ghana: Institutionalist approaches to understanding urban collective action'. *International Journal of Urban and Regional Research* 27(1): 11-23.

MOLONY, T.S.J. (2007), '"I Don't Trust the Phone, It Always Lies": Social capital and information and communication technologies in Tanzanian micro and small enterprises', *Information Technologies and International Development* 3(4): 67-83.

MOLONY, T.S.J. (2008), 'Non-developmental uses of mobile communication in Tanzania'. In: J.E. Katz, ed., *The handbook of mobile communication studies*, Cambridge, MA: MIT Press, pp. 339-352.

PONTE, S. (2002), *Farmers and markets in Tanzania: How policy reforms affect rural livelihoods in Africa*, Oxford: James Currey.

QIANG, Z.W.C., G.C. CLARKE & N. HALEWOOD (2006), 'The role of ICT in doing business'. In: W. Bank, ed., *World Information and Communication for Development Report (WICDR): Trends and Policies for the Information Society*, Washington, DC: World Bank.

RHEINGOLD, H. (2005), 'Farmers, phones and markets: Mobile technology in rural development', accessed 7 March 2006 at: http://www.thefeature.com/article?articleid=101423

SAMUEL, J., N. SHAH & W. HADINGHAM (2005), 'Mobile communications in South Africa, Tanzania and Egypt: Results from community and business surveys'. In: D. Coyle, ed., *Africa: The impact of mobile phones*, Newbury: Vodafone, pp. 44-52.

SEBASTIANI-KUOKO, S. (1998), 'Potential production systems in the northern hHighlands of Tanzania: A Study of the yield potential and associated constraints', Unpublished PhD Thesis, University of Reading.

THE ECONOMIST, 8 November (2007), 'Does not compute'.

THE ECONOMIST, 12-18 March (2005), 'The real digital divide'.

THOMSON, J. & N. TERPEND (1993), 'Promoting private sector involvement in agricultural marketing in Africa', *FAO Agricultural Services Bulletin*, FAO: Rome.

TRULSSON, P. (1997), *Strategies of entrepreneurship: Understanding industrial entrepreneurship and structural change in Northwest Tanzania*, Linköping: Department of Technology and Social Change, University of Linköping.

UN-HABITAT (2002), 'Human settlements statistical database', accessed 16 April 2004 at: http://www.unhabitat.org/habrdd/conditions/eafrica/tanzania.htm

UN-HABITAT (2004), 'Human settlements statistical database version 4: Dar es Salaam', accessed 16 April 2004 at: http://www.unhabitat.org/programmes/guo/data_hsdb4.asp

UNDP (2001), *Human Development Report: Making New Technologies Work for Human Development*, New York: OUP.

UNFPA (2007), *The state of world population 2007*. New York: United Nations Population Fund.

URT (1997), *Iringa region socio-economic profile*, Dar es Salaam: Planning commission and regional commissioner's office, Government of the United Republic of Tanzania.

WORLD BANK (1998), *World Development Report: Knowledge for development*. Washington, DC: World Bank.

WORLD BANK (1999), *Social sector review: Tanzania*, Washington, DC: World Bank Group.

WORLD BANK (2004), 'Country indicator tables: Tanzania', accessed 2 May 2005 at: http://www.worldbank.org/cgi-bin/sendoff.cgi?page=%2Fdata%2Fcountrydata%2Faag%2Ftza_aag.pdf

WORLD BANK (2007), 'Developmen indicators: Tanzania', accessed 10 December 2007 at: http://devdata.worldbank.org/external/CPProfile.asp?PTYPE=CP&CCODE=TZA

Acknowledgement

The research was funded by a doctoral studentship (R42200134339) awarded by the United Kingdom's Economic and Social Research Council. The chapter was written during a post-doctoral fellowship at the School of Geography, Archaeology and Environmental Studies, University of the Witwatersrand, Johannesburg, South Africa.

6

Téléphonie mobile. L'appropriation du sms par une « société de l'oralité »

Ludovic Kibora

Introduction

Le téléphone portable a connu depuis son arrivée en Afrique un développement spectaculaire. Une telle situation serait due au fait que son usage s'adapte au contexte de la "culture de l'oralité" qui a cours dans les sociétés africaines. Au Burkina Faso cependant, on constate que, contrairement à cette assertion, l'utilisation du SMS qui fait appel à l'écrit prend de l'ampleur dans toutes les couches de la société aussi bien en milieu urbain que rural. L'arrivée du téléphone portable dans la seconde moitié des années 1990 dans ce pays classé parmi les plus pauvres du monde a entraîné un engouement surprenant des populations pour cette nouvelle technologie. Des initiatives sont localement développées par les consommateurs pour la possession et l'utilisation du téléphone portable en l'adaptant aux réalités socioculturelles et économiques.

Le Burkina Faso est un pays sahélien de l'Ouest africain, comportant une soixantaine de groupes socioculturels, qui constituent une population d'environ 13 730 258 d'habitants (INSD 2007). Il s'agit d'un pays agricole arriéré dont environ 80% de la population vit en milieu rural. Selon le ministère de l'économie et du développement, le taux de pauvreté est de 40,8% (MED 2007). Malgré ces conditions économiques peu favorables, le téléphone fixe qui est installé dans le pays depuis la période de l'indépendance politique du pays en 1960 a, en moins d'une décennie, été dépassé par le téléphone portable dont l'acquisition est faite de nos jour par les paysans des campagnes les plus pauvres.

A travers ce processus d'adoption, voire d'appropriation (Miller 1995; Hast & Miller 2004, 2005.) du téléphone portable, un phénomène a marqué notre attention, celui de l'adoption du système de message court (SMS) par les usagers. Le Burkina Faso a l'un des plus bas taux de scolarisation (60,5%) et d'alphabétisation (26%) du monde (MEBA, annuaire statistique 2005-2006). Or, il est surprenant de constater un certain engouement des populations pour cette forme d'expression toute particulière faisant appel à l'écriture qui n'est pas forcément la chose la mieux partagée dans le pays.

Méthode et technique de recherche

Cet article, qui vise à montrer comment le téléphone portable a été adopté par les populations burkinabè mais surtout comment l'un de ses modes d'utilisation, l'envoi de SMS, est en train de se développer dans un contexte social qui n'est pas favorable, est le résultat d'enquêtes menées au Burkina Faso. En plus de l'observation participante dont nous avions usé depuis l'arrivée du téléphone portable dans ce pays où nous vivons (étant nous même consommateur et usager courant du SMS), nous avons aussi mené des enquêtes orales à Ouagadougou, la capitale, Bobo Dioulasso, la seconde ville du pays, et dans des villes et villages (Pô, Tiébélé, Kaya-Navio, Dakola) de la province du Nahouri de façon discontinue depuis l'année 2005 à nos jours. Au total, nous avons eu des entretiens directs et systématiques avec 100 usagers du téléphone portable en milieu urbain et 100 autres en milieu rural avec une grande disparité d'âge et de sexe.

La synthèse des informations recueillies a été enrichie par une recherche documentaire pour donner lieu à cet article qui présente dans un premier temps l'engouement des populations burkinabè pour le téléphone portable et ensuite le développement extraordinaire du SMS.

Téléphonie portable, une technologie mondiale qui s'installe facilement dans un milieu Africain

Le téléphone portable s'est introduit en Afrique dans des contextes sociaux particuliers comme l'a bien su souligner J-A. Dibakana (Dibakana 2002, 2006).

En effet dans de nombreux pays, bien que les pouvoirs publics aient bien compris la nécessité du téléphone, cette technologie est restée pendant longtemps inaccessible à la majorité des populations, compte tenu des lourdeurs qui entourent sa mise en place. C'est pourquoi, au-delà de toute autre considération, l'engouement actuel des populations pour le téléphone portable peut être compris comme une coïncidence avec la nécessité, celle de communiquer oralement, en rendant présent l'interlocuteur dans son environnement immédiat. Ce qui constitue un facteur de vitalité important pour les relations sociales.

En 2004, le nombre approximatif de 400 000 abonnés au téléphone mobile au Burkina a été atteint (source Wikipédia). Cela correspondait à environ 4% de la population de ce pays.

De nos jours, bien que les opérateurs rechignent à donner le nombre exact de leurs abonnés, on peut de façon empirique estimer que ce chiffre est largement dépassé. Rien qu'en avril 2008, le seul opérateur Celtel fêtait son millionième abonné. Cependant, vu l'usage communautaire (plusieurs personnes peuvent profiter d'un seul appareil) qui est fait d'un appareil, on peut estimer que les statistiques officielles sont en deçà de la réalité du nombre d'utilisateurs.

Dans une étude sur les perspectives économiques en Afrique, l'OCDE affirme que « *le téléphone mobile en Afrique a un taux de pénétration de 39%* » A défaut d'étude spécifique sur le Burkina Faso ceci donne une idée sur la situation. Sur le continent africain qui selon la même source a une ligne pour 100 habitants pour le téléphone fixe, on trouve 15 abonnements au téléphone mobile pour cent habitants. Pour une technologie qui s'est véritablement imposée au début de ce millénaire, ce boom du

Photo 6.1   Un jeune homme entrain d'écrire un sms.

portable pourrait s'expliquer par le fait que cette technologie nouvelle a trouvé un terrain favorable. Contrairement à la situation du téléphone fixe évoquée plus haut, le mobile grâce à une antenne de relais peut couvrir une plus grande zone. Même le système fixe via le satellite qui est en train d'être développé au Burkina Faso ne parvient pas à remplir les mêmes fonctions que le cellulaire (comme on l'appelle couramment au Burkina) parce que son utilisation nécessite que le poste soit en permanence branché sur une prise électrique, or jusqu'à présent, l'électricité demeure une denrée rare dans de nombreuses localités du pays.

Au Burkina Faso, la téléphonie mobile s'est installée véritablement en 1996 avec la création de la société nationale TELMOB. A l'époque, le coût exorbitant des appareils, ajouté à la cherté de l'abonnement des postes post-payés (le système de prépayé n'existait pas encore), ne permettait qu'à une élite de posséder ce nouvel outil de la technologie mondiale. Alors privilège des hommes politiques, opérateurs économiques ou simples frimeurs, le téléphone portable était l'apanage d'une certaine élite dans une société où le téléphone fixe par nombre d'habitants était loin d'atteindre les normes internationales. Mais l'arrivée du portable a eu comme avantage de permettre aux populations de contourner les difficultés liées à l'acquisition du fixe. En tout cas, malgré le coût des premiers abonnements, l'intérêt des populations pour cette nouvelle technologie est allé crescendo. En effet le téléphone portable, nouvel instrument de communication, allait connaître dans le cadre de la globalisation un essor fabuleux auquel ne résisteront pas les campagnes les plus reculées de la civilisation fortement imprégnée de la culture occidentale. Passés les premiers moments d'observation et de questionnement divers, le boom du portable au Burkina Faso sera à l'image de celui de nombreux pays d'Afrique et du monde.

Le début du troisième millénaire allait coïncider avec l'accréditation de deux opérateurs privés en plus de celui national. Ainsi, entre 2000 et 2003 deux autres compagnies ont commencé à opérer au Burkina. La concurrence entre les différents fournisseurs de téléphonie mobile est souvent profitable au consommateur qui peut ainsi bénéficier de technologies de pointe à des prix que peut supporter son pouvoir d'achat. L'interconnexion intervenue entre les trois opérateurs (Telmob, Celtel, Télécel) en 2001 va accroître l'engouement des habitants des villes et progressivement celles des campagnes pour ce nouveau mode de communication. Il s'est développé ainsi au sein des populations locales une stratégie d'appropriation de cet outil qui remplace de loin les modalités traditionnelles de transmission de messages, tels que le griot qui se baladait de porte à porte ou le héraut qui à la criée relayait les informations importantes.

En effet le téléphone portable a pu s'insérer dans la dynamique de communication de cette société qui a par le passé développé une tradition de l'oralité. Ceci explique-t il cela?

La réalité pourtant est que le téléphone portable, au-delà des aspects liés à son coût qui peut paraître démesuré pour les habitants d'un des pays les plus pauvres du monde, n'a pas eu de mal à s'installer au « Pays des Hommes intègres ».

De la date de son apparition au Burkina Faso à nos jours où il a atteint un niveau d'expansion important, on peut estimer que le téléphone portable s'est imposé en un temps relativement court, en s'intégrant dans les réalités quotidiennes des populations des villes et des campagnes. Comme le dit si bien A. Nyamba « *L'expansion des nouvelles technologies de communication a entraîné une grande restructuration, irréversible à mon sens, des services traditionnels de télécommunication, tant dans les pays dits développés que dans ceux dits sous-développés. Tout cela annonce à l'aube du 21e siècle ce que d'aucuns ont appelé la bataille pour la révolution planétaire de la communication* » (Nyamba 2000 : 6)

Le téléphone portable a certes un coût que les Burkinabè pauvres parmi les pauvres ne sauraient supporter, diront ceux qui ne voient pas un avenir à l'expansion du téléphone mobile dans ce pays. On est fondé à leur donner raison si l'on tient compte des différentes statistiques nationales qui situent près de la moitié de la population en dessous du seuil de pauvreté, c'est-à-dire vivant avec moins d'un dollar US par jour. Faire une telle déduction, c'est oublier que lorsque les populations décident de s'approprier un objet de consommation provenant d'une autre culture, elles en exploitent le côté bénéfique dans une sorte de réinvention de l'objet. Elles développent des initiatives leur permettant de l'intégrer dans leurs possibilités économiques.

C'est ainsi que, depuis l'introduction du téléphone portable au Burkina Faso, une nouvelle dynamique s'est développée d'abord autour du mode d'acquisition de cet objet de consommation. De jeunes opérateurs économiques nationaux qui avaient commencé à écumer les capitales occidentales et asiatiques à la recherche de produits de consommation meilleur marché, ont axé leur séjour à l'extérieur sur la recherche de téléphones mobiles commercialisables sur le territoire national. Ces appareils sont souvent revendus à crédit sur plusieurs mensualités à ceux qui le désirent.

Certains de ces revendeurs récupèrent des téléphones usagés dans les dépotoirs en Europe, jetés pour des pannes diverses que les réparateurs locaux se feront le plaisir de remettre à neuf. Ces téléphones « *au revoir la France* »[1], cédés à bon prix, font le bonheur de nombreuses personnes dont le pouvoir d'achat ne permet pas de s'offrir un appareil neuf.

Ce circuit de vente a transformé de nombreux travailleurs immigrés, voire des étudiants nationaux en Europe, en marchands occasionnels de téléphone mobile. Certains étudiants rentrés en vacance parviennent grâce à la vente des téléphones portables rapportés de l'Occident à récupérer leur frais de voyage et de séjour.

---

[1]   Cette expression désigne tout objet ou appareil usager en provenance de l'Europe.

Au delà de ce circuit d'achat-vente qui permet à la population de s'approvisionner en téléphone mobile, il y a aussi cette tradition de cadeaux offerts par les voyageurs de retour, qui a aidé de nombreuses personnes à posséder un portable. Ainsi, il n'est pas rare que des personnes restées au pays sollicitent de la part de parents ou amis séjournant à l'extérieur, un téléphone mobile en guise de cadeau.

Certes il existe de nombreuses personnes, surtout chez les jeunes gens, pour qui la possession d'un téléphone portable est semblable au fait de porter un habit à la mode. Mais, ce côté « frime » n'est pas la chose la plus partagée. De nombreuses personnes adultes qui au début des années 2000 disaient *« je n'ai pas besoin de portable parce que ça coûte cher et je n'en vois pas la nécessité,* ont fini par en posséder pour des raisons professionnelles où même simplement sociales. Des dames qui n'ont généralement pas de poche dans leurs vêtements et qu'on accuse de toujours oublier leur téléphone dans les sacs à main, ont trouvé l'astuce d'accrocher leur portable au cou tels des médaillons au bout d'une chaîne, tout en exerçant leurs activités quotidiennes.

Il n'est pas rare de voir des pères de famille qui ne sont pas particulièrement nantis doter leurs enfants, (souvent de jeunes élèves) de portables pour pouvoir les joindre en toutes circonstances.

Les différents modes d'acquisition du téléphone portable qui font appel à des initiatives qui contournent les lois traditionnelles du marché rejoignent les méthodes d'utilisation et d'entretien du téléphone portable.

L'usage du téléphone se fait de façon parcimonieuse. Certaines personnes ne rechargent leur abandonnement prépayé que lorsqu'elles courent le risque d'être « coupées » par l'opérateur. Les quelques unités[2] que l'utilisateur achète ne sont utilisées qu'en cas de nécessité absolue. Il peut même arriver qu'il garde un peu « d'unités », juste de quoi « biper »[3].

C'est en cela que l'arrivée du SMS en 2003 chez les différents opérateurs a constitué une autre aubaine pour les usagers du téléphone portable.

Téléphone portable et envoi de messages courts

Au mois d'avril 2007, la presse burkinabé s'est fait l'écho de l'histoire rocambolesque de cette jeune élève de 15 ans que les parents avaient destinée à un mariage forcé. Grâce aux SMS qu'elle envoya à ses amis et professeurs, la police fut alertée et cette jeune fille fut ainsi sauvée. Ce fait divers est un exemple qui montre les différentes possibilités qu'offre le SMS à la jeunesse burkinabé surtout dans sa frange scolarisée ou déscolarisée.

---

[2] Le temps de communication est dénommé en nombre d'unités de sorte que les vendeurs ambulants de cartes prépayées utilisent ce terme pour désigner leurs cartes vendues à la criée.

[3] Biper consiste à composer le numéro d'un correspondant et faire sonner son appareil sans lui laisser le temps de décrocher. Il pourra identifier votre numéro et vous rappeler s'il le veut.

Photo 6.2   La devanture d'un *télecentre* privé. L'indication sur la plaque montre que dans ce lieu ou
peut non seulement téléphoner sur un téléphone fixe moyennant paiement, mais
s'acheter des carte de recharge pour téléphone mobile des trois compagnies qui sont
dans le pays

Aucun peuple ne vit sans communication. L'échange de parole précède celui des
biens et services dans la société, toutes choses qui entretiennent et renforcent les
relations sociales entre les hommes. Ainsi, les systèmes d'obligations nés de ces
échanges ont besoin d'être entretenus pour donner en permanence vie au groupe.
Dans les sociétés qui ont développé une culture de l'oralité comme celle du Burkina
Faso, l'importance de la parole demeure encore très forte malgré les transformations
subies par les apports culturels de l'Occident. Aujourd'hui encore, « on ne dit pas
n'importe quoi à n'importe qui ». La hiérarchisation de la parole de même que les
conditions de son utilisation demeurent soumises à des codes non écrits, connus de
ceux qui appartiennent à une même culture. Cette importance de la parole ne serait-
elle pas en elle-même un atout favorable à l'introduction du téléphone dans un tel
milieu social ?

S'il est loisible d'estimer que le téléphone portable préserve le langage oral, d'où
son efficacité, force est de constater que dans l'utilisation de cet outil de communication, l'arrivée du SMS, avec son coût abordable et son caractère discret a

aussi été très vite intégré dans les modes de communication d'une grande partie des usagers de la téléphonie mobile, aussi bien en ville qu'à la campagne, pourvu qu'ils sachent écrire quelque chose de déchiffrable par leurs interlocuteurs. Ce fait remarquable peut donner lieu à des discussions sur des questions variées : l'utilisation du langage, l'origine sociale, etc.

Au Burkina Faso, la langue officielle est le français. C'est la langue de l'administration et de l'enseignement. Cependant, selon des études menées par des linguistes, seulement 0,13% de la population (Barretau, 1998) de ce pays s'exprime correctement en français et environ 13% selon les mêmes sources peut être jugée capable de s'exprimer en français. Le Burkina Faso disposerait de 59 langues nationales (Kedrebeogo, 2006) ce qui fait du français une langue secondaire pour la plupart des Burkinabè. Pourtant, en tant que langue première de l'enseignement, le français conserve ce même rang au niveau de l'écrit. Lors des discussions que nous avons pu avoir avec de nombreux utilisateurs de téléphones portables, il est ressorti que l'envoi de message court par le mobile se fait majoritairement en français.

Il est donc plus facile pour un locuteur de se faire comprendre à l'écrit en français en ayant quelques notions seulement dans cette langue, que dans une langue nationale. Il est alors surprenant de constater que de nombreuses personnes qui communiquent difficilement et rarement en français, lorsqu'il s'agit de l'oral, envoient couramment des SMS dans cette langue.

Le SMS qui ne sanctionne pas les fautes est devenu un moyen d'expression très prisé, non seulement des jeunes gens, mais aussi des gens d'un certain âge et d'un certain rang social qu'on ne soupçonne pas toujours de savoir l'employer. Le tout est de savoir griffonner quelque chose qui puisse être déchiffré par le destinataire du message, l'essentiel étant de se faire comprendre.

« PPS de fati samdi o vilag ». Voilà un exemple de message qui peut être envoyé d'une ville ou d'un village vers des destinataires situés à des centaines de kilomètres, pour informer d'un rituel important dans l'accomplissement d'une alliance matrimoniale. « PPS » est une abréviation du mooré « pug puusum » qui littéralement signifie « salutation de la femme. » Il s'agit d'un des moments charnières dans le processus d'un mariage. La délégation des parents du futur époux doit se déplacer (quelle que soit la distance) pour aller dans le village de la future épouse y demander sa main. C'est cette cérémonie qui scelle l'union entre les deux groupes de parenté. Dans les différents groupes socioculturels burkinabé, on trouve des manifestations similaires dans le cadre du mariage, d'où l'utilisation fréquente de cette abréviation générique qui s'adapte bien au système de message court. Cette abréviation qui a été développée par les jeunes de la capitale (Ouagadougou) s'est répandue dans plusieurs régions du Burkina Faso, notamment celles ayant une grande population de moréphones (7 régions sur les 13 que compte le Burkina). Son existence est certes antérieure à l'entrée du portable au Faso, mais son aspect pratique en fait un des types de messages adaptés au SMS.

De tels messages, mêmes envoyés sur le téléphone portable d'un habitant illettré d'un village donné, peuvent être décodés par l'infirmier ou l'instituteur du village. Ces mêmes personnes, qui étaient sollicitées par les villageois pour lire leurs courriers reçus de l'extérieur, doivent en plus intervenir pour déchiffrer des SMS. Selon les dires de nombreuses personnes rencontrées, on constate que progressivement l'arrivée de lettres écrites en provenance de la ville vers certains milieux ruraux se fait de plus en plus rare, en raison de ce côté pratique du SMS. Une fois le SMS lu, le bouche-à-oreille fait le reste et toute la communauté concernée par l'information est touchée. Jadis, il aurait fallu envoyer un émissaire pour apporter l'information sur plusieurs sites différents. Car, dans les cultures locales, il est inconcevable que certains événements importants, tels que les différents rites de passage, soient effectués à l'insu ou sans la participation de certaines personnes du réseau étendu de parenté. Or, avant l'arrivée des technologies nouvelles comme le SMS, il fallait envoyer soit une lettre écrite qui nécessitait qu'il y ait quelqu'un qui se déplace ou aille à un bureau de poste dans la ville la plus proche, soit envoyer un émissaire sur plusieurs sites différents pour informer les proches parents qui se chargeaient à leur tour de relayer l'information.

Le coût relativement bas de ce canal de communication a milité en faveur de son appropriation par les populations burkinabè. Il est ainsi entré dans les habitudes d'une frange importante de la population : ceux qui savent lire et écrire et ceux qui se débrouillent tout simplement dans l'écriture et la compréhension de la langue. Il arrive qu'à la manière des écrivains publics de jadis, les propriétaires de téléphones portables soient sollicités par un proche qui leur demande d'envoyer un SMS à un correspondant pour le prévenir d'un événement. « Envoie-lui un message pour lui dire de me rappeler ». De telles demandes de service sont courantes, d'autant plus que le « bipage » ne fait plus recette.

Comme la lettre que l'on se fait écrire et qui à l'arrivée est lue par l'instituteur du village, le message peut ainsi transiter par des intermédiaires. En effet, dans de nombreuses villes du Burkina Faso, dans l'enceinte des bureaux de postes, il existait jadis des écrivains publics. Toute personne pouvait requérir leur service pour se faire écrire ou lire une lettre moyennant paiement. Ces dernières années, ces écrivains publics ont presque disparu, certainement parce que le nombre de ceux qui savent lire et écrire s'est accru. Pendant que cela avait cours en ville, dans les campagnes où généralement il n'existe pas d'école ou s'il y en a, uniquement des écoles primaires, les jeunes fonctionnaires (qui sont généralement l'infirmier et/ou l'instituteur du village) jouent ce rôle d'écrivain public. Cela est valable encore de nos jours et le service offert par ces jeunes agents du service public est gratuit au profit des villageois. Cela facilite parallèlement leur intégration dans leur milieu d'accueil.

Le processus de circulation de la parole semble être bouleversé par ce mode de communication. Une invitation pour un mariage, l'information d'un décès ou de simples salutations sont effectuées par SMS.

Dans de nombreuses sociétés burkinabè, la moindre cérémonie qui concerne un membre du lignage nécessite que l'on informe certaines personnes du réseau de parenté quel que soit leur lieu de résidence. Qu'elles soient informées et ne puissent pas faire le déplacement, ne constitue pas en soit un problème. Cependant, l'absence d'information peut être dramatique pour la cohésion au sein du groupe social. C'est là que le SMS joue un rôle important dans la transmission de l'information en milieu rural.

Il est vrai que toutes les zones rurales du Burkina ne reçoivent pas de signal de téléphonie mobile dans le cas où une antenne de téléphonie ne s'y trouve pas. Cependant, il est possible de recevoir par moments, sur ses sites non couverts par un opérateur, des bribes de signaux qui à certains endroits permettent d'envoyer et/ou de recevoir des SMS, mais la communication orale devient pénible voire impossible. Alors un message envoyé sur le portable d'un habitant d'une zone rurale peut lui parvenir plusieurs heures plus tard, dès qu'il « retrouve le réseau » selon l'expression consacré au Burkina.

Un jeune infirmier de brousse de Santidougou, un village situé à 35 kilomètres de la seconde ville du Burkina, nous a confié avoir identifié un arbre du haut duquel il pouvait envoyer et recevoir des SMS. Alors, avant de commencer le travail dès 7 heures du matin, il montait sur l'arbre pour envoyer des messages en ville ou pour en recevoir. Il faisait ainsi autant de fois que besoin était. Il lui arrivait d'obtenir des cartes prépayées de la part de villageois qui le sollicitaient régulièrement pour l'envoie de SMS. Des cas similaires sont légion dans les différents villages du Burkina.

Le SMS est de nos jours beaucoup utilisé par les paysans et autres producteurs pour écouler leur récolte. Le signal, consistant en un ou plusieurs mots en langue nationale ou dans un français appris pour la circonstance, avertit l'acheteur installé en ville, afin qu'il vienne récupérer les produits. La transaction première peut aussi se faire à distance, en écrivant le prix au kilogramme s'il s'agit de produits agricoles ou à l'unité pour les autres choses.

Un restaurateur qui excelle dans la vente de porc au four à Ouagadougou, a l'habitude de se rendre dans des villages souvent très éloignés de la capitale pour aller chercher ses bêtes qu'il parque, une fois revenu, dans un quartier périphérique de la capitale. Il renouvelle sa tournée à chaque fois que son stock s'amenuise. Pour éviter de revenir bredouille de ses déplacements, il a entrepris de doter ses principaux fournisseurs de téléphone portable et les a initiés à l'écriture de messages courts et simples, du genre : « ya 10 por ». Ce qui signifie que ce fournisseur dispose d'une dizaine de porcs. Quelle que soit la réponse qu'il enverra au dit fournisseur, il est sûr d'être compris, car de l'élève du collège à l'infirmier du village en passant par l'instituteur, les « décodeurs » de message ne manquent pas dans un village.

Lorsqu'on parvient à apprendre aux paysans à manipuler le téléphone, le reste n'est qu'un jeu d'enfant. Cette solution par le SMS permet même au vendeur de charcuterie d'approvisionner toujours son stock pour satisfaire sa clientèle citadine.

Autant d'événements qui dans la culture locale exigeaient le transfert de l'information par voie orale avec souvent une présence physique de l'informateur, transitent désormais par SMS. Le SMS c'est le règne du pragmatisme en matière de communication. Il a démontré son efficacité en matière de mobilisation dans de nombreuses circonstances.

Les moyens d'annonces traditionnels des événements sociaux que sont les you you, les sons de tambours et autres instruments traditionnels, ne permettent pas d'aller au-delà des limites des habitations du village. Dans les villages où on les utilise encore, ils ne peuvent servir qu'à prévenir les seuls résidents du moment de la tenue d'un événement. Le plus souvent les personnes qui sont dans les champs de culture à plusieurs kilomètres des habitations ne peuvent être averties que par l'envoi d'un émissaire. Toutes ces situations rendent nécessaire l'utilisation d'autres moyens de communication ayant une plus longue portée. La jeune génération qui apporte le portable au village parvient aisément ainsi à coller à une réalité existentielle. Il n'est pas rare de voir des paysans illettrés remettre leur téléphone à une personne sachant écrire en français, afin que celle-ci envoie par SMS une information à un destinataire lointain avec l'assurance que ce dernier même s'il ne lit pas le français, trouvera quelqu'un pour lui déchiffrer le message. En outre, le nombre de plus en plus croissant d'adultes alphabétisés favorise l'utilisation de ce système de message.

Tout le monde sait que le SMS existe et qu'il est d'un coût abordable quel que soit l'opérateur de téléphonie mobile. Les réalités économiques ont fait adopter ce canal de communication par de nombreux consommateurs même si par ailleurs sa discrétion est aussi dans certaines circonstances un atout non négligeable.

De façon empirique, on peut dire que le nombre d'utilisateurs de ce canal de communication est en croissance du fait de son aspect pratique. Pour effectuer l'enterrement d'une femme par exemple chez les Kasina du Burkina Faso, il est indispensable que ses parents viennent ou donnent leur avis avant qu'on ne procède à la mise en terre. Ce groupe du lignage des parents constitue une sorte de « co-lignage » du mari, et, s'il n'est pas considéré dans une telle situation, la cohésion sociale peut en être affectée. Or, de nos jours, de façon très pragmatique, ces personnes acceptent d'être informées par SMS et par personne interposée. Les réponses : « vous pouvez faire » ou « attendez on arrive », peuvent aider à mieux organiser les obsèques et éviter certains désagréments liés à la conservation du cadavre. Cela est valable pour des situations où pour une personne décédée et enterrée en ville on doit transférer les « restes » au village. Pour de tels enterrements mobilisant de nombreux citadins, l'utilisation d'une telle technologie résout bien le problème de coordination.

Pratique pour son coût, discret pour la transmission de certains messages ou pour diverses autres sollicitations, le SMS connaît un grand succès au Burkina Faso. L'utilisation du SMS est désormais intégrée dans les habitudes de communication des populations à telle enseigne que lorsqu'on n'informe pas un proche de la tenue d'une cérémonie quelconque alors qu'on aurait pu le faire par simple envoi de SMS, il est difficile d'avoir une excuse. Il n'est pas rare d'entendre dans de tels cas, des plaintes du genre « tu aurais pu m'envoyer au moins un message. » Ce qui montre que le SMS introduit un nouveau système d'obligations. En effet, comme nous le disions plus haut, il est important d'informer voire d'impliquer certaines personnes à l'organisation de certaines cérémonies sociales. Cependant, malgré la volonté des premiers concernés d'envoyer courriers et émissaires partout, il arrive qu'on ne puisse pas toucher tout le monde à temps. L'arrivée du SMS réduit cette marge de gens non informés, et donne l'occasion de transmettre l'information à temps. Cela est important car tout déplacement dans le but de prendre part à un rituel ou tout autre cérémonie nécessite qu'on «se prépare» à l'avance. Pour certaines situations il y a des contributions financières ou en nature, coutumièrement fixées, pour d'autres « on donne ce qu'on peu ». Dans tous les cas il y a nécessité d'être informé à l'avance pour savoir la conduite à tenir et éviter toute surprise désagréable. L'usage du SMS contribue à accroître le nombre de participants «bien préparés», ce qui est d'un grand apport à la réussite des cérémonies coutumières.

Pour des populations qui étaient habituées à ce que toute information soit trans-mise oralement, le fait de se contenter de nos jours des messages écrits via SMS, traduit une certaine transformation des canaux traditionnels de communication. Elle démontre aussi la capacité de ces populations à s'approprier une technologie qui peut paraître aux antipodes de leurs réalités culturelles. La capacité d'adaptation des populations à cette nouvelle façon de communiquer est à notre avis, une traduction de la flexibilité des cultures africaines par rapport aux technologies importées, surtout lorsque celles-ci correspondent d'une certaine façon à leurs attentes.

En plus de son aspect pratique, le SMS contribue au développement d'une sorte de métalangue qui permet de cerner cette concordance syntaxique qui mêle, dans un style original, français et langues nationales pour enrichir l'expression courante .tout en faisant court.

Conclusion

L'adoption du téléphone mobile par les populations du Burkina Faso - y compris celles du milieu rural, comme on l'a vu - tient au fait qu'il se situe au prolongement de leur « culture de l'oralité ». Les messages, jadis relayés de village à village au rythme des instruments traditionnels de musique, se trouvent plus efficacement transmis de nos jours par le biais d'un appareil qui permet d'entendre la voix à des milliers de kilomètres. En outre, dans cette situation de communication, informateur et informé, émetteur et récepteur peuvent échanger, se poser des questions, discuter.

Tout se passe actuellement dans les sociétés burkinabè aussi bien dans celles rurales qu'urbaines, comme si le téléphone mobile avait su prendre sa place dans les relations sociales sans pour autant entraîner un bouleversement en profondeur des dispositions culturelles. Ainsi, bien que ses conditions d'obtention et d'entretien soient compliquées pour ces populations pauvres, celles-ci ne lésinent pas devant les opportunités qui leur permettraient d'entrer en possession de cette technologie mondiale

Dans une telle situation, l'attrait exercé par le SMS paraît tout de même contradictoire avec les réalités culturelles. Pourtant il répond à une autre logique, celle qui consiste à exploiter la nouvelle technologie dans le sens de ses intérêts propres. Certes cela ne fait pas forcement l'affaire des opérateurs de téléphonie mobile compte tenu du faible coût d'utilisation de ce service (6% de leur chiffre d'affaires en Afrique selon l'agence Reuter, mai 2006). Cependant, cet intérêt d'une population à majorité analphabète pour un canal dont l'utilisation nécessite un certain niveau d'instruction, devrait inciter les opérateurs de téléphonie mobile à développer des services tels que le SMS vocal, qui permet de traduire le message dicté oralement en texte écrit. Selon l'agence Reuter, «Des experts réunis à Naïrobi au Kenya, à l'occasion d'une conférence sur la téléphonie mobile, ont déclaré que les opérateurs africains auraient plus à gagner à développer l'utilisation du SMS ou de services tout simplement en phase avec les besoins des Africains plutôt qu'à gaspiller des millions de dollars dans la construction de nouveaux réseaux télécoms » (Reuter 18 mai 2006)

L'alphabétisation des adultes qui permet une formation accélérée des populations surtout en milieu rural à la lecture et à l'écriture dans leurs langues locales, pourrait accroître leur niveau d'utilisation du SMS.

Ce qui semble intéressant, c'est le fait que l'appropriation de cette technologie par les populations locales se réalise telle quelle. Il ne s'agit pas d'une transformation voire d'une réinvention de l'objet physique pour l'adapter à leur capacité technique et économique, il s'agit plutôt d'une appropriation des modalités d'utilisation.Les populations, dans leur façon pragmatique de consommer les technologies nouvelles, conservent toujours les éléments fondamentaux de leur culture tels que le respect de la hiérarchie sociale, le déroulement des rites de passage, la façon dont ils échangent les biens et services, etc., même si elles ne peuvent empêcher des transformations introduites par celles-ci.

Les populations africaines semblent raisonner dans le sens d'une interrogation du genre : « quel est l'aspect de cette nouvelle technologie dont nous pouvons tirer un quelconque profit ? ». Certes, cela n'est pas particulier aux seuls africains, mais compte tenu du faible niveau de développement économique de certains pays comme le Burkina Faso, les populations essayent toujours de maximiser l'exploitation des technologies venues d'ailleurs. Ce faisant, l'utilisation de certains appareils ou outils par ces populations dépasse le plus souvent les prévisions du fabricant.

C'est dans ce sens que le SMS est utilisé au Burkina Faso. Même s'il peut être jugé comme allant à l'encontre de la « tradition de l'oralité » parce que c'est de l'écrit, il permet paradoxalement de maintenir, voire développer l'esprit de solidarité, en permettant comme nous le montrions plus haut de mobiliser facilement et rapidement plus de gens autour d'événements sociaux. Mieux vaut garder le contact, ne serait-ce que par SMS, que de rester longtemps sans nouvelles de ses proches. Aussi, on peut plus facilement emprunter le téléphone d'autrui pour envoyer un SMS que pour effectuer un appel. Des appels à la mobilisation autour d'un phénomène social sont plus facilement relayés via un SMS et le transfert du message se fait plus aisément que s'il s'était agit de le relayer par appel oral.

Le téléphone mobile en lui-même peut paraître un luxe pour les populations du Burkina Faso si l'on s'en tient à des déductions purement économiques. Il semble pourtant dans la réalité répondre à un besoin réel. C'est ce qui explique qu'en même temps que son coût rebute les populations des villes et des campagnes, celles-ci tiennent toutefois à se l'approprier. Ce côté onéreux du téléphone mobile, mis cependant en rapport avec ses différentes utilisations possibles, le fait considérer autrement. Il n'est donc pas rare de nos jours que les parents vivant au village, qui par le passé demandaient à ceux restés en ville de vieux vêtements, leur demandant maintenant « leur ancien téléphone portable ». Quant à l'utilisation de l'appareil acquis, les stratégies les plus inouïes sont développées pour réduire les coûts.

En conclusion, on peut affirmer que l'appropriation du SMS est utile aux populations burkinabè non seulement pour passer les informations dans le cadre de cercles économiques, mais aussi pour l'organisation de cérémonies culturelles indispensable à la survie de la société. L'augmentation vertigineuse du prix des hydrocarbures qui entraîne par ricochet celle des coûts des transports en commun et de certains moyens de locomotion (le SMS permettant de supprimer voire réduire les déplacements souvent inutiles), sont actuellement autant d'arguments utilisés par ceux qui estiment que l'appropriation de cet appareil qui permet de toucher des milliers de personnes en dépensant moins d'argent et sans bouger de chez soi est la bienvenue.

Références

BARRETAU, DANIEL (1998), 'Système éducatif et multilinguisme au Burkina Faso', Recueil d'articles ORSTOM, Ouagadougou.

DIBAKANA, JEAN-AIMÉ (2002), 'Usages sociaux du téléphone portable et nouvelles sociabilités au Congo', *Politique Africaine* 85: 133-150.

DIBAKANA, JEAN-AIMÉ (2006), 'L'usage du téléphone mobile à Brazzaville. La consommation comme analyseur d'enjeux de pouvoir en milieu urbain africain. L'exemple du téléphone portable au Congo Brazzaville', http://www.argonautes.fr/sections.php?artid=351

HAHN, HANS P. (2004), 'Global goods and the process of appropriation'. In: P. Probst & G. Spittler, eds, *Between resistance and expansion. Explorations of local vitality in Africa.* (= Beiträge zur Afrikaforschung, 18), Münster: LIT Verlag, pp. 211-230.

HORST, HEATHER & DANIEL MILLER (2005), 'From kinship to link-up. Cell phones and social networking in Jamaica', *Current Anthropology* 46(5): 755-779.

INSD (2007) 'Recensement général de la population et de l'habitat, Rapport provisoire, Ouagadougou', INSD.

KEDREBEOGO, GÉRARD (2006), 'Critère: Critère de choix des langues d'enseignement au Burkina Faso', Ouagadougou, séminaire de l'INSS.

MEBA (Ministère de l'enseignement de base et de l'alphabétisation) (2006), *Annuaire statistique de l'enseignement de base 2005-2006*, Ouagadougou.

MILLER, D. (1995), 'Consumption and commodities', *Annual Review of Anthropology* 24: 141-161.

MED (=Ministère de l'Economie et du Développement) (2007), 'Revue annuelle du CSLP, rapport provisoire', Ouagadougou: MED.

MELKOTE, DRINIVAS R. & H.L. STEEVES (2004), 'Information and communication technologies for rural development'. In: C. Okigbo & F. Eribo, eds, *Development and communication in Africa*, Lanham: Rowman & Littlefield, pp. 165-173.

NYAMBA, ANDRÉ (2000), 'La 'parole du téléphone'. Significations sociales et individuelles du téléphone chez les Sanan du Burkina Faso'. In: A. Chéneau-Loquay, eds, *Enjeux des technologies de la communication en Afrique. Du téléphone à Internet*, Paris: Karthala, pp. 193-210.

7

The healer and his phone:
Medicinal dynamics among the
Kapsiki/Higi of North Cameroon

Wouter van Beek

What influence is the mobile phone having on indigenous medicine? This contribution presents the case of a *tradi-praticien* (an indigenous healer) and discusses the way he uses his mobile phone and the continuities and discontinuities of such use in the practice of traditional medicine among the Kapsiki/Higi[1] in the Mandara Mountains of Cameroon. Fieldwork was done in January 2009 and reflects the current state of medicinal development and care in the area.

The new doctor

Haman Tizhé is his name and he is an important man among healers. His present position came about from a complicated life history. Growing up in Roufta, one of the outlying Kapsiki villages, he was a personal friend of the 'prince', the son of Djoda, who was the Lamido (Fulbe chief of the district) at the time. When he was about twelve, he became involved in a brawl and threw a stone at a certain Bereme

---

[1] The Kapsiki of northern Cameroon and the Higi in northeastern Nigeria who live in the Mandara Mountains along the border between the two countries form one ethnic group. I use the term Kapsiki for both groups. I have been carrying out field research in the area since 1972/73, with regular return visits every three to five years, the latest being in 2008/2009.

from Mogodé who was hit in the groin and subsequently died. Haman was arrested by the Lamido, a distant kinsman of Bereme's, who then put himself *in loco parentis* to collect the *kelehu* (the blood price). This is not a fixed price and the victim's party can take anything they can lay their hands on that belongs to the culprit's kinsmen. The young Haman and his father were chased by the people of Roufta and went to Teki in the northeast of the Kapsiki area. After some time, his father went to Guili among the Hina in the south and Haman himself was taken to the house of his friend, the Lamido's son. After a few years he left for Nigeria where he became an apprentice to the Lamido's servants in Michika, the Nigerian counterpart of Djoda, and learnt to fix machinery. From there he ventured out into the bush where he made the acquaintance of the healers in the area, usually blacksmiths or hunters. Investing much time, money and energy in those relations, he was gradually introduced to the secrets of Kapsiki medicine. What was important, he said, was to look carefully at what animals ate and in particular what food they spurned. Then one took that plant and showed it to someone who knew about them in order to gain extra medicinal knowledge. He still spends a lot of time in the bush with old hunters and healers but has also met them in Sokoto, Aba, Gaitan (all in Nigeria) and in Niger, even communicating with *grand marabouts* from Mali when he was in Sokoto. One needs to travel a lot as a healer and Haman was, therefore, frequently away, though more so in the past than today because now that he is established, people come to him.

Photo 7.1   The sign of the practice

After twenty years, he returned to Cameroon and settled in Mogodé, the central village of the Cameroonian Kapsiki, and set himself up as a *tradi-praticien*. Particularly adept at networking (and at wooing officials), he initiated the *Association pour les tradi-praticiens de Mayo Tsanaga*, and realized its membership of the national umbrella organization of traditional healers in Cameroon, and also received recognition from the OISA, the *Organisation Internationale pour la Santé en Afrique* (see Photo 7.5, p. 132).

Once installed in Mogodé, he also initiated a *tontine* (a classic kind of rotating savings association) for all the women in Mogodé who were from the Kama, a sub-group of villages around Roufta, to help them promote their own interests in Mogodé. Using his organizational skills, he made this *tontine* into a thriving business and at the same time benefiting himself, as a healer, from the many contacts he made through these women.

Haman has also built up a practice in Mokolo, the regional capital of the *préfecture*. He divides his week between the two places – three days a week in Mokolo and four in Mogodé – spending market day in Mogodé in his residence just across the road from the dispensary while his house in Mokolo is just around the corner from the hospital. These choices of location indicate his desire for respectability and cooperation with the western medical system.

Photo 7.2   Haman Tizhé and his credentials

Photo 7.3   Haman Tizhé's other organization

The phone and new medicines

I will not go into details here about Haman's pharmacopoeia but instead highlight some generalities relating to his use of the mobile phone in his treatment of patients. His array of medicines, which are stored in a special hut, is built up in three categories, all of which can be described by the generic Kapsiki term *rwhj*. One is the general cultural knowledge of *material medica* that the Kapsiki have about plants whose medicinal properties most people are aware of, folk medicine in fact. Examples of common knowledge are trees whose bark is used to treat 'fever' (usually meaning malaria) and medicines to fight scabies, intestinal parasites and hepatitis. A prescription from another Kapsiki specialist

> In the case of hepatitis, take the bark of the *ndeweva vèra* (Ziziphus mauritiana), and boil it with lemon and acacia leaves for two hours. Two calabashes with the bitter potion have to be filled. From one the patient drinks in the morning, from the second in the afternoon, for four days. Then recovery has to be done without further medication.

The second group of medicines is typical of traditional medication. The Kapsiki tend to link one plant species, or even *specimen*, to one affliction. The most important medicines come from two species: *Crinum sp.* and *Cissus Quandrangularis.*[2] *Cissus*

---

[2]   The latter has a wide distribution as a ritual, symbolic and medicinal plant across the whole Mandara area.

(*ha'/₂gedle* in Kapsiki) has a broad symbolic meaning but *Crinum* (*hwį°ĭ* in Kapsiki) is the most important medicinal species. In principle any of these native onion variants, and usually individual specimens of *hwį°ĭ*, are medication for a specific affliction, as each *Crinum* plant can heal its 'own' illness. Which specific plant helps which affliction is something only the specialist knows and he keeps this highly lucrative information secret. Sometimes the specific aim of the onion depends on its surface characteristics: a *Crinum* against smallpox has to be an onion with brown spots on its leaves.[3] However in the majority of cases, only the plant's owner knows its use, as this information cannot be gleaned from the plant's appearance alone. Some specific medicinal plants (other than the two mentioned above) are part of this group, and one illness can then be correlated to one species. These correlations are, however, strictly secret and the healer's own private information.

The third sector is the new one, and it is here that the phone is important. This is the area of combinations of medicines, the cocktails, the multiple medications. These are the medicines to be used when all other prescriptions fail, and these are the ones that establish the healer's reputation.

Haman has developed a new array of medication. More than in traditional settings and more than the usual medicine men (the blacksmiths), he is addressing new problems in his daily encounters: how to pass exams, how to achieve success at work or how to get revenge on one's enemies, using also the word *voyance* (knowing the future). Traditionally this resides in divination, usually by crab or pebbles, but Haman does not perform divination himself, he just makes diagnoses, basing his assessment on the client's somatic complaints. But not all new problems are somatic. For example, to have good luck in your car, you have to take some chameleon eggs and then you will not have any accidents and people will see you coming.

It is with this third type of medication that the phone comes in. Haman has not only built up an additional pharmacopoeia but also an extensive network and a good reputation. A growing number of Kapsiki have migrated to the cities in the south, like Douala and Yaoundé, the national capital, often forming *tontine*-like associations of *Ressortissants de Kapsiki* in those cities, and these people form a natural clientele for the new doctor. Haman actively seeks clients and advertises by word of mouth within this group and beyond. This means that he has to perform his diagnoses, prescribe medication and complete all the financial transactions at a distance, hence the need for a phone.

How does the phone operate in the medical world? New clients are now found by telephone, and many appointments and treatment sessions are held by phone. The patients describe their ailments, Haman asks where the pain or problem is, and

---

[3]   This homology between symptom and medicine is normal and well known in African medication: the medicine to fight *damara* (smallpox) has to be drunk from a calabash with 'smallpox', *kwetlekwe damara*. But in fact this is already specialist territory.

then they have to pay his fees by transferring money by telephone. After he has received the money, he sends the products to the post-office box indicated, with each package bearing a different number. Once the patient has received the parcel, they call him and have to convince him that they are the patient in question: he again asks about their ailments and checks whether these are the same. He then tells them what the numbers stand for and how to use the various products – in what order, at what time, with what drink or food – and explains at some length the way they have to take medicine. They have to repeat it back to him, during the same phone call, and should not write the information down but retain it in their head in order not let anyone else know the details. Once they are healed, they are expected to phone him again; if not, he checks up on them by phoning them, about every two weeks. Once they appear healed, he sends no bill but asks them to 'send whatever Allah has provided them with', and to send it via Western Union, Moneygram or MTA transfer, which, of course, has to be done by phone as well. But just what they can afford, as – in his words – a patient should not become poor because of medical treatment. This way he has built up a wide circle of patients in the south of Cameroon, and even in Norway and Paris – all of them Africans.

For these treatments by phone and at a distance, Haman has developed what he calls a *passe-partout*, a general medication with a broad spectre. This is a composite medication made up of five plants, which have to be taken within five minutes of each other. When a new patient calls on the phone, he asks what the ailment is: where it hurts and what the problem is. However he has to check what people have eaten recently and whether women are menstruating as this precludes certain

Photo 7.4   Part of Haman Tizhé's medicine cabinet

products. If the patient has no diarrhoea, he sends him/her his *passé-partout* and waits for its arrival. In the subsequent call, he indicates which product has to be taken first, what the waiting time between products should be and then tells the patient to call back within four hours. If the problem abates a little, he instructs the patient what to take for the rest of the week and to call back in six days. If the medicine appears to have had no effect, another product is tried but this evidently takes time. He is now also using this *passe-partout* with patients at home where the feedback is quicker. Such a *passe-partout* is not an easy thing to come by and he is proud to have it in his collection. But like anything in medicine, one has to exert oneself to get it or develop it. In his words: 'Only a real healer who has genuinely "suffered" has such a *passe-partout*.'

The mobile phone: Change in continuity

Haman Tizhé operates both within and beyond the confines and definitions of Kapsiki medicine. He does not belong to the habitual healer's category – the black-smiths – but bears all the characteristics of the second category, that of the *ndekel*, the 'night-walker' or clairvoyant.[4] Kapsiki society knows people with a different *shinankwe* (shadow) that go out at night to battle with 'shadows' from other villages. One of their assets is that they know something about the future, about 'hidden things', and as such many *kelj¹/ze* are healers.

The crucial characteristics of Kapsiki medication are the privatization of know-ledge, the increasing surrender of the patient to the healer in the process of diag-nosis, as well as a growing distance between patient and healer. The first, secrecy, is important. Beyond the well-known general folk medication – which does not call for a specialist – patients have no idea what medication they are using or need. This privatization of knowledge is facilitated by the peculiar focus on specimens instead of species: it is the individual plant that has the relevant characteristics and, beyond the incidental homology cited above, no stranger can be sure of the medicinal pro-perties of a Crinum plant except its proprietor, i.e. the specialist. The same holds for the *rhwi* of the third category but in a different way. Here the plants themselves, and especially their combinations, are kept secret. The phone plays straight into these mechanisms of secrecy: by using a phone, separating the product from its use is made easier. The plants bear little information as to their use and by sending them and phoning afterwards, this separation is enhanced. The same holds true for the combinations of medicines. Here too the medication sent carries no information at all and the phone provides the option of sending the relevant information piece-meal.

---

[4]   He denies being one but his neighbours emphatically state that he is. Being a *kelj¹/ze* is nothing to be ashamed of although being a *mete* (witch) would be – but this is rarely acknowledged in conversation.

This increases, not diminishes, the patient's dependence on the healer, a sur-render which is part of the pathway of healing in which the somatic aspects of the ailment is stressed. Specialists' healing cases have to do with the length of an illness, as the specialist is usually not the first to be consulted. In divination sessions, when a diviner looks for the hidden causes of a persistent illness, the client is actively involved but the illness is clear, it is the treatment which is intensified not the diagnosis. And Haman operates in this trajectory of intensified treatment; with a more complicated treatment that is usually in the third category of medication. The agency of the client is reduced in favour of that of the specialist. The patient has a reduced grip on what is happening to and with him. The distancing of the phone, with its possibility of parcelling information and the single-stranded communication between healer and patient, increases that surrender, defining the healer as ever more a specialist, someone who 'really knows'. And the newer the ailments or the problems being addressed, the greater the client's dependency: new services enhance surrender.

Photo 7.5   New services!

The third element is the distance between healer and client. Healing involves danger. A serious and persistent illness is a force in itself, and healing means that the illness has to go elsewhere, possibly to the healer. To paraphrase Mary Douglas: 'illness is evil out of place'. Just as in sacrifices, evil is chased from the compound to the potential detriment of neighbours, so too healing a patient implies risk for a bystander, primarily for the specialist. So a specialist maintains a distance from his patients to avoid this 'contamination', and again the phone helps: a distant patient remain distant and any risk is borne by his/her immediate neighbours and not by the healer.

The telephone has reinforced cultural continuities in medicine but has simulated changes as well. Especially in the third category of medicine, the telephone has been a catalyst for change in the pharmacopoeia, in particular in the development and use of the broad spectre of *passe-partout* medication. Though this *passé-partout* is used in face-to-face medication too, it is especially useful in diagnoses made at a distance. It is also a reinforcement of a typical aspect of African medication, the 'try-out'. Haman explains that he often prescribes medication such as the *passe-partout* to try it out and that the reaction to the medication is part of the diagnostic process: give a combination of medicines and see what happens. If healing occurs, continue the whole mix. If no improvement in the patient's condition is discernible, the process of trying out is repeated till the right mix is found. Whatever the first diagnosis, it is not the anamnesis that counts here but the healing. Payment by phone presents a clear distance, adding an impersonality to the transaction that plays into the hands of the healer.

Finally, even in cultural continuity things change. A healer such as Haman Tizhé has patients in a large range of localities and his network has grown in size and intensity. He can now, thanks to the mobile phone, reach and treat patients over a far wider geographic range than was possible in the past. He benefits as a healer and this ties in with the Kapsiki system of healing that is much closer to the cosmopolitan system of medication, as is signalled by Haman's proximity to dispensaries and hospitals. Despite clear cultural continuities, Kapsiki healing has become part of a wider world, a wider community of healing and one of the instruments facilitating this change is the mobile phone.

We are witnessing history in the making through similar ongoing histories that can be observed in many places in Africa where new areas are being connected to mobile phone networks. These include regions like the Mandara Mountains that could be labelled 'marginal' and where people have always lived in very mobile communities, the 'mobile margins'. However these mobile margins are being transformed by the arrival of new means of communication and relations over large distances are becoming a part of people's daily social lives, thus reintroducing old continuities in economic, social and cultural spheres. The healer's practice is just one example of a typically global enterprise.

8

The mobility of a mobile phone: Examining 'Swahiliness' through an object's biography

Julia Pfaff

It is not just humans that have a memory and oral history, things too can tell us something about their past and our possible future
(Hetherington 2001: 40)

Mobile phones and their cultural and spatial mobility

Thousands of mobile phones, mobile-phone accessories, SIM cards and top-up vouchers.... In Aggrey about a hundred shops sell mobile phones and items connected to their usage and appropriation. Most of the shops, being only a few square metres, have a glass cabinet at the front displaying mobile phones, with one lying next to the other. Different brands in different rows, arranged by price or the length of time they have been on display. This road is full of mobile-phone shops offering a broad (if not complete) range of models that are available in stores all round the world today, from the latest Sony Ericsson design to the Motorola flip phone in all different colours and also some of the old and simple Nokia and Siemens phones.

Looking at the collection in this small road in Kariakoo, one of the main business areas in the centre of Dar es Salaam, Tanzania, it is obvious that thousands of processes of acquisition and exchange are involved, stretching across space and time. As Hill (2006: 340) points out, collections 'carry a multitude of meanings that are intimately linked to the biographies of the collected objects', hinting at the spatial and cultural dimenions of their existence. In this respect, I argue that taking a closer look at the mobile phones on display opens up a window through which to examine the spatial and cultural practices in which the objects are embedded as well as to see how mobile phones influence 'Swahiliness'[1] and vice versa.

Concentrating on the object's mobility, I explore here the ways mobile phones are being appropriated and incorporated into the lives of many Swahili and are playing an important role in contemporary trading practices.

Outlining central aspects of Swahili culture and especially the crucial role of trading practices for processes of identification, I highlight the ways in which the specific connections between people and objects are vital to an understanding of socio-cultural as well as socio-spatial processes. Putting this in the context of recent debates on mobile phones in Africa as well as cultural geographic research, I introduce some conceptual and methodological ideas of object biographies and 'follow the thing-geographies'. The chapter then returns to one of the shops in Aggrey, presenting phases in the life course of a particular mobile phone on display to explore its meanings in different relations and the ways in which it has been circulated and appropriated over the last eighteen months. In doing so, I attempt to give a much-needed empirical impression of the varying encounters between different owners, users, traders and the mobile phone and offer insight into the ways in which its biography tells us a lot about 'Swahiliness' and how it is constantly being negotiated, (re)created and practised by engaging.

The Swahili as merchants

Although the trading history of the 'Swahili Corridor' and Zanzibar in particular (with its two main islands of Unguja and Pemba) is far more complex, the following briefly sketches some of the central aspects of an ideology and culture of trade. Having controlled most of the intercontinental commerce between the interior of Eastern and Southern Africa and the Gulf, the Indian subcontinent and Indonesia for more than thousand years, the Swahili have long inhabited and fashioned transnational spaces of trade (Topan 1998, Middleton 1992, Mbembe 2001, Gilbert 1999: 10). People from Zanzibar are therefore often characterized (and see themselves) as 'a seafaring and merchant people, nurtured by contact' and it is their engagement in commercial practices that has essentially contributed to a Swahili culture and iden-

---

[1]   The term 'Swahili' is generally used to refer to people from the East African coast who have a way of life characterized by the region's long-standing Afro-Arabic relations and the influences of the Indian Ocean, speak Kiswahili as their vernacular language and are Muslim (see Constantin 1989, Le Guennec-Coppens 2002). However most people who come under this term would first consider themselves as a member of the city or region they originate from, for example, Waamu (a Swahili from Lamu), Wamvita (a Swahili from Mombasa), Wapemba (a Swahili from Pemba). This article concentrates on Swahilis from Zanzibar (Wazanzibari) and Pemba who call themselves either *mpemba* or *mwarabu* (Arab).

tity (Le Guennec-Coppens 2002: 56). Trade in Zanzibar has been regarded for a long time as a guarantor of wealth, and much of its success has been related to the familiar role of merchant adventurer. Flexibility and mobility have played a crucial role in trade journeys along the coast and into the interior, but the trading voyage has been neither a specialized nor a regularized business (Villiers 1948; 400-404). Under the Oman Empire, Zanzibar was part of a network of ports with shared commercial interests. Recognizing the importance of Zanzibar, it was Seyyid Said bin Sultan, the most active Omani trader of all, who moved his capital to the island (Cooper 1977: 32-42). The traders enjoyed political power and economic supremacy and formed an aristocracy of merchants including religious leaders and learned men, effectively dominating all aspects of life (Le Cour Grandmaison 1989: 179; Constantin 1986-1989: 56). As Middleton (2003: 519) emphasizes, although 'the Swahili merchants view of their worlds never exactly mirrored the commercial and political actuality, (...) it gave reason and order to what they saw as their central position in world society as they knew it'. It is difficult to estimate the economic dimensions of the contemporary Zanzibari trading networks that are revitalizing and expanding old routes through transnational connections in the diaspora. Nevertheless, it is evident that their imaginary and ideological basis, which is especially relevant to the processes of identification, is still present (Freitag 2004: 79). The general feeling is that, to be rich, one has to engage in commerce, and that those who engage in trade also become rich, not only financially but also by moving up the social hierarchy.[2] In this respect, trading practices are still recognized as a worthwhile activity, not only for the anticipated profit trade brings but primarily to see oneself as a part of a society that is based to a large extent on this very ideology. Almost all the young people I have spoken to claimed that whatever they might do to earn a living, they would also definitely engage in some kind of trading activity.[3]

Mobile phones are a primary material form in contemporary Swahili trading networks, both as objects of exchange and as technologies of communication. They are of vital importance not only as a trading good but also for organizing trading practices. And as mobile phones have come to play a crucial role in everyday life more generally, they are not just 'anything' but a 'good' that is closely linked to the traders' processes of identification. They represent, therefore, an object through which to analyze the ways economic and cultural practices are intertwined, and provide valuable material to explore contemporary 'Swahiliness'.

---

[2] In Kiswahili the word *tajiri* (from the Arabic *tāğer* and translated as 'trader'), refers to a rich person or someone who engages in commerce (Kamusi ya Kiswahili sanifu 2004). To be a rich person (*mtajiri*) does not only mean having money but also refers to being rich in social status.

[3] This paper is based on my PhD research on 'Mobile Networks, Trading Practices and Translocality among the Swahili'. With mobile ethnographic research, especially among young *wazanzibari* and *wapemba* in Zanzibar, Dar es Salaam, mainland Tanzania, Dubai and London, I explored mobile trading connections and the flows of people, ideas and objects and their contribution to an understanding of a 'translocal Swahili space'.

Researching mobile phones in Africa

Focusing on the everyday practices and meanings attached to the circulation and adoption of a particular mobile phone across space and time, I present an impression of mobile-phone biographies in Africa. To date, very few studies have systematically considered the key factors of mobile ICT use in developing countries using data collected directly from individual consumers (Meso *et al.* 2005: 120; Horst & Miller 2006). There is a lack of qualitative and ethnographic work on mobile-phone use in Sub-Saharan Africa and, as Castells *et al.* (2007: 138) point out, the specific ways mobile phones are used, especially among young people in Africa, are largely undocumented. For this reason, the section in their book 'Mobile communication and society' which deals with mobile phones in Africa is not only rather short but also repeatedly refers to the anecdotal nature of many of the assumptions. As they put it (Ibid: 138), 'some have argued that so far most stories about mobile phones in Africa are anecdotal, everyone comes across an event or a situation in which he or she is struck by the omnipresence of mobile phone advertisements, by different kinds of usage (Phone sharing etc.), but academic debates on mobile phones in Africa only seem to start'.

However these anecdotes hint at a variety of meanings and roles of the mobile phone, and Castells *et al.* (2007: 156) emphasize the importance of exploring the ways in which people adopt and appropriate mobile phones in ways closely linked to the construction of their own culture. In his article 'Cell phones, social inequality and contemporary culture in Nigeria. Smith (2006) provides an important contribution by analyzing the social and cultural changes generated by the proliferation of mobile phones and the way the spread of the technology has accentuated already prevalent cultural dynamics and intensified perceptions and discontents about inequality in contemporary Nigeria. Considering mobile phones not only as a catalyst for change but also as objects that shed light on important dimensions of long-standing features of people's social life and culture, he emphasizes the roles and meanings of mobile phones for people in different situations (Ibid: 499). Laurier (2001: 489) argues that a mobile phone can range from being 'a designer plastic box with buttons' to 'a battery-operated machine' or a 'rental agreement between Orange and the customer' or much more. While the complex 'agreements and the heterogeneous engineering nesting in the space that we ordinary observers would [nevertheless] consistently recognise as a mobile phone' (Ibid: 490) are frequently forgotten by users, the mobile phone appears to be an everyday object that may even have certain human characteristics or merge with people (Oksman & Rautiainen 2002: 25; Gell 1998: 12). In their rich ethnographic study of mobile phones in Jamaica, in which Horst & Miller (2006: 65ff) examined the impact of mobile phones on poverty among low-income Jamaicans, they argue that mobile phones are far more than just a phone. This paper offers an insight into everyday relations between people and mobile phones by examining the different ways of relating to, using, disposing of and acquiring mobile phones. Asking how links are created, how they are maintained and why they fall apart is seen as a way of exploring the identifications, practices and symbolization arising from these manifold connections and what they say about the mobile phone as well as about what it means to be Swahili.

Rematerializing cultural geography: A focus on travelling objects

There have been several calls in the past few years for a 'rematerialization' of human geography (e.g. Jackson 2000). With similar trends in the social sciences more generally, geographers have started to 'rethink the object' as well as the ways in which the 'material' and the 'social' intertwine and interact (Thrift 1996: 24; Whatmore 1999: 27). Following the idea that the social is as much constituted by materiality as the other way around (Miller 1998: 3; Bingham 1996), a number of researchers are seeking to account for the 'sensuous, concrete and polyvalent nature of commodities as they inhabit our daily lives' (Leslie & Reimer 1999). As Engstroem & Blackler (2005: 310) argue, 'it would be a mistake to assume that objects are "just given". (...) Objects are [not] constructed arbitrarily on the spot; objects have histories and built-in affordances, they resist and "bite back"'. 'Instead of seeing commodities simply as being produced, existing and observed to circulate through an economic system, this perspective usually entails understanding objects as an effect of stable arrays of relations (Latour 1993: 390, Law 2000: 1). As active constituents of social relations in this regard, the meanings of an object are 'not only plural and contested, but also mutable over time and space' (Bridge & Smith 2003: 259).[4] It is, therefore, the biographies and geographical lives of commodities that have gained geographers' attention and are seen to provide a unique window through which to understand their social and cultural contexts.

Building on the ideas of Appadurai (1986) and Kopytoff (1989), tracing 'the forms, uses and trajectories of 'things-in-motion'" (Dwyer & Jackson 2003: 270) has become a means of exploring negotiations of culture, questions of mobility, translocal commercial networks and the complex connections between places. Tracing English royal letters'; journeys, Miles Ogborn (2002) for example, has concentrated on the production, carriage and the use of texts as material objects to understand their place in early modern trading networks. Another example of current cultural geography is the work on food by Ian Cook et al. (2004, 2006) and their recent publication (Cook & Harrison 2007) on West Indian pepper sauce. Bringing to the fore debates on 'conducting "follow the thing" geographies', Cook & Harrison (2007: 40) present how 'in, and through, that bottle of sauce, an amazing array of

---

[4] See Law (1996) and Law & Hetherington (1999) for empiricial examples of ANT on travelling objects.

complex connectivities and mobilities' seems to be being mobilized on different scales (Ibid: 58).

Acknowledging the importance of the engagement between people and material objects in everyday life, it is evident that exploring the life course of an object provides valuable insight into the diverse encounters between things and people on the move and offers a unique opportunity to highlight the diverse meanings of an object over time and space. However, putting objects at the centre of interest also creates new challenges for the ways in which empirical research is done and how information is presented.

Accompanying a mobile phone

Getting to grips with aspects of mobility requires an understanding of the 'things-in-motion' and the ways in which people try to deal with these mobilities (van Binsbergen 2005: 24). Whereas on the one hand this means understanding the actual movement of an object and, with it, the relationships between people as well as the connections between places, on the other hand, it entails developing an understanding of its mobility in the sense of its adaptability and the different ways in which it becomes appropriated, the change of the object itself (Benfoughal 2002: 113). Exploring the connections through which mobile objects move shows, as Law (1994: 102) puts it, that some materials 'travel better than others'. As this study tries to show, mobile phones travel quite well, despite changes on their routes as their connections change. Despite the importance of the technological dimension of making a mobile phone a mobile phone, this does not result in technological determinism. Instead, it is of interest to tease out the differences in the use made of the varied potentialities of the technology (Horst & Miller 2006: 5). With respect to De Laet & Mol (2000), the mobile phone can be regarded as fluid technology, holding its shape in a fluid manner and enacted in practices.

To contextualize the object within prevailing cultural practices and understand its utilities, meanings and symbolism from within the frame of reference of those who interact with it (Bridge & Smith 2003: 259), one particular mobile phone is at the centre of the ethnographic material presented here. Instead of seeing the mobile phone as a 'travelling companion' (Thrift 1995), different people will be seen as the phone's temporary travelling companions.

People clearly cannot communicate with objects in the same way that they communicate with other people. Nevertheless, the different meanings that a mobile phone incorporates express themselves in the practices in which they are embedded. Accompanying this particular mobile phone entails examining the phone's relationships to the different people to whom it has belonged on its journey and to see what it becomes in respect of the different ways in which it is dealt with. Instead of characterizing the person who owns or uses it, it means concentrating on the mobile phone itself to see what it embodies, what it does and what it becomes. The focus is not on the person and what s/he thinks and does to the mobile phone but what they make of the mobile phone. Embodying the desires and ideas of its users, it mirrors them, causes and influences actions and plays an important role in processes of identification and the development and negotiation of ideas, cultural practices and ideologies.

In the first half of 2006, a particular mobile phone aroused my interest in Tanzania as I became involved in the first processes of its adaptation in Zanzibar. Casually following its career, I was struck by its mobility within a relatively short period of time but it was only when I came across the same mobile phone again in 2007 that I decided to consider its biography as a way of opening a different window to analyze contemporary trading practices. As a part of my ethnographic research, I engaged in conversations about this particular phone with its different owners and users and tried to trace and reconstruct as detailed a path for it as possible. Although not covering its whole life, I focus on the period in which it is most closely linked to and part of the Swahili culture of trade. Without having to cross national borders or travel long distances, I concentrated on the everyday practices and meanings associated with its adaptability and circulation across Zanzibar and Tanzania over the last eighteen months.

Extract from a mobile-phone biography

When I last visited the mobile-phone shops in Kariakoo in August 2007, I was also able to meet again a particular phone on display in one of the shops in Aggrey, the road mentioned in the beginning. This is the phone – a Siemens CF62 – I knew, accompanied and traced over the last year and a half from its first arrival in Zanzibar to its inclusion in the collection in the shop's glass cabinet. Based on fieldnotes and interviews from ethnographic research, I describe its mobility and the changes in relation to the meanings and roles attributed to it by the different people using and dealing with it.

Connecting to Africa

This mobile phone came to Africa in the hands of a young Canadian woman who was doing voluntary work in a primary school in Zanzibar. During the first weeks of her stay, the phone spent most of its time in her room in one of the flats in Michenzani[5] where she was living with a host family. Without a local SIM card the phone was not much use to her and she hardly used it. Not having been appro-

---

[5]   Michenzani is an area of Zanzibar Town with mainly six-storey apartment buildings put up between 1964 and 1977 as a part of the 'New Zanzibar' public-housing project with financial support from the German Democratic Republic.

priated to the new environment, it turned out to be an object hinting at the temporary nature of her stay, being on a break and waiting to take up its old connections after her return. Soon a Celtel[6] SIM card was inserted to improve its connectivity in its new surroundings but was mainly used to communicate with family and friends abroad, allowing her to stay in touch with friends and family regularly and spontaneously regardless of the distance involved.

Due to the generally high costs of international calls from Tanzania, the phone was usually called instead of being used to call someone. The most important aspect was to be reachable at all times and this reachability provided a certain feeling of safety on both sides. The phone, allowing the transmission of important news and for use in cases of emergency, was seen as a promoter of security and remained to a certain extent in the sphere of control with its centre at home.

With respect to connections within Zanzibar, the insertion of the Celtel SIM card had a significant influence on the mobile phone, triggering the important step from being a 'foreign phone' to a 'local phone'. Being connected through a Tanzanian Celtel number makes the phone a member of the Tanzanian or even East African network and the number ensures that it is impossible to see who the phone belongs to and where the owner or user comes from. It simply tells people that the user is a Tanzanian resident. In the same way, the Tanzanian number significantly contributes to the phone's and the Canadian woman's process of 'going native'. From her point of view, she has now become more than just a tourist, as tourists generally do not change their SIM cards while on holiday. By staying for three months, the phone has enabled her to communicate with friends and acquaintances in Zanzibar and feel part of a Zanzibarian way of life. And as a Tanzanian number, the phone has entered phonebooks and communication networks and created a sense of belonging to its new environment.

Instead of taking it home, the Canadian woman decided to leave the phone with the woman in her host family and the phone entered a sphere of exchange in which values were negotiated and situational factors played a decisive role. As Gregson *et al.* (2007: 188) point out, by focusing on ordinary commodities, giving things up 'entails not just habit, routine or even competence, (...) but relations between artefacts, conduits and meanings'. For her, leaving the phone in Zanzibar seems to have opened up a more appropriate future career than re-appropriating it to its former environment and connections. The phone can even be considered a kind of personal 'development aid'. It becomes an object which is seen to do some good to its new owner and, in the process, will make the previous owner feel good about having given it up.

---

6   Celtel is currently operating mobile-phone networks in 15 African countries. Celtel Tanzania was launched in 2001 and is known for its reliability and wide coverage, even reaching remote areas of the country.

Becoming Zanzibarian

While the new relations come into being, the shape of the mobile phone holds itself constant (Law 2000: 8). Nevertheless, a number of reconfigurations take place as well as the establishment of a set of new connections. The Celtel SIM card is exchanged for a Zantel[7] card as connections to other Zantel lines are now at the centre of communication. In a way, the phone becomes even more Zanzibarian as its tasks become completely related to an understanding of Zanzibarian culture. The phone's ringtone was immediately changed to one of the famous Arabic songs to express its owner's personal style. The new Zanzibarian (woman) owner of the phone usually spends the equivalent of US$1 a day on the phone, mainly using it to communicate with her female friends and relatives.

Although this sort of communication existed before the widespread use of mobile phones, they facilitate the exchange of news between women as the mobile phone allows for communication to take place in different spaces. For Muslim women, who usually need to have a reason to leave the house, the phone allows easy communication with others while each remains in her own private space. The latest gossip is delivered by phone and with it too the news that this phone was received as a gift from her *mzungu*.[8] Showing off this particular connection, the phone brings something new to her life. Although neither its appearance nor its features are particularly attractive to the owner, it is its newness that is appealing.

As the 'women's exchange' involves the sending and receiving of wedding pictures and religious messages too, it is perceived as a 'deficiency' to be unable to take and send pictures. Not being a model that attracted any admiring attention from her friends, she soon decided to sell it together with her old phone to buy the long-desired 'must have'. The acquisition, use and replacement of a mobile phone can be related to its fashion and style (Katz & Sugiyama 2006: 321) and this surely has to be seen alongside its financial capabilities. In this case, it is the additional selling of the 'unfashionable phone' that allows for an expression of the woman's sense of self through having a phone that is seen to accurately represent her social and cultural embeddedness. Despite its deficiencies, it is its exchange value that gives this phone its power.

While waiting to be sold, the phone is regularly lent to friends and theirs borrowed in return. By doing so, the phone moves between different users, thus retaining its newness. As the Zanzibari woman stated, it is completely undesirable to have the same phone for a long time. Instead, it is important to express the connectedness that allows her to arrange this kind of deal, showing that she does not

---

[7]   Zantel refers to Zanzibar Telecom Ltd, a joint venture between the government of Zanzibar, ETISALAT (UAE), Kinbary Investment (Channel Islands) and Meeco International (TZ). Originally operating only in Zanzibar, it has now expanded its services to the Tanzanian mainland and Eastern Africa.

[8]   *Mzungu* is generally translated as a European or white person.

need to stand still in life. Changing mobile phones can therefore be regarded as a way of avoiding stability and uniformity. The mobile phone becomes an expression of an imagined adaptability and part of striving for 'improvement' while, at the same time, being unsatisfactory in the longer term. To succeed and realize a 'better' phone by selling her old one, the Zanzibarian woman asks her younger brother to help her. He is known for trading mobile phones and is given the phone to arrange a deal.

Extending mobile connections

This trader is one of the many young people in Zanzibar who have decided to engage in trade to earn a living. Born in Pemba, he still spends most of his time here but he tries to travel to Zanzibar once a month and goes to Dar es Salaam as often as possible to look for business opportunities, orders and possible customers. Responding to the way these phones have become a crucial and very mobile part of everyday life in Zanzibar, he is now concentrating on mobile phones. To him, a mobile phone is a bulk commodity, omnipresent and never failing to be in need of a new owner. His task is to create new owners by tempting people to buy and sell, with mobile phones always being at the centre of the exchange process.

Receiving the phone from his sister, it is immediately included in a network of trading practices and added to a pool of mobile phones that are for sale. With a different SIM card in the phone, it becomes connected to a number of potential buyers or people who might be able to find one. Apart from extending its connections, the phone also becomes more mobile. Not having a shop, the trader is generally looking to find potential buyers or sellers. His job involves following people to get and deliver money that is often paid in instalments. This high degree of activity and mobility can be seen as a type of resistance to the routine of everyday life. Engaging in trade is considered one of the few alternatives to hanging around a *maskani*[9] the whole day. In this respect, the mobile phone becomes both an opportunity and an occupation. Although the trader cannot afford to buy an expensive phone, his job enables him to use and be seen with the best phones around. From his point of view, this temporary enjoyment contributes to his reputation as a trader and raises interest in his goods in general.

Still owned by the Zanzibarian woman but on its way to a new owner, the phone now inhabits a more explicit trading space. Being neither cheap nor attractive to people with little financial means or being one of the latest models to attract people who can afford more, the phone takes up a middle position, which makes it less appealing to a potential customer. Along with other phones, it goes with the trader

---

[9] In this context *maskani* (generally translated as dwelling place) refers to a place where (young) men meet and hang out. Usually, every young man has 'his' *maskani* that he visits regularly. But spending a lot of time at a *maskani* is seen as an expression of having nothing to do, being unemployed, being lazy and is sometimes relatd to an increased use of drugs.

who usually carries two or three phones with him to show to any potential customers he might meet. Its ability to travel well is therefore important both for the
user and the mobile trader as it can be carried easily and allows for spur-of-the-
moment business and exchange on the move (Bender 2004). However, many
phones in the hands of a young person might lead to accusations of theft and as it is
complicated to prove one's authority to trade, the phone is sometimes left behind to
wait its turn. Sometimes it may be left with someone who has a phone of similar
value to sell and the trader is able to borrow it to present to a potential customer.
Over the course of these different trading activities, nobody is ever left without a
phone. Depending on its attractiveness, the phone is taken and shown to certain
people, or left behind with other people to be able to present another model instead. It soon becomes obvious that, among the things contributing to a successful
deal, the mobile phone itself is one of the most indispensable and essential. It is
made a central object of the communication between the people involved and
becomes an active participant in the trading network. In the phase when the phone
moves from one owner to the next, it does so by passing through the hands of
numerous users and other phones. Instead of a one-phone-one-user relationship,
the phone is part of and embedded in complex connections that complement each
other but are mobile and changing. After a while, the trader benefits from these
connections and finds someone in Pemba to buy the phone at a acceptable price.
The phone may not have generated a huge profit but in his opinion it has contributed to his new career as a trader and to asserting himself in the traders' world.

Moving to 'Bongo'[10]

The phone has now been bought by a young man in Pemba and has become his
first mobile phone. In his hometown of Wete, his everyday life has been characterized by the close proximity between his home, family, workplace and *maskani* so
that a mobile phone had not seemed important. People knew where to find him so
he preferred to save money instead of spending it on 'superfluous additional communication'. In contrast to most of his friends, he did not yet share the view that
not having a phone marked an individual as particularly lacking (see Horst & Miller
2006: 59) but he admitted to a recent desire to own one himself, instead of having
to use his friends' phones. When he decided to leave his business for a while to go
to Dar es Salaam and look for new business opportunities there,[11] he decided to buy
a phone. He is convinced that he will need to contact people in Dar es Salaam
without knowing where to find them and he therefore chose a simple phone that

---

[10]   The word *bongo* means brain. In slang it is used to refer to Dar es Salaam.
[11]   Extending their business activities to Dar es Salaam and the Tanzaniaan mainland because trade is
        thought to be more profitable there can be observed as a general trend among young people from Zan-
        zibar and Pemba.

would enable him to connect to people in an environment less known and characterized by distances rather than proximity.

This phone has thus become a 'necessary accessory' (Fortunati 2002: 54) on his trip to Bongo allowing for the new distances and being able to cope with them. The mobile phone creates proximities by bringing people closer and replaces a proximity to certain places by a proximity to the phone. In Dar es Salaam, the young man is found via the phone and it is the names and numbers of people he knows or has heard of or are saved on the phone by previous users that help him to contact and meet people. The phone has become a memory preserving and reminding its user of useful connections and communications. In addition, it gives the impression of having been in use for many years by having some scratches and looking more hackneyed. Its appearance makes it easy for the young man to appear as somebody who has had a phone for a long time. This corresponds with Katz & Sugiyama's idea that phones actively influence the ways in which they are incorporated into the self-images of their users (Katz & Sugiyama 2006: 325).

While in Dar es Salaam, the young man lives in Kariakoo, sharing some rooms in a Swahili house with other young men he knows from Pemba. With a Tigo[12] SIM card, the phone becomes appropriated to this 'ghetto life',[13] and its ability to record sounds is now used to record the young men's voices, their jokes and sayings in their street language (*kiswahili cha mtaani*). And at night when tariffs are lower,[14] the phone is used to catch up with friends and talk to girls without being disturbed. These conversations emphasize the importance of establishing and confirming interpersonal relationships through talk and, as already observed by Abrahams (1983), pursuing friendships is often more important than just passing on a message.

With respect to relationships with girls, communication by phone allows for a certain kind of intimacy even though the two people do not see each other. Despite this verbal intimacy, the young man states that relationships often remain non-committal 'as you never know who else the other one is flirting with apart from you'. While social control makes secret encounters very difficult, romantic engagement on the phone is far less easily detected which can be seen as both an advantage as well as a disadvantage for those involved.

It is generally felt that the phone plays a crucial role for young men in adapting to and leading a 'bongo life'. For young men who are always on the go, it makes them feel reachable while on the move and allows them to be part of a mobile society.

As most of the time the phone's new owner is either in the company of friends or in public, text messages offer a welcome means of communicating more private-

---

[12] Tigo is a mobile-phone network belonging to Mobitel and operating in fourteen countries, seven of them in Africa. In Tanzania it has wide coverage and has offered the cheapest tariffs for a long time.

[13] The term 'ghetto' is generally used to refer to a space occupied by unmarried young men.

[14] Tigo has been famous for two years, especially among young people, for its tariff 'longer longa time' (*longa* means chatting) from 11pm-5am with one minute costing only TSh1.

ly. He thus uses this service to express more personal concerns or critical points about his new surroundings. It is obvious how the phone embodies different ways of life, moods and interests and becomes a mediator bringing them together. During the day he strolls around in Kariakoo visiting friends in their shops, helping out and considering where it might make sense to open his own shop. Overt use of the phone in public is restricted due to the dangers of theft so the phone spends most of its time in his pocket and becomes something worth protecting.

Before going back to Pemba, the young man sold the phone to a friend who owns a mobile-phone shop in Aggrey. Having failed to start another business, he decided to return to his shop in Pemba and sold the phone to raise cash to buy other goods to sell at home.

Becoming a story

Kariakoo is the part of Dar es Salaam where Zanzibari and Pembans are most visible (Saleh 2006: 354). It is where their economic investments are most considerable, where they have opened shops and, even more visibly, acquired land and are replacing old Swahili houses with high-rise buildings. Although Aggrey is still characterized by small houses, numerous shops have opened in its shopping centres and along Uhuru Street all specializing in mobile phones. Numerous young people from Zanzibar who were previously engaged in the trade of mobile phones have decided to settle down and are now renting one of the small spaces mentioned at the beginning of the chapter. When I was in Dar es Salaam interviewing some of the owners of these shops, I enquired about the mobile phone sold by the young man from Pemba. It was still on display in the glass cabinet of his friend's shop and has become part of a wide collection of mobile phones waiting to continue their mobile lives. For many of the shopkeepers, mobile phones have become an investment: they offer the opportunity of establishing a more settled life while still allowing mobility. Instead of the kind of mobliity lived by the young trader in Pemba, many of the traders are looking forward to trips to Asia and Dubai to buy new goods. It is important for the mobile phone not to stay on sale in a shop for too long as the mobility of the objects in the cabinet reflects the success of the business. Because of its age and few functions compared to more recent models, the phone has now become physically immobile for the first time since being bought by the Canadian woman. Over time, if it turns out to be hard to sell, it will change from being a 'welcome addition to the collection' to a 'difficulty' and a 'hindrance' and finally, after we have talked about its biography, it becomes a 'story'.

Conclusion

The academic debate on mobile phones in Africa is still in its infancy. This chapter promotes object geographies as a fruitful way of engaging with the multitude of meanings and roles of mobile phones in everyday life in Africa. It has been shown that analyzing an object's biography reveals a wealth of information, not only about economic relations but especially about its social and cultural contexts. In many parts of Africa, the mobile phone is not an object which is imported, sold and then consumed by only one person. Instead, it is involved in complex practices of exchange and processes of acquisition, appropriation, abandonment and selling that influence its different meanings and the role of mobility.

It is evident that the mobile phone is much more than just a tool for calling, text messaging, music, photos and phone numbers. It is the device itself as well as its attributes that play a role in processes of individual expression and identification. The relationship of the Zanzibari woman to the phone and the phone as 'imagined adabtability', 'temporary enjoyment' and 'bongo life' point out how the mobile phone works to demonstrate the importance, financial situation, style and 'trendiness' of its user. Nevertheless, this extract of the phone's biography provides a unique window through which to understand that a mobile phone is becoming even more than that. The phone is 'reachability', a 'women's exchange', an 'active part in a trading network' and a 'memory' and its importance is to facilitate social relations while on the move. The variety of relationships between people and the object – despite their mobility – affirms its meaning as 'social glue' (Hil 2007: 72) and reinforces its active participation in the making and holding together of social relations regardless of distance (Pels *et al.* 2002: 11).

Insight into the diverse encounters between people and a thing on the move exemplifies how links are created, how they are maintained and why they break. As its biography has shown, the mobile phone changes from being 'welcome' to 'unsatisfactory', from being a 'necessary accessory' to a 'hindrance'. And in contrast to the expectation that with each resale an object tendentially loses value, the phone constantly moves back and forth between the extremes of different values. Biographies of things are not linear or one directional, but instead ups and downs are incorporated into the idea of a life course.

While the varying meanings of an object develop out of the particular relationships between people and things, examples of individual encounters also shed light on the important dimensions of people's social lives and culture more generally. The ways in which the mobile phone is used and dealt with constitutes the making and management of hierarchies, ideologies and cultural negotiations. Looking at the ways in which the phone and different people perform together, relationships can be characterized by their mobility and flexibility. Arguing that mobility is not only a

matter of physical distance, it is especially these ever-changing, spontaneous relations represented in the fluid space of a mobile phone that play a crucial role in the
understanding of 'Swahiliness'.

Engaging in trading practices can be considered as 'going native' as many regard
it as 'the proper occupation for a Swahili'. Trade, therefore, is not only worth
protecting but also omnipresent, creating proximity in a translocal space and a
means to negotiate 'Swahiliness' over distance. In this respect, it is striking that the
mobile phone moves through a variety of different trading practices. Having entered
the network as 'development aid', everyone involved in its biography can somehow
be seen as a trader representing different visions and ideas of trade. As well as the
mobile phone itself, diverse trading practices are considered an opportunity, an
investment and an occupation and, constituting connections, they (actually and
imaginatively) are a crucial mediator between Swahili in different places. Accompanying a mobile phone, the mobility, multiple connections and diverse cultural practices in which it is embedded have become visible. And it is through engagement
with an object that stories about the mutual constitution of the biographies of the
people, objects and places involved can be revealed.

References

ABRAHAMS, R.D. (1983), *The man-o-words in the West Indies: Performance and the emergence of creole culture*,
    Baltimore: Johns Hopkins University Press.
APPADURAI, A. (1986), 'Introduction: Commodities and the politics of value'. In: A. Appadurai, ed.,
    The social life of things, Cambridge: Cambridge University Press, pp. 3-63.
BENDER, E. (2004), 'Social lives of a cell phone', Technology Review
    www.technologyreview.com/articles/print_version/wo_bender071204.asp (12.07.2004).
BENFOUGHAL, T. (2002), 'Ces objets qui viennent d'ailleurs'. In: H. Claudot-Hawad, ed., *Voyager
    d'un point de vue nomade*, Paris: Editions Paris-Méditerranée, pp. 113-135
BINGHAM, N. (1996), 'Objections: From technological determinism towards geographies of
    relations', *Environment and Planning D: Society and Space* 14: 635-657.
BRIDGE, G. & A. SMITH (2003), 'Intimate encounters: Culture-economy-commodity', *Environment
    and Planning D: Society and Space* 21: 257-268.
CASTELLS, M., M. FERNÁNDEZ-ARDÈVOL, J. LINCHUAN QIU & A. SEY (2007), *Mobile communication
    and society*, Cambridge, Ma.: MIT Press.
CONSTANTIN, F. (1986-1989), 'Fin des races ou debut des classes? Inegalites, representations et
    pouvoir sur la Cote Swahili Est-Africaine', *APOI* XI: 43-63.
CONSTANTIN, F. (1989), 'Condition Swahili et identité politique'. In: J-P. Chretien & G. Prunier,
    eds, *Les Ethnies on Tune histoire*, Paris: Karthala, pp. 337-356.
COOK, I. *et al.* (2004), 'Follow the thing: Papaya', *Antipode* 36(4): 642-664.
COOK, I. *et al.* (2006), 'Geographies of food: Following', *Progress in Human Geography* 30(5): 655-666.
COOK, I. & M. HARRISON (2007), 'Follow the thing: West Indian Hot Pepper Sauce, *Space and
    Culture* 10(1): 40-63.
COOPER, F. (1977), *Plantation slavery on the east coast of Africa*. New Haven: Yale University Press.
DE LAET, M. & A. MOL (2000), 'The Zimbabwe bush pump: Mechanics of a fluid Technology',
    Social Studies of Science 30: 225-263.
DWYER, C. & P. JACKSON (2003), 'Commodifying difference: Selling eastern fashion', *Environment
    and Planning D: Society and Space* 21: 269-291.
ENGESTROEM, Y. & F. BLACKLER (2005), 'On the life of the object', *Organization* 12(3): 307-330.

FORTUNATI, L. (2002), 'Italy: Stereotypes, true and false'. In: J.E. Katz & M. Aakhus, eds, *Perpetual Contact*, Cambridge: Cambridge University Press, pp. 42-62.

FREITAG, U. (2004), 'Islamische Netzwerke im Indischen Ozean'. In: D. Rothermund & S. Weigelin-Schwiedrzik, eds, *Der Indische Ozean. Das afro-asiatische Mittelmeer als Kultur- und Wirtschaftsraum*, Wien: Promedia, pp. 61-81.

GELL, A. (1998), *Art and agency: An anthropological theory*, Oxford: Oxford University Press.

GILBERT, E. (1999), 'Sailing from Lamu and Back: Labor migration and regional trade in colonial East Africa', *Comparative Studies of South Asia, Africa and the Middle East* 19(2): 9-15.

GREGSON, N., A. METCALF & L. CREWE (2007), 'Moving things along: the conduits and practices of divestment in consumption', *Transactions of the Institute of British Geographers* 32(2): 187-200.

HETHERINGTON, K. (2001), 'Phantasmagorial/phantasm agoria: Materialities, spatialities and ghosts', *Space and Culture* 1(11/12): 24-41.

HILL, J. (2006), 'Travelling objects: The wellcome collection in Los Angelos, London and beyond', *Cultural Geographies* 13: 34-66.

HILL, J. (2007), 'The story of the amulet', *Journal of Material Culture* 12(1): 65-87.

HORST, H.A. & D, MILLER (2006), *The cell phone – an anthropology of communication*, Oxford: Berg.

JACKSON, P. (2000), 'Rematerialising social and cultural geography', *Social and Cultural Geography* 1: 9-14.

KATZ, J.E. & S. SUGIYAMA (2006), 'Mobile phones as fashion Statements: Evidence from student surveys in the US and Japan', *New Media and Society* 8(2): 321-337.

KOPYTOFF, I. (1986), 'The cultural biography of things: Commoditization as process'. In: A. Appadurai, ed., *The Social Life of Things*, Cambridge: Cambridge University Press, Cambridge, pp. 64-91.

LATOUR, B. (1993), 'Ethnography of a "high-tech" case: About Aramis'. In: P. Lemonnier, ed., *Technological choices: Transformation in material culture since the Neolithic*, London: Routledge, pp. 372-398.

LAURIER, E. (2001), 'Why people say where they are during mobile phone calls', *Environment and Planning D: Society and Space* 19: 485-504.

LAW, J. (1994), *Organising modernity*, Oxford: Blackwell.

LAW, J. (1996), 'Traduction/trahision: Notes on ANT', Lancaster: Lancaster University, Centre for Science Studies,
http://www.comp.lancs.ac.uk/sociology/papers/Law-Traduction-Trahision.pdf

LAW, J. & K. HETHERINGTON (1999), 'Materialities, spatialities, globalities', Lancaster: Lancaster University, Centre for Science Studies
http://www.comp.lancs.ac.uk/sociology/papers/Law-Hetherington-Materialities-Spatialities-Gobalities.pdf

LAW, J. (2000), 'Objects, spaces and others', Lancaster: Lancaster University, Centre for Science Studies
http://www.comp.lancs.ac.uk/sociology/papers/Law-Objects-Spaces-Others.pdf

LE COUR GRAND MAISON, C. (1989) Rich cousins, poor cousins, hidden strafitication among the Onem arabs in eastern Africa, *Africa* 59(2), 176-184.

LE GUENNEC-COPPENS, F. (2002), 'Les Swahili: Une Singularité Anthropologique en Afrique de l'Est', *Journal des africanistes* 72 (2): 5-70.

LESLIE, D. & S. REIMER. (1999), 'Spatializing commodity chains', *Progress in Human Geography* 23: 401–20.

MBEMBE, A. (2001), 'At the edge of the world. Boundaries, territoriality, and souvereignity in Africa'. In: A. Appadurai, ed.; *Globalization*, Duke University Press, Durham, pp. 22-51.

MESO, P., P. MUSA & V. MBARIKA (2005), 'Towards a model of consumer use of mobile information and communication technology in LDCs: The case of sub-Saharan Africa', *Information Systems Journal* 15: 119-146.

MIDDLETON, J.F.M. (1992), *The world of the Swahili. Africcan – an African mercantile civilization*, New Haven: Yale University press.

MIDDLETON, J. (2003), 'Merchants: An essay in historical ethnography', *Journal of the Royal Antropological Institute* 9: 509-526.

MILLER, D. (1998), *Material cultures: Why some things matter.* London: University College London
    Press.

OGBORN, M. (2006), 'Streynsham Master's Office: Accounting for collectivity, order and authority
    in 17th Century India', *Cultural Geographies* 13: 127-155.

OGBORN, M. (2002), 'Writing travels: Power, knowledge and ritual on the English East India
    Company's early voyages', *Transactions of the Institute of British Geographers* 27: 155-171.

OKSMAN, V. & P. RAUTIAINEN (2002), 'Perhaps it is a body part. How the mobile phone became
    an organic part of the everyday lives of Finnish children and adolescents'. In: J. Katz, ed.,
    Machines that become us, New Brunswick: Transaction Publishers.

PELS, D., K. HETHERINGTON & F. VANDENBERGHE (2002), 'The status of the object:
    Performances, mediations, and techniques', *Theory, Culture and Society* 19(5-6): 1-21.

SALEH, M.A. (2006), 'Les Zanzibari à Kariakoo'. In: B. Calas, ed., *De Dar es Salaam à Bongoland*,
    Paris: Karthala, pp. 353-368.

SMITH, D.J. (2006), 'Cell phones, docial inequality, and contemporary culture in Nigeria',
    CJAS/RCEA 40(3): 496-523.

TAASISI YA UCHUNGUZI WA KISWAHILI (2004), *Kamusi ya Kiswahili sanifu*, Oxford University Press,
    East Africa Ltd.

THRIFT, N. (1995), 'Inhuman geographies: Landscapes of speed, light, and power'. In: P. Cloke *et
    al.*, eds, *Writing the rural: Five cultural geographies*, London: Sage, pp. 191-248.

THRIFT, N. (1996), *Spatial formations*, London: Sage.

TOPAN, F. (1998), 'Langue et culture swahili à Zanzibar'. In: C. Le Cour Grandmaison & A.
    Crozon, eds, *Zanzibar aujourd'hui*, Karthala, Paris, pp. 246-257

VAN BINSBERGEN, W.M.J. & P. GESCHIERE (2005), *Commodification: Things, agency & identifications,
    The social life of Things revisited*, Münster: LIT Verlag, pp. 9-51.

VILLIERS, I.A. (1948), 'Some aspects of the Arab dhow trade', *Middle East Journal* 2(4): 400-404.

WHATMORE, S. (1999), 'Hybrid geographies: Rethinking the 'human' in human geography'.
    In D. Massey, J. Allen & P. Sarre, eds, *Human geography today*, Cambridge: Polity Press, pp. 24–39.

9

Could connectivity replace mobility?
An analysis of Internet café use
patterns in Accra, Ghana

Jenna Burrell

International mobility is a privilege unevenly distributed among the world's population. I was reminded of this reality again and again when conversations with young Internet users in Accra, Ghana turned towards travel experiences, applications (accepted or denied) for travel visas to the US or Europe, money lost to 'connection men' who claimed to have back-door contacts at the embassies, and any number of other travel and migration-related topics. Mobility was treated as a highly desirable commodity by young Internet users. It can be bought with money but the visa requirements and immigration policies of foreign governments have meant that mobility is not entirely subject to free market forces. Mobility is also experienced as a form of capital, one that migrants found could be leveraged for monetary gain, to realize advantages in business, a better education and/or a broader, more prosperous social network.

This all-consuming focus on migration and mobility among Internet users in Accra illustrates the central point of this chapter, that beliefs in opportunity, about pathways to development and even the concept of development itself may be perceived quite differently by citizens of a developing nation than they are by development institutions. By contrast, the role technology plays in facilitating migration was notably absent from the speeches and documents produced at the recent UN-sponsored World Summit on the Information Society (WSIS). WSIS is a useful point of reference because of its enormous scale (attracting more than 11,000 participants) and the diversity of the groups involved, from government agencies and corporations to NGOs and academics. Part of the WSIS proceedings, the WSIS Africa regional conference was held at the Accra International Conference Center concurrently although not connected to the activities taking place in the Internet cafés of Accra.

A central focus of WSIS, encapsulated in its title, was the key role of information in realizing progress towards development. Africa and other developing regions are being encouraged to build up their telecommunications infrastructure and use these capabilities to become connected to the global economy. The model of a worldwide, information society envisages farmers, school teachers, craftsmen and chiefs pulling information into their communities to improve local conditions. It implicitly de-emphasizes physical mobility through its vision of space-transcending networks crisscrossing the globe that make everyone virtually co-located in one global village[1] (McLuhan 1962, Rheingold 1993). Distance and travel, where referenced, were described as barriers. For example, in the WSIS Declaration of Principles it is stated that new technologies 'may reduce traditional obstacles, especially those of time and distance … for the benefit of millions of people in all corners of the world' (WSIS 2005). In a UN-produced document that was distributed via the WSIS website, new technologies were favourably described as 'killing off the concept of distance' (Papadakis 2005). Technology-enabled connectivity was also presented as a substitute for local travel, a way of avoiding the time-consuming and risky nature of Third-World road transport (Dufborg 2005). A theme that therefore emerged through the WSIS was mobility, both local and international, which was considered to be something that could ideally be supplanted by new information and communication technologies.

However, at Internet cafés in Accra, rather than reducing the desire to migrate, for many users the Internet is further feeding this drive and makes it seem more attainable. The Internet has provided opportunities for engaging fantasies about foreign lands and international travel. Pragmatically, users have also used the Internet to make contact with family living abroad to negotiate assistance with migration, to search for foreign contacts who would provide 'invitations' that would improve

---

[1] Voices critical of the 'global village' formulation include Ess (1998), who notes that expectations of an underlying 'common humanity' and adequate communication will resolve political differences. These are not universal, but distinctively Western, ideological positions. Halavais (2000) argues that the topography of the Internet reasserts rather than transcends national boundaries. Hampton & Wellman (2002) provide an empirical study on a 'wired suburb' that demonstrates that a greater improvement in social relations has been realized among those who were already geographically proximate, emphasizing the continuing significance of physical distance. Fortner (1993) similarly argued for the significance of ongoing proximity in the creation of group intimacy and felt that 'global metropolis' was a better metaphor for global media spaces like cyberspace than 'global village'.

their chances of getting visas, and to seek information about schools and scholarship programs.[2] Ultimately, access to the Internet has not transformed young Ghanaians' migratory impulses into the kinds of information practices often promoted by governments and development institutions. Instead, the Internet has provided new resources for seeking migration opportunities and increasing one's mobility.

Besides their use in building global connections, the research noted that Internet cafés were being occupied by young people in reaction to local socio-cultural structures of kinship, authority, status and social obligation. This is related to mobility in another form, as the freedom of movement experienced by individuals within their home society. New technologies like the Internet present alternative ways of indicating status, new ways of constructing and maintaining social networks and of distinguishing oneself from one's peers and other social groups. Social mobility is the capacity to realize a change in socio-economic standing. Young Internet users from modest backgrounds also yearned for this kind of upward mobility, seeing it as something that could be realized through access to new technologies like the Internet. This chapter deals with the role users envisaged for technology in addressing their sense of marginality (in relation to older authorities in particular) and for realizing a more central position within their home society as well as greater mobility through international travel.

The findings of this research are based on an eight-month period of ethnographic fieldwork on Internet café use. Conducted in 2004 and 2005, it involved a combination of observation and interviewing in Internet cafés and a variety of other settings. I frequented six Internet cafés in four different areas in or adjacent to the city. The neighbourhoods where these Internet cafés were located ranged from the impoverished, largely residential neighbourhood of Mamobi to the central business district north of Nkrumah Circle along Ring Road. All of the Internet cafés studied operated as for-profit businesses. During the first phase of fieldwork, basic personal data (such as ethnicity and age) were collected and in-depth interviews (lasting from 30 minutes to 3 hours) were held with 75 Internet café users, operators and owners. Of these interviews, 57 were with individuals under the age of 30 so the population of users was very clearly skewed. A subset of these interviewees (12 in total) emerged as key informants and, in keeping with ethnographic techniques, were interviewed several times and visited in multiple settings. In addition to the interviews, I observed online and offline activities in Internet cafés, visited families, shared meals, attended church, visited informal hangouts and organized social gatherings, went to workplaces, and attempted to grasp the everyday lives of users and the role the Internet played in their daily routines.

---

[2]   Pragmatic practices of negotiating with family members in the diaspora were also observed by Horst (2006) among mobile phone users in Jamaica.

In 2004 it was estimated that there were between 500 and 1000 Internet cafés in Accra. These cafes were an emerging trend in Ghana and driven primarily by local players working on a small-scale (Foster *et al.* 2004). The number of cafés has fluctuated since and it is unclear whether the number is growing or shrinking, but they remain a popular and highly visible type of small business in Accra. Typically, these spaces were run as small for-profit businesses and existed largely outside of institutional development efforts and government programmes.[3] A small but diverse set of Internet cafes was selected for this research. At one extreme was BusyInternet, a 100-screen café that charged almost twice the hourly rate for Internet use as smaller cafés. BusyInternet was far from typical: it was much larger, had a more elaborate and expensive décor, faster connections, many more additional services, and a much higher hourly rate than the typical café. It was a profit-generating business with an underlying social mission of building up technology skills and entrepreneurial activity in Ghana. It attracted foreigners and a somewhat older clientele as well as many white-collar professionals in technology and media industries. Its location in a central business district, its fast Internet connection and the many services it provided on site (photocopying, scanning, business cards, desktop publishing, business registration, etc.) encouraged this type of customer base. The smaller Internet cafés in LaPaz and Mamobi were more typical, the former a middle to lower-middle income neighbourhood on the outskirts of the city and the latter an impoverished, densely populated, centrally located neighbourhood with a large Muslim population. These cafés offered 10 to 20 Internet-connected computers and few other services in addition to typing, printing and scanning. In addition, the café in LaPaz was notable for providing webcams with each computer. Another in Mamobi offered a music search and CD-burning service using Kazaa peer-to-peer network software. These smaller cafés tended to attract students and the unemployed or underemployed youth but very few business people. Finally, an Internet café at the prestigious University of Ghana at Legon was selected to see what differences in use would emerge and what similarities there still were with a client base with an atypically higher education and from a more privileged socio-economic background.

Delving into the background of Internet users in Accra through individual and family interviews, their personal histories were found to challenge past assertions about for-profit Internet cafés in Africa. In the context of development discussions, Internet cafés are sometimes dismissed as the domain of the elite and an example of an emerging digital divide within countries, compounding those existing between countries (Robbins 2002, Alhassan 2004, Mwesige 2004, Mercer 2005). It should, however, be acknowledged that the term 'elite' is not an objective category but one with a variety of subjective connotations and put to use for rhetorical purposes. The

---

[3]   Although it could be said that they are, by extension, the outcome of government efforts at liberalizing the telecommunications industry and other infrastructure building projects.

elite are depicted as the very small segment of society in a developing nation that already possess the wealth, education, social connections and political power to do well in life.

Photo 9.1   Busy Internet café's interior

Photo 9.2   A typical small Internet café in the La Paz neighbourhood

If the life circumstances of Internet café users in Accra are considered holistically, it becomes difficult to maintain the notion that this group represents an elite segment of Ghanaian society. For example, in the typical, small, neighbourhood Internet café, young Internet users, on the whole, experienced very little privilege. Many people in the Mamobi and La Paz neighbourhoods had parents who were without work, marginally employed or dead. The father of a 16-year-old Internet user named Bernice, who was employed as an electrician, lamented in an interview that 'here [in Ghana] if you're an electrical contractor, you don't get the job, there's no job. You only call yourself an electrical contractor, but there's no job for you.' Bernice's six family members were tenants in a single unit within a compound house that they shared with seven other families. It had an outdoor toilet and no running water. Other Internet users lived with parents who were bakers, drivers and did other types of work that required no more than a low-level secondary school education and sometimes less. Young Internet users had often managed to obtain more education than their parents, up to a senior secondary school certificate or even additional vocational training at a tertiary school. They were also literate (to varying degrees) in English. What made Internet users better off than the general population was their relatively advanced level of educational attainment, but little else beyond this.

How young people provisioned money for Internet use reflected both the value they placed on the resource as well as their lack of financial means. The money young people managed to collect to pay for Internet use was often skimmed from the daily 'chop money' their parents gave them for food and transportation. Saadiq, a senior secondary school student who lived in Mamobi, said he received 2000 cedis (approx US$ 0.20) each day from which he was able to save about 1000 cedis. Over several days he could scrape together enough to use the Internet for an hour. He was also able to get a little extra money from friends. Fauzia similarly described the circulation of scarce resources among friends noting that, 'sometimes I use my own money, I save for it because I want to use the café. Sometimes I too go there, and when I see friends I ask them to buy me the code. I just say, "Oh, Charley, you know what, I want you to buy me a code, I'm broke. You know I'm broke."' Internet cafés are frequented in poor neighbourhoods not in spite of poverty but *because of* this lack of privilege. They represent one of very few avenues of opportunity open to local people that require only minimal financial outlay and (unlike mobile phones) no obligation to continue paying for the resource.

The demographic profiles of Internet users bore a relationship to their patterns of Internet use. The cafés were not exclusively the domain of youth but older users generally had quite different patterns of use and reasons for frequenting these spaces. It became clear in the course of this research that Internet activities roughly correlated to age, gender and education level. Young people tended to fixate on certain forms of use – collecting foreign pen pals and seeking romantic partners, chatting and hanging out – usually to the exclusion of all else. The term 'pen pal' was used to refer to an extremely wide range of relationships including same-age peers, boyfriends, girlfriends, older patrons, mentors and business partners. Collecting pen pals is an activity that predated the Internet in Ghana and used to be carried out using the postal system. Some young people valued these relationships for the enlightening conversation and the creation of social bonds, while others saw them primarily as strategic affiliations for realizing material gain. Daniel, a former Internet scammer who was teaching at a primary school, saw his pen pal collecting activities as similar to credit card fraud noting that, 'apart from using the credit card I take pen pals just to exchange items and actually I don't take my size, I take sugar mommies and sugar daddies because if you take your size they are unemployed. So if you ask them for something which is very huge, they wouldn't get it for you. So you have to go in for the grown-ups like 50 year olds, 40 and above so they are actually working and they have the money so they can buy whatever you ask.' Abiba, a 16-year-old senior secondary school student, described the focus of her peers on pen pals as an addiction, observing that, 'some people they like friends. You see they are addicted … to getting Net pals and letting them send them things. You see some people, they are fashion crazy.' In these examples, through the mediation of the chat room, foreign chat partners were completely objectified as suppliers of niceties, fashion items and mobile phones. These examples point to a form of acquisition-driven play within a range of recreational activities that is described in subsequent sections.

Young users (particularly students) also spent more time than older users visiting Internet cafés in groups as a social activity pursuing entertainment and fun on the Internet. They watched music videos, found lyrics from songs and designed inventive competitions. Older users were more often versed in information searching and were typically more effective in using the Internet for research. Several young people described or demonstrated difficulty in identifying whether the information they had found was valid and were, therefore, susceptible to falling victim to online scams. It should be noted that older users tended to be quite affluent and well-educated and for this reason their patterns of use cannot be disentangled from these aspects of their background. University students, although young, used the Internet to do research and acquire information with great expertise.

Many young Internet users had never used or heard of Google or other search engines. Instead of using search engines, several web users mentioned memorizing or even guessing URLs. Some received URLs from friends via email or chat clients. This meant that the range of media young people accessed on the web (outside of email and chat) was quite limited. The sites most often mentioned included a few news websites, archives of music lyrics, and e-cards. However, these Internet users did not see that their Internet skills were lacking: for them, chatting and email, and collecting foreign pen pals in particular, were what the Internet was all about. It was through personal contacts, not depersonalized information, that both entertainment and real opportunities for personal development could be found.

Limited use of the World Wide Web and search engines did not mean that young people did not formulate questions and seek answers on the Internet. Instead of search engines, many used their foreign chat partners to collect information about educational opportunities abroad, international news and life in other societies. This could provide some added advantages. In a few cases, users were able to borrow the media and technology literacy of chat partners who had more experience with the technology. For example, Charles, a teenager who was preparing for his senior secondary school exams, described how a friend of his had lost US$100 to someone who claimed to be a representative of a school in Sweden. Charles himself noted of such Internet scams: 'I really have a difficult time. Actually yes I'm not able to tell.' He admitted to being somewhat blinded by his hopefulness commenting, 'sometimes you are eager for something and you come across it, wow you are happy. You want to go into it. You don't even take your time to explore it....' Luckily for Charles, he had developed a long-lasting friendship with an American physician who had spent a short period of time in Ghana and who checked out education and scholarship opportunities that Charles came across online to prevent him from falling for a scam.

Education itself was also something that Internet users sought through interaction with human sources. A young man called Moscow by his friends said that on the Internet he 'would want to meet an educative person. Someone who is educated, a teacher or a scientist ... so that he could tell me more about this science course, it will be easy for me when I go to school.' When asked what benefits there were to knowing people living outside of Ghana, he added, 'when you've got a friend either from America or London, he teaches you English'. The digital information young people received could often not be de-personalized and was embedded within their online interactions. It was not always data that these Internet users sought but a learning process, a 'sounding board', or someone who could pave the way for them to migrate abroad, get an education or find employment.

What distinguished the Internet café use of university students was the greater degree of mobility they experienced due to their more privileged backgrounds. The Internet supported their movements in pragmatic ways. Prince, for example, was using the Internet to check his bank account in London when I encountered him in the café. He had also been working on an online application for a job with the multinational company Maersk. He had previously spent time in London working for a florist and living with his aunt while on a work holiday visa and was considering returning to London for a postgraduate course. Several university students also described how access to the Internet made up for an inadequate and outdated university library. Manuela, a 22-year-old biology student, had also spent time in London. She was working on a research project and used email to communicate with the professors on the project, including one at Johns Hopkins University in the US. The Internet allowed these students to get around inefficient national infrastructure (such as the slow postal system) to engage with European and American institutions. Yet their greater mobility and capability with the Internet did not necessarily preclude an interest in meeting foreigners online. There was still a fascination among some of these well-educated users with everyday life in foreign lands. Some of the Internet users at the Volta Hall Internet café on campus described chatting with foreign chat partners. A young woman named Adama, who was studying English and drama at the university, was particularly involved in these activities. Much like the Internet café users from modest backgrounds in Mamobi or La Paz, she prized her vast foreign social network boasting that, 'I have so many friends in Europe'. Her main chat partners included a Norwegian, a Swede and a Nigerian. However, the social relationships university students maintained were typically valued for the sociability and possible status they provided and less explicitly for material gain or the migration opportunities they might offer. Often these university students were able to navigate through formal channels for such opportunities. Users from poor communities, by contrast, pursued informal methods such as seeking invitations to obtain visas from strangers in chat rooms or even, in extreme cases, carrying out Internet scams.

Youth in Accra

Having established some of the use patterns of Internet users in Accra, Ghana, this chapter now focuses on the younger generation, those in their teens and twenties who made up the dominant proportion of Internet users in this study. Young Internet café users in Accra expressed a sense of double marginality: firstly, by the migration restrictions of foreign states that immobilized the young more than the older generation and, secondly, by a social order in their own society that still draws heavily on traditional gerontocratic principles and invest social authority in the older generation. Their marginality was, therefore, related to a lack of access to and control of social space in their home society. The activities of Ghanaians in Internet cafés were not simply a case of resistance among African citizens to Western powers and political regimes. Instead, these young people, individually and in groups, negotiated the constraints they faced within their own society by innovating technological practices. The Internet was enrolled to address concerns about access to global processes helping users to expand into an international social network, but the technology and its café milieu also played a role in mediating local interpersonal relations between peers and the older and younger generations.

A gerontocratic ordering of society persists in Ghana despite the uprooting processes of rural to urban and international migration. This ordering is played out in the everyday lives of young people in a variety ways. For example, Miriam had a younger sister living with her who swept the room they shared every morning, fetched water for Miriam's bath and sat at a drink-selling kiosk all day while Miriam was free to come and go. In exchange, Miriam was expected to take care of her sister's financial needs, including her education. Similarly, Abiba, a 16-year-old senior secondary school student, was the youngest member of her household that was made up of her grandmother and several aunts and uncles. Her family was Muslim and she was an Internet user, liked listening to American rap and hip-hop artists, dressed in Western clothes (often trousers rather than skirts) but also wore a headscarf when out in public. She slept in her grandmother's room at night in case the grandmother needed anything (a glass of water was given as an example) and she did chores (cooking, cleaning, errand running) around the compound. Abiba, like many young people, was expected to work for the family and was almost constantly being supervised.

The structure of Abiba's home life was continuous with the school environment which similarly held students to exacting standards of good behaviour. Schools were oriented towards discipline and orderliness, values that were emphasized by the annual competition between schools that perform in uniformed marching squads at the annual Independence Day celebrations on 6 March. These squads compete for awards based on their precision and conformity. Young people were not expected to argue with, question or talk back to their elders and supervision and the enforcement of good behaviour was not limited to home and school but could also be witnessed on the streets. Although these checks on behaviour were limited by the unavoidable anonymity of urban living, it was socially acceptable and expected that older members of the community would monitor and regulate the behaviour of young people whether or not they were kin.

The particular restrictions youth faced varied according to gender and religious affiliation. Abiba, the Muslim girl described above, was among the most restricted. During her interview she noted that, 'I'm not even allowed out more times. I'm always restricted. Before I go out I seek permission, the time is given, go and come at this time. Don't stay long, so I'm being restricted.' She described these constraints as an effort to prevent her from getting mixed up with bad people and disreputable activities. Her grandmother expressed suspicion about Internet cafés being spaces where fraudulent activities were taking place, and although she paid for Abiba to take a computer course, she was unsure about the reasons behind Abiba's visits to the Internet café. While it was not stated explicitly by Abiba or her family, gender probably played a role in these restrictions and Abiba herself complained about how boys at Internet cafés 'will just disturb you. They say, "Oh, I want you to be my girlfriend.'" By contrast, Frank lived in the same area as Abiba but noted that his father 'used to laugh. He said, one day they will arrest you. Maybe he [read] a paper about fraud.' His father, who affectionately referred to him as 'Internet man', added: 'I advise him that if you want to use the Net, you have to use it [in the] correct way, not a devious way.' While aware that fraudulent activities were sometimes taking place in Internet cafés and even indicating suspicion that his son might be involved with such activities, Frank's father allowed him a great deal of autonomy.

In light of the discipline expected from young people by the older generation, the Internet café served as a space to escape the surveillance of elders. Internet cafés also offered a sense of purpose to many young people who faced periods of boredom and inactivity after completing a level of schooling. Typically, students faced long gaps where they were not actively enrolled in school but were preparing for exams or waiting for exam results to come out. An exam was taken after junior secondary school at the age of 15 and again at age 18 many students took the Senior Secondary School Certificate Examination or university entrance exams. Students sat these exams in the autumn but did not receive their results until the spring. Those who did not do well enough had to re-sit them and then wait again for their results. Some young people were also forced to wait until they or their family members could find the money to fund their next level of education. Many were eager to find a way to fill the extra time. Isaac was offered the position of driver's mate on a tro-tro bus[4] by his father while he was waiting for his exam results. He readily agreed to the job noting that: 'I was lonely at home doing nothing'. Many young people took computer and software courses while waiting and spending time at Internet cafés was another way to fill this void. As Fauzia, an unemployed 23-year-old noted, 'sometimes instead of sitting in the house, making a noise, it's better to go to the café and chat'. Visiting an Internet café was not only an enjoyable way of passing the time but the skills and foreign contacts gained might prove beneficial in the future, thus justifying the investment of time and money.

Fantasies of foreign travel

Young Internet users addressed the constraints on their mobility, their desires and inability to travel internationally (due to visa restrictions or a lack of funding) through various forms of online activity. Some treated the time they spent at the Internet café as an engaging diversion and a way of exploring fantasies of foreign travel. For these users, connectivity was a sort of substitute for mobility, a 'make-do' strategy (but certainly not mistaken for the real thing). Others took a more purposeful and goal-oriented approach, attempting to arrange real travel opportunities

---

[4]   The driver's mate is the person who collects money, announces the bus route to those waiting at bus stops and arranges seating. Tro-tros are the primary form of low-cost public transportation in Ghana. The vehicles and routes are not government funded or organized but are privately owned and operated.

through the Internet. For example, Stephen, an unemployed 21-year-old who had recently completed secondary school, was like many other young aspiring migrants from an unprivileged background. He treated immigration regulations as a system to be outwitted, having heard that embassies ask about 'travel experience' and deny visas to those who have none. So he was collaborating with a friend to obtain a visa for South Africa, a country that was known as a destination that was relatively easy to get into from Ghana. He was hoping to take this trip solely to acquire travel experience. Every interaction Stephen had in online chat rooms was focused on securing an 'invitation' as quickly as possible from a foreigner. He believed this would also help him to get a travel visa. He noted that many of the people he contacted 'want to know you for some time before … they will give you their email address, they will ask you to write to them, to communicate with them for some time before [giving an invitation]'. Having no patience for such time-consuming efforts and seeing no redeeming value in the process itself, Stephen noted that 'when I chat and I see that you are not willing, I have to quit.' He had, however, been unsuccessful so far in realizing his dream of travelling abroad.

Kwaku, Daniel and three other friends from secondary school saw the Internet more as a device for recreational pursuits. However, like Stephen, they similarly directed their attention to foreign destinations and fantasies of travel. They regularly visited the Internet café together and ended up forming a club, formalizing it by going online on the British Airways website where they signed up for the frequent flyer programme and received membership cards by post. The British Airways programme was called the 'Executive Club' and they adopted this name for their group. Although they never planned to use the cards, they were pleased to note that they could charter flights and receive other benefits thanks to their membership. Kwaku, Daniel and their friends also invented a competition where they would order things free online and see who could collect the most. They did this with a CD of computer games: the goal was not the computer game itself but the accumulation of CDs.

The theme running through these activities online and offline was a fascination with abroad and whatever evoked travel and connectivity with distant locales. Airline membership cards and CDs or books by mail, personalized with a name and address, provided this sense of global interconnectivity that was far more compelling for young people than the gambling games the CDs contained. The Internet provided opportunities to make faraway places tangible and personal – marked with the most intimate of labels, one's name. Accumulating mail was a way of demonstrating power spanning great distances with whoever collected the most material declared the winner. This thrill was also evident in the most popular of Internet activities among youth – collecting pen pals. This was often conducted with such brevity and lack of attention by Internet users in Accra that it was clear that a moment of contact rather than the content of extended conversations had value in and of itself for some users (Slater & Kwami 2005).

One can imagine ways in which desired economic or educational opportunities might be channelled through new technologies like mobile phones and the Internet to reduce the necessity of travel. However, as was illustrated by the activities of Kwaku and his friends in the Exccutive Club, a desire for greater mobility was rarely motivated by such instrumentalist motives alone. In Ghana, there is powerful symbolic value to having been abroad and chatting with and collecting foreign pen pals in Yahoo chat rooms, and having contacts abroad can lend status to young Internet users. Many aspiring migrants talked about travel as an experience they valued as a form of enrichment and saw as identity forming. A diversity of perceived benefits went along with the material gains expected from moving outside Ghana's national borders.

Internet cafés as the territory of youth

Internet cafés are spaces where technology is contextualized socially (by customers and staff) and materially (by furniture, decor and other technologies). It is, therefore, important to consider not only the use of the Internet but also the use of the space of the Internet café. For young people, the Internet café served to build social cohesion among peers and in strategies for coping with inter-generational relations. Internet cafés held an appeal as spaces where the youth could escape the surveillance of their elders and, in contrast to home, school and most public spaces, were spaces dominated by young people where there was limited, if any, supervision by elders. Internet café owners were typically absent most of the time and operators were often of a similar age to the customers, acting more as peers than supervisors. Young people would arrange to visit cafés when they knew older people would not be around. For example, Gabby noted that he and his friends from boarding school would 'leave the school around 10 or midnight because by then the price is low and older people will not be on the net. They will tell us to stop watching pornography.' Internet cafés were therefore spaces for forms of mischievous, youth-centred and peer-oriented behaviour that would undoubtedly be disapproved of by authority figures. These activities included watching and emulating music videos, flirting with foreign chat partners, trying to hack the computers to get free browsing time, and finding ways to obtain free things such as pamphlets, bibles or CDs of computer games. Activities could be configured by users to fill the space of the Internet café. For example, on one occasion I walked into an Internet café where everyone was watching the movie *Top Gun* on a computer monitor. On another, I observed a young man with some friends studying a video by the hip-hop artist Usher and emulating his dance routines. The ability to escape parental supervision and create personal space is described as similarly motivating teenagers in the West to spend time on MySpace and other popular spaces online (Boyd 2006), consume music and television in private spaces such as bedrooms (Livingstone 2002), use mobile phones (Green 2002) and spend time in Internet cafés (Laegran & Stewart 2003).

Group activities in Internet cafés illustrate that the use of the Internet was not motivated solely by a desire to engage in global processes and have contact with foreigners. This global technology providing worldwide connectivity also served a role in the face-to-face activities of local groups. For youth in groups, visits to the Internet café served as a way to build social cohesion within peer groups, as well as to establish individual status and roles. The formation of organized youth groups was not a product of the Internet but a pre-existing social practice. For example, in the impoverished and densely populated neighbourhood of Mamobi in the centre of Accra, young men came together to form 'bases' that were composed of friends who were associated with a certain informal hangout spot such as an unfinished building or a street corner. Many groups competed against one another in football matches and some of these groups' activities included entrepreneurial ventures and/or community service. In addition to the bases, mixed-gender groups came together to form youth clubs concerned with education and community service. As further evidence of the symbolic potency of connections to foreign lands, bases and youth groups had certain naming conventions, often favouring place names in the West, frequently in the United States. For example, among the names mentioned were the Alaska Youth Club, Nebraska Youth Club, Dallas Base and the Canadian Academy. This naming convention was reflected in the nicknames used within the groups. One young man who admired the Soviet's resistance against the West in the Cold War era was called Moscow. Another, whose brother lived in Italy, was nicknamed Alitalia after the Italian airline. Finding a space of their own was a concern for these groups who often laid claim to interstitial spaces by posting a painted banner or sign with their name and motto on the side of a dirt path or the wall of a building (see Photos 9.3 and 9.4). Similarly, the Internet café was emerging as a new, initially unclaimed space that was well suited to the desires among the young for a space they could inhabit on their own terms.

The prevalence of porn watching in Internet cafés was exaggerated in alarmist accounts in the local media, informal publications[5] and sometimes in my casual conversations with older Ghanaians. However, it was possible on occasion to

---

[5]   A self-published book titled *The Word of God on Sex and the Youth* was handed to me by its author Victor Olukoju at a career development event for young people that was sponsored by an evangelical church based in Nigeria. It contained a chapter on the Internet and this warning about Internet pornography: 'Thousands of youth worldwide are already addicted to this ungodly practice. ... People keep ungodly appointments to go and chat with boyfriends and girlfriends on the Internet. They occupy their time with such chats and do not have enough time to sleep early so they come to Church anytime they want. What sort of world are we living in? People pay money to commit sin! ... The youths now steal and borrow money to browse the net just to 'enjoy' these nude pictures and other immoral acts or films.'

Photo 9.3   A youth group in Mamobi in front of their signboard

Photo 9.4   A base claims this unfinished building as their hangout

witness individuals and groups (usually young men) watching porn in Accra's Internet cafés. Sadia, a secondary school student from Mamobi described how some of her classmates – both male and female – went to an Internet café to watch obonsam cartoons. Obonsam means 'satan' in Twi (a widely spoken local language) and the phrase was a coded and humorous reference to porn videos. These school mates would discuss and tease each other about what they had seen when back in class. Young people were certainly aware that this activity was considered transgressive and did not defend it. As Sadia warned, 'there's a saying that anything that the eye sees enters the mind and what enters the mind wants to be practised. They are looking at pornographic pictures ... and they want to practise and at their age I don't think you should do that.' These activities depended on elders expressing alarm or disapproval since such a reaction was seen as a sign of having escaped the hold such authorities had on young people's minds and behaviour.

Young people in Accra's Internet cafés leveraged their proficiency with technology to make claims on new territory beyond the Internet café itself. Internet use affected the way they occupied the space of the school yard, classroom and dormitory. As Sadia mentioned above, young people discussed their forays online in the classroom and school yard, thus subversively expanding this terrain of youthful independence into spaces where they were highly supervised. Computer printers and scanners made it possible to do so in multiple formats, as Gabby noted of his early Internet experiences, 'I followed my seniors to town and we went to the café and then you see, when we got there ... the pornographic pictures, sites, we have them plenty .... We go, scan them then we paste them up in our dormitories.' Through these actions, youth found new ways to challenge authority. The conversations about their transgressive activities and displays of illicit media in the institutional setting of the classroom or dormitory was one way that young people could claim new spaces, thus extending the domain of the Internet café into places that they were obliged to inhabit but ordinarily on the terms of the school authorities rather than their own.

There was a difference between the new and unclaimed space of the Internet café and the classroom and home where the roles of youth were clearly demarcated. The Internet café had less history, fewer interconnections with social processes in the larger society and was consequently subject to 'takeovers'. Over a period of time, for example, groups of rowdy young men known as 'Nima Boys' from the impoverished Nima neighbourhood took hold of the space at BusyInternet, the largest café in town, by their noise and numbers. Their exclusionary claim on the space alienated other patrons such that management instituted new policies to regain a sense of the space as equally open to men, women, the young and the old. These new policies included limiting to two the number of people sitting at a single computer and enforcing the consumption of food or beverages at the next-door café/restaurant to prevent the space from being monopolized by young trouble-makers. The intrusive and suggestive comments made by young men to young women (as noted above by Abiba) also served in these takeover activities by establishing the space on young men's terms. The overt nature of these takeovers contrasts with the obedient behaviour of young people at school and in other similar spaces. In these institutional domains they were forced to rely on surreptitious means (such as posting porn in concealed dormitory spaces) to claim and re-territorialize space.

The activities of young people in Internet cafés that their elders would likely consider frivolous or outright harmful quite clearly served youth as a way to claim personal territory, flouting social norms and exploring alternatives, and establishing themselves as individuals distinct from the expectations of parents, teachers and older relatives. It served as a reaction to what Willis (1990) describes as 'institutional and ideological constructions of youth which privilege certain readings and definitions of what young people should do, feel or be'. Internet cafés were spaces where young people were able to contravene these constructions and their activities there served as attempts to realize greater physical and social mobility in both local and global contexts.

Reflecting on an institutional development discourse

Scholars who analyze the social impact of new technologies have treated the simple substitution of connectivity for mobility as highly problematic (Marvin 1988, Nakamura 2002, Urry 2002). The examples in this chapter bear out the complexity of such a relationship. The Internet has certainly prompted much thought among young Ghanaians about their place in the world, their society's relationship with the West, and its ties (or lack thereof) to the global economy, The Internet has provided new tools for realizing aspirations to migrate abroad. However, the activities taking place in the space of the Internet café have demonstrated that the technology has also served as a mediator in local interpersonal relations. The Internet café was well suited to peer socializing and competition and a place for young people to address intergenerational tensions. The ongoing engagement and enthusiasm with the technology was tied to the role it has played in these local relations. Through these compatibilities, the Internet and the Internet café have found a place in Ghanaian society but this process has also been responsible for the often asymmetrical adoption of the Internet by young men whose Internet café 'takeovers' have discouraged some young women, and perhaps also older people, from participating.

The question of what motivates individuals in different societies to engage with new technologies is of ongoing interest. It is particularly worthwhile to do research into the understudied regions of Sub-Saharan Africa where new technologies are rapidly diffusing. The draw of the Internet for users in Accra has frequently been related to a desire for personal development. Recreational activities such as watching music videos exist alongside the more focused search for opportunities that are taking place in Internet cafés. Often, instrumentalist activities directed at self-improvement have not been entirely distinguished from recreational pursuits. Users chat with pen pals for the sake of sociability and conversation while at the same time seeing this as a chance to network and build rapport with foreign contacts who might be able to help provide a migration opportunity or finance an education or business opportunity in the future. Future research could evaluate the way notions of 'information' and 'communication' are culturally defined and how these categories are distinguished (or in the case of Ghana have collapsed together) in different societies. In contrast to the centrality of information at WSIS and other technology for development events, it was communication and migration that were the most compelling 'development' concepts shaping Internet use in Accra in 2004. As this chapter has demonstrated, the promise of technologies like the Internet is being reconceived and reinvented in different regions of the developing world.

References

ALHASSAN, A. (2004), 'Development communication policy and economic fundamentalism in Ghana', Unpublished PhD Thesis, University of Tampere.

BOYD, D. (2006), 'Identity production in a networked culture: Why youth heart my space', presented at the American Association for the Advancement of Science.

DUFBORG, A. (2005), 'Preface'. In: S. Danofsky, ed., *Open access for Africa: Challenges, recommendations, and examples*, New York: United Nations ICT Task Force Working Group on the Enabling Environment.

ESS, C. (1998), 'Cosmopolitan ideal or cybercentrism? A critical examination of the underlying assumptions of "The Electronic Global Village"', *APA Newsletters* 97(2).

FORTNER, R. (1993), *International communication: History, conflict, and fontrol of the global metropolis*, Belmont, CA: Wadsworth.

FOSTER, W., S. GOODMAN *et al.* (2004), 'Global diffusion of the Internet IV: The Internet in Ghana', *Communications of the association for Information Systems* 13(38): 1-47.

GREEN, N. (2002), 'On the move: Technology, mobility, and the mediation of social time and space', *The Information Society* 18(2): 281-92.

HALAVAIS, A. (2000), 'National borders on the World Wide Web', *New Media and Society* 2(1): 7-28.

HAMPTON, K. & B. WELLMAN (2002), *The not so global village of netville. The Internet and everyday life*. Oxford: Blackwell.

HORST, H. (2006), 'The blessings and burdens of communication: Cell phones in Jamaican transnational social fields', *Global Networks* 6(2).

LAEGRAN, A.S. (2002), 'The petrol station and the Internet café: Rural technospaces for youth', *Journal of Rural Studies* 18: 157-68.

LIVINGSTONE, S. (2002), *Young people and new media*, London: Sage Publications.

MARVIN, C. (1988), *When old technologies were new: Thinking about electric communication in the late 19th Century*, New York: Oxford University Press.

MCLUHAN, M. (1962), *The Gutenberg Galaxy: The making of typographic man*, Toronto: University of Toronto Press.

MERCER, C. (2005), 'Telecentres and transformations: Modernizing Tanzania through the Internet', *African Affairs* 105(419): 243-64.

MWESIGE, P.G. (2004), 'Cyber elites: A survey of Internet café users in Uganda', *Telematics and Information* 21: 83-101.

NAKAMURA, L. (2002), *Cybertypes: Race, ethnicity and identity on the Internet*, New York & London: Routledge.

PAPADAKIS, S. (2005), 'Open access: How good is it for Africa?'. In: S. Danofsky, ed., *Open access for Africa: Challenges, recommendations and examples*, New York: United Nations ICT Task Force Working Group on the Enabling Environment.

RHEINGOLD, H. (1993), *The virtual community: Homesteading on the electronic frontier*, Reading, MA: Addison-Wesley.

ROBBINS, M.B. (2002), 'Are African women online just ICT consumers?' *Gazette: The International Journal for Communication Studies* 64(3): 235-249.

SLATER, D. & J. KWAMI (2005), 'Embeddedness and escape: Internet and mobile use as poverty reduction strategies in Ghana', Working Paper Series, Information Society Research Group, London.

URRY, J. (2002), 'Mobility and proximity', *Sociology* 36(2): 255-274.

WILLIS, P. (1990), *Common culture: Symbolic work at play in the everyday cultures of the young*, Milton Keynes: Open University Press.

WSIS DECLARATION OF PRINCIPLES (2005), Geneva: International Telecommunication Union (ITU).

List of authors

Wouter van Beek is Professor of Anthropology of Religion at the University of Tilburg and a senior researcher at the African Studies Centre in Leiden. His main thematic interests are religion, cultural ecology and tourism and he has worked for many years on the ethnography of the Mandara Mountains in Cameroon, in particular the Kapsiki/Higi, as well as on the Dogon of Central Mali. His recent publications include, with P. Lemineur & O. Walther, 'Tourisme et patrimoine au Mali. Destruction des valeurs anciennes ou valorisation concertée?' in *Geographica Helvetica* (4): 249-58, 'Agency in Kapsiki Religion, A Comparative Approach' in M.E. de Bruijn, R. van Dijk & J-B. Gewald (eds) *Strength beyond Structure. Social and Historical Trajectories of Agency in Africa* (Brill, 2007) and 'Boys and Masks among the Dogon' in S. Ottenberg & D.A. Binckley (eds) *Playful Performers. African Children's Masquerades* (Transaction Publishers, 2006).

Hisham Bilal (MA) is an anthropologist who graduated at the University of Khartoum. At present he is an assistant lecturer in Anthropology at the University of Khartoum. Hisham Bilal has been involved in research on technology and society, and on social change in urban environments. He is presently working on his PhD programme focussing on the effects of large-scale dam construction in the Northern part of Sudan.

Inge Brinkman was awarded her PhD at Leiden University in 1996 and then did research on southeast and northern Angola at Cologne University, Germany and Ghent University, Belgium before working on the socio-cultural history of a Dutch development organization. She has also done research into communication technologies in Sudan and is currently attached to the African Studies Centre in Leiden where she is working on the 'Mobile Africa Revisited' programme which is studying the relationship between mobility, communication technologies and social hierarchies, (with Mirjam de Bruijn & Francis Nyamnjoh). Her publications include *A War for People, Singing in the Bush* (Rüdiger Köppe, 2005) and, with Axel Fleisch, *Grandmother's Footsteps* (Rüdiger Köppe, 2005).

Mirjam de Bruijn is Professor of Contemporary History and Anthropology of West and Central Africa at Leiden University and a senior researcher at the African Studies Centre in Leiden. Focusing on the interrelationship between agency, marginalization and mobility, her work has a clearly interdisciplinary character. She has published widely on nomadic societies, the relationship between culture and poverty, crisis and identity. One of her current research programmes, together with Francis Nyamnjoh & Inge Brinkman were funded by a NWO/WOTRO grant, 'Mobile Africa revisited' is a comparative study of the role of ICT and its interrelationship with agency, marginality and mobility patterns in Central and West Africa. Her recent publications include, with R. van Dijk & J-B. Gewald (eds), *Strength beyond Structure. Social and Historical Trajectories of Agency in Africa* (Brill, 2007), 'Mobility and

Society in the Sahel. An Exploration of Mobile Margins and Global Governance' in G. Klute & H. Hahn, *Cultures of Migration: African Perspectives* (LIT, 2007) and, with H. van Dijk, 'The Multiple Experiences of Civil War in the Guera Region of Chad, 1965-1990' in *Sociologus* 57(1): 61-98 (2007).

Jenna Burrell is an Assistant Professor at the School of Information at the University of California-Berkeley. She is currently undertaking research on patterns of mobile phone gifting and sharing in rural Uganda. She obtained her PhD from the Sociology Department of the London School of Economics and has forthcoming publications in *Information Technology and International Development* and *Field Methods*. Her article on Ghanaian transnationals entitled 'I Have Great Desires to Look beyond My World' appeared in *New Media and Society, 2008*.

Ludovic Ouhonyiquè Kibora has been the Head of the Department of Socio-economic and Development Anthropology at the INSS since 2004. In 2006 he was a visiting research fellow in African Studies at the University of Bayreuth and he is currently Associate Professor at the University of Koudougou. His most recent publication, with Hans Hahn, is 'The Domestication of the Mobile Phone. Oral Society and New ICT in Burkina Faso' in *Journal of Modern African Studies* 46: 87-109 (2008).

Thomas Molony is a research fellow at the Centre of African Studies at the University of Edinburgh where he is working on the social, cultural, health, economic and political applications of ICT in Africa. His PhD on 'Food, Carvings and Shelter: The Adoption and Appropriation of Information and Communication Technologies in Tanzanian Micro and Small Enterprises' is one of the earliest detailed studies of the effects of mobile phones and the Internet on business in an emerging economy. He has published widely on the everyday acquisition and use of ICT, with his most recent publication being 'Running out of Credit: The Limitations of Mobile Telephony in a Tanzanian Agricultural Marketing System', which appeared in the *Journal of Modern African Studies* 46(4): 637-658 (2008).

Walter Gam Nkwi is doing his PhD in social history at the University of Buea, Cameroon and the African Studies Centre in Leiden. Entitled 'Mobility and Information Communication Technology in Kom, Cameroon 1928-1998: A Socio-Historical Perspectives', it examines the link between communication technology, mobility and hierarchy in Kom proper and Kom in the diaspora. He is also interested in the history of phones and the arrival of the first cars in Cameroon and how they affected mobility. His publications include 'Boundary Conflicts in Africa: The Case of Bambili and Babanki-Tungoh, of Northwest Cameroon, c.1955-1998' in *Journal of Applied Social Science: A Multidisciplinary Journal of the Faculty of Social and Management Sciences* 6(1 & 2): 6-41 (2007) and 'Folk-songs and History amongst the Kom of Northwest Cameroon: The Pre-colonial and Post Colonial Periods' in *Humanities Review Journal* 30(4): 125-150 (2006).

Francis B. Nyamnjoh has taught sociology, anthropology and communication studies at universities in Cameroon, Botswana and South Africa and is currently Head of Publications at the Council for the Development of Social Science Research in Africa (CODESRIA) until 2009. He was recently appointed professor in Anthropology at the University of Cape Town. He has published widely on globalization, citizenship, media and the politics of identity in Africa, with his recent books including *Africa's Media, Democracy and the Politics of Belonging* (Zed Books, 2005) and *Insiders and Outsiders: Citizenship and Xenophobia in Contemporary Southern Africa* (CODESRIA/ZED Books, 2006). He has also published various novels, the most recent being *Souls Forgotten* (2008), *The Travail of Dieudonné* (2008) and *Married but Available* (2009). One of his current research programmes is 'Mobile Africa revisited' (with Mirjam de Bruijn & Inge Brinkman).

Lotte Pelckmans is an anthropologist who is currently doing her PhD at the African Studies Centre in Leiden on the dynamics of social hierarchical relations in mobile Fulbe society and modern translations of hierarchy in different contexts through the practice of remembering, with case studies from rural and urban Mali (Douentza/ Bamako) and urban Europe (Paris). Her most recent publication is 'Negotiating the Memory of Fulbe Hierarchy among Mobile Elite Women' in M.E. de Bruijn, R. van Dijk & J-B. Gewald, eds, *Strength beyond Structure: Social and Historical Trajectories of Agency in Africa* (Brill, 2007).

Julia Pfaff has studied at the University of Bayreuth, Germany, as a DAAD scholar at the State University of Zanzibar and at Royal Holloway, University of London. At present she is doing her PhD at the University of Bayreuth on 'Translocality, Mobility and Trade: Imaginative Geographies of the Swahili'. Her most recent publication is 'Finding One's Way through Places – A Contemporary Trade Journey of Young Zanzibari Traders' which appeared in G. Klute & H. Hahn; eds, *Cultures of Migration: African Perspectives* (LIT, 2007).

Printed in the United States
148170LV00003B/2/P